African American Anti-Colonial Thought 1917–1937

Key Texts in Anti-Colonial Thought
Series Editor: David Johnson, The Open University

Available titles
The Revolutionary and Anti-Imperialist Writings of James Connolly 1893–1916
Edited by Conor McCarthy
African American Anti-Colonial Thought 1917–1937
Edited by Cathy Bergin

Forthcoming titles
Beyond 1968: Anti-colonial Texts from Central American Student Movements 1929–1979
Edited by Heather Vrana

African American Anti-Colonial Thought 1917–1937

Edited by Cathy Bergin

EDINBURGH
University Press

Edinburgh University Press is one of the leading university presses in the UK. We publish academic books and journals in our selected subject areas across the humanities and social sciences, combining cutting-edge scholarship with high editorial and production values to produce academic works of lasting importance. For more information visit our website: www.edinburghuniversitypress.com

© Cathy Bergin, 2016

Edinburgh University Press Ltd
The Tun – Holyrood Road, 12(2f) Jackson's Entry, Edinburgh EH8 8PJ

Typeset in 10.5/13 Sabon by
Servis Filmsetting Ltd, Stockport, Cheshire

A CIP record for this book is available from the British Library

ISBN 978 1 4744 0968 1 (hardback)
ISBN 978 1 4744 0958 2 (webready PDF)
ISBN 978 1 4744 0957 5 (paperback)
ISBN 978 1 4744 0959 9 (epub)

The right of Cathy Bergin to be identified as the editor of this work has been asserted in accordance with the Copyright, Designs and Patents Act 1988, and the Copyright and Related Rights Regulations 2003 (SI No. 2498).

Published with the support of the Edinburgh University Scholarly Publishing Initiatives Fund.

Contents

Series Editor's Preface	x
A Note on Primary Material	xi
Acknowledgements	xiii
Introduction	1

Part I: Red, Black and Green: The Emergence of Left Black Radicalism 1917–1929

1 Bolshevism   23

Bolshevism and World Democracy, Editorial in *The Messenger* (1918)	23
Get out of Russia, Editorial in *The Messenger* (1919)	24
The Bolsheviki, Editorial in *The Crusader* (1919)	26
We Want More Bolshevik Patriotism, Editorial in *The Messenger* (1919)	26
Make their Cause your Own, Editorial in *The Crusader* (1919)	27
Socialism the Negro's Hope by W. A. Domingo (1919)	28
Did Bolshevism Stop Race Riots in Russia by W. A. Domingo (1919)	31
Bolshevist!!! Editorial in *The Crusader* (1919)	34
Bolshevism and Race Prejudice, Editorial in *The Crusader* (1919)	35
Bolshevism's Menace: To Whom and To What by Cyril Briggs (1920)	36
Bolshevism in Barbados by Hubert Harrison (1920)	38
Everywhere Bolshevism Brings Terror to the Heart of Imperialism by W. A. Domingo (1920)	39

	A New International by Hubert Harrison (1920)	40
	The Negro and Radical Thought by W. E. B. Du Bois (1921)	41
	Reds Seek Negro Recruits to Help Start Revolution (1921)	44
	Negroes in Soviet Russia, Editorial in *The Messenger* (1923)	46
	Soviet Russia and the Negro by Claude McKay (1923)	46
2	**Irish Anti-Colonial Struggle and Black Radical Politics**	58
	Friends of Irish Freedom, Editorial in *The Messenger* (1917)	58
	England, Editorial in *The Crusader* (1919)	59
	Internationalism, Editorial in *The Messenger* (1919)	60
	Approaching Irish Success, Editorial in *The Crusader* (1919)	62
	Negro Police Captains, Editorial in *The Messenger* (1919)	62
	Forward by W. E. B. Du Bois (1919)	64
	England Again by W. E. B. Du Bois (1920)	65
	Heroic Ireland: Irish Fight for Liberty the Greatest Epic of Modern Times and a Sight to Inspire to Emulation all Oppressed Groups by Cyril Briggs (1921)	66
	Irish Boycott on British Goods, Editorial in *The Crusader* (1921)	67
	Bleeding Ireland, Editorial in *The Crisis* (1921)	68
	How Black Sees Red and Green by Claude McKay (1921)	69
	Hon. Marcus Garvey, as Spokesman for 400,000,000 Negroes, Telegraphs Arthur Griffith and Premier Lloyd George on the Settlement of The Irish Question and Creation of a Self-Governing Irish Free State (1921)	74
	Irish Free State, Editorial in *The Messenger* (1922)	78
	The Irish and the Negro by J. A. Rogers (1924)	79
3	**The New Negro: Anti-Colonialism/Anti-Capitalism**	82
	Africa for the Africans by Cyril Briggs (1918)	82
	The Call by W. Francis Jr. (1918)	84
	Would Freedom Make Us 'Village Cut-Ups' by Cyril Briggs (1919)	85
	Africa Speaks! Editorial in *The Crusader* (1919)	87
	Capitalism the Basis of Colonialism by W. A. Domingo (1919)	88
	Loaded Dice by C. Valentine (Briggs) (1920)	90

The New Negro – What is He? Chandler Owen and A. Philip Randolph (1920)	93
The Black Man's Burden (A Reply to Rudyard Kipling) by Hubert Harrison (1920)	96
A New Negro for a New Day by W. A. Domingo (1920)	97
Wanted a Colored International by Hubert Harrison (1921)	100
Enslaved by Claude McKay (1921)	102
Frightful Friendship vs Self Defense by Hubert Harrison (1921)	103
Liberating Africa, Editorial in *The Crusader* (1921)	108
Hands Across the Sea by Hubert Harrison (1921)	109
Negroes have Slumbered for Centuries by Marcus Garvey (1922)	111
Birthright by Claude McKay (1922)	114
The Colonial Congress and the Negro by Richard B. Moore (1927)	118

4 Responses to Garveyism — 122

Marcus Garvey by W. E. B. Du Bois (1920)	122
Lessons in Tactics for the Liberation Movement by Cyril Briggs (1921)	125
Will Not Co-operate, Says Garvey, Editorial in *The Crusader* (1921)	128
Garvey Turns Informer by C. Valentine (Briggs) (1921)	130
Black Zionism by A. Philip Randolph (1922)	131
Garvey as a Negro Moses by Claude McKay (1922)	137
Garvey Unfairly Attacked, Editorial in *The Messenger* (1922)	141
Hon. Marcus Garvey Tells of Interview with Ku Klux Klan (1922)	143
A Symposium on Garvey by Negro Leaders (1922)	150
The Only Way to Redeem Africa by A. Philip Randolph (1922)	158
W. A. Domingo and Chandler Owen's Debate (1923)	163
To All Oppressed Peoples and Classes (1927)	171

Part II: Anti-Colonialism and Anti-Racism 1929–1937

5 Transnational Anti-Racism — 177

ANLC Organizes Labor Unions in West Indies by O. E. Huiswoud (1929)	177

Lenin, Editorial in *The [Harlem/Negro] Liberator* (1930)	179
The Negro and the Struggle Against Imperialism by James W. Ford (1930)	180
The Revolutionary Movement in Africa by George Padmore (1931)	182
Increase and Spread the Scottsboro Defense, Editorial in *Negro Worker* (1931)	185
What is the International Trade Union Committee of Negro Workers? (1931)	188
Trouble in the West Indies by George Padmore (1932)	189
For Self-Determination in the Black Belt, Editorial in *The [Harlem/Negro] Liberator* (1932)	190
How the Empire is Governed by George Padmore (1932)	192
A New Song by Langston Hughes (1932)	199
Equality Land and Freedom: A Program for Negro Liberation (extracts from a pamphlet), League of Struggle for Negro Rights, 1933	201
A Century of Emancipation, Editorial in *Negro Worker* (1934)	203
Negroes Speak of War by Langston Hughes (1934)	204
Going South in Russia by Langston Hughes (1934)	206
The Role of Proletarian Fraternalism in the Liberation Struggle of the Negro People by Louise Thompson (1934)	210
From the Colonies (1934)	212
The Same by Langston Hughes (1935)	213
The Negro and the Century of Alexander Pushkin by William L. Patterson (1937)	215

6 Anti-Colonialism and Anti-Fascism — 220

Southern Terror by Louise Thompson (1934)	220
Ethiopia Unity Rallies Harlem, Editorial in *The [Harlem/Negro] Liberator* (1935)	226
Ethiopia and World Politics by George Padmore (1935)	228
The Abyssinian Situation and the Negro World by William L. Patterson (1935)	236
Boycott Hearst, Editorial in *The [Negro/Harlem] Liberator* (1934)	239
Stay Out of the Nazi Olympics, Editorial in *The Crisis* (1935)	240

A Stirring Ballad of Ethiopian People by Langton Hughes (1935)	241
Political Highlights of the National Negro Congress by James W. Ford (1936)	243
I Visited Spain by Edward E. Strong (1936)	247
Walter Garland Tells what Spain's Fight against Fascism Means to the Negro People by Richard Wright (1937)	252
Support the Spanish People, Editorial in *Negro Worker* (1937)	255

Conclusion 257

Index 259

Series Editor's Preface

Key Texts in Anti-Colonial Thought re-publishes selections of anti-colonial texts and locates them in their colonial/neo-colonial contexts. Leading scholars in Postcolonial Studies introduce a wide variety of hitherto hard-to-access anti-colonial writings. Each volume opens with a substantial introduction contextualising the selected texts, setting out the specific forms of colonial governance, economic exploitation and cultural imperialism they wrote against, as well as the communities of resistance, the solidarities and the distinctive political cultures that sustained them. In addition, the volumes provide extensive explanatory notes, annotated guides to further reading, and concluding discussions of the texts' relevance today. The series aims to counter the dependency of Postcolonial Studies on a narrow range of theorists and literary texts, and to provoke reflection on the connections between anti-colonial thought and contemporary resistance to global inequalities.

David Johnson

A Note on Primary Material

This collection re-publishes articles on anti-colonialism from a number of remarkable left-wing African American magazines and Communist Party publications of the interwar period:

The Communist [1919–1921] a weekly magazine of the Communist Party of America (CPUSA) edited by Italian-born Communist Louis C. Fraina.

The Communist [1927–1944] a theoretical monthly magazine of the CPUSA which was renamed *Political Affairs* in 1944. Its original editor was the German-born Communist Max Bedacht. The magazine is notable for its long and often exhaustive articles.

The Crisis [1910–present] the monthly magazine of the National Association for the Advancement of Colored People (NAACP) edited by W. E. B. Du Bois until 1934 when Roy Wilkins became editor. In addition to its campaigning journalism *The Crisis* also had extensive arts and culture coverage.

The Crusader [1918–1922] a monthly newspaper founded by Cyril Briggs in 1918, which eventually became the magazine of the African Blood Brotherhood (ABB). Briggs was a founding member of the ABB, went on to join the Communist Party and edited *The [Negro/Harlem] Liberator* (1929–1935).

The Emancipator [1920] was launched in March 1920 and edited by the Jamaican Socialist W. A. Domingo (1889–1968). It was a short-lived publication, closing down on 24 April 1920.

The [Harlem/Negro] Liberator [1929–1935] a weekly and bi-weekly newspaper of the American Negro Labor Congress edited by Cyril Briggs until September 1933 (subsequently it was edited by Maude White, an African American Communist and organiser until July 1934, and the radical African American lawyer and Communist

Benjamin Davis). Originally called *The Liberator* the newspaper changed its name twice – to the *Harlem Liberator* in 1933 and to the *Negro Liberator* in 1934. It is named in this volume as *The [Harlem/Negro] Liberator* to avoid confusion with *The Liberator* [1918–24].

The Liberator [1918–1924] an important and influential monthly socialist magazine which attracted some of the finest writers on the Left in the USA. It was edited by the Socialist Max Eastman and co-edited for a time by the Jamaican writer Claude McKay. It became a Communist Party publication in 1922.

The Messenger [1917–1928] a monthly newspaper founded and edited by A. Philip Randolph and Chandler Owen. Randolph was the most successful black trade unionist of the period, founding the Brotherhood of Sleeping Car Porters and Maids in 1925. He joined the Socialist Party in 1910 and his antipathy towards the Communist Party becomes more pronounced in the early 1920s. Chandler Owen joined the Socialist Party in 1916 though by the end of the 1920s he had become a member of the Republican Party.

Negro World [1918–1933] was the official organ of Garvey's United Negro Improvement Association. Its early issues were decidedly more influenced by left-wing politics though, as Chapter 4 details, relationships between Garvey and other black activists disintegrated swiftly in the early 1920s.

Negro Worker [1928–1937] was a monthly journal of the International Trade Union Committee for Negro Workers (ITUCNW). It was edited by George Padmore from 1931–1934, and attempted to provide an internationalist vision of both pan-African and interracial anti-colonial struggle.

The radical press of the time was gloriously unstandardised in terms of spelling and punctuation. To maintain clarity throughout I have corrected minor errors in spelling, otherwise the texts are reproduced as they were at the time. Certain articles have been abridged, this is clearly signposted in the extracts themselves.

Acknowledgements

David Johnson has been an invaluable support in the writing of this book. I am very grateful for his enthusiasm, rigour and patience. Jackie Jones, Adela Rauchova and Rebecca MacKenzie at Edinburgh University Press have been a pleasure to work with; I thank them for their insights and professionalism.

Susan Bergin's assistance in the transcribing of these documents was generously offered and delivered. I am grateful to her for this and much else besides.

My colleagues and friends on the Humanities Programme in the University of Brighton continue to provide as close to an ideal work environment as is possible in these neo-liberal times. Particular thanks are due to Anita Rupprecht and Tom Hickey for their interest in and support of my work and of course for their valued friendship and shared political commitment.

I am grateful to the University of Brighton for granting me a research sabbatical which was essential to completing this project. The staff at the University of Brighton library couldn't have been more helpful. Chris Davies was especially notable in this regard. My head of school Paddy Maguire is always, without fanfare, supportive of all my teaching and research endeavours.

I am often reliant on Patricia McManus's friendship and her brilliant mind, no less so in relation to this project than many others. Thanks are also due to these excellent people: Naomi Ashman, Daisy Asquith, Brendan Donohoe, Anne Duffy, David Featherstone, Brian Hanley, Brian Kelly, Shad Khan, Theodore Koulouris, Geetha Jayaramen, Ian McDonald, Mark McGovern, Eugene Michail, Jason Porter, Louise Purbrick, Kevin Reynolds, Sallie Richards and Lucy Robinson.

Many thanks to my family Fiona, Susan and Barbara Bergin, Clare

Murphy, Kit and Ella Connolly, and most especially my wonderful mother Marie Bergin. I deeply regret that my peerless father Johnny Bergin (1938–2014) did not see the publication of this book but his love and encouragement remain ever present.

John Duffy is essential to everything. This book is dedicated to him.

The author wishes to thank the Crisis Publishing Co., Inc., the publisher of the magazine of the National Association for the Advancement of Colored People (NAACP), for the use of material first published in the December 1923, July and October 1927, June and November 1934, May and September 1935 and December 1936 issues of *Crisis*. For help and advice in relation to permissions, the author would also like to thank David Featherstone, Robert Hill, Maira Liriano, Kenneth Robinson, Holger Weiss, Tehra Williams and the Marxists Internet Archive.

For John Duffy

Introduction

Bolshevism is the Banquo's ghost to Macbeth capitalists of the world whether they inhabit Germany, England, America or Japan.
  The Messenger editorial, July 1918

Among these volunteers who have offered their lives in defence of Spain from fascist barbarism are a number of Negroes and other colonials. These colonials, fighting for the ranks of the Government forces realize that the fight for freedom in Spain is very closely connected with their own struggles against tyranny and the ever increasing world fascist menace. They realize further that a defeat of fascism in Spain, means not only a victory for the Spanish people, but a decisive curb to the fascist ambition of war for colonial annexation and a tremendous setback in Mussolini's attempt to consolidate his occupation of Abyssinia.
  The Negro Worker editorial, February 1937

For at least two generations of black activists in the USA the concept of internationalism was one which not only enabled a very particular type of anti-colonial politics, it was a concept which placed race[1] at the centre of a visionary anti-capitalism. *The Messenger's* (1917–1928) literary reframing of Marx's opening lines to the *Communist Manifesto* – where a 'spectre is haunting Europe – the spectre of communism' – is here mobilised to place Bolshevism at the centre of world revolution. The editorial from the *Negro Worker* (1928–1937) in which the Spanish Civil War is imagined as the locus for an international anti-colonial and anti-fascist struggle in which the African diaspora has a vested interest, is not a random and isolated moment of Utopian sloganeering. It is

---

[1] Race should be understood throughout this text as 'race', i.e. a socially constructed category.

the culmination of an anti-colonial politics which emerged in the wake of the Bolshevik revolution, the race riots of 1919, the US occupation of Haiti, the anti-colonial struggles in Ireland and India, the horrors of racism in the USA, Mussolini's invasion of Ethiopia and the experiences of a variety of black activists and intellectuals living in the USA between the wars.

This introduction will trace the historical contexts of these writings. This history is so rich and multifarious that I can only refer readers to the important historiography that is listed in the bibliography of this introduction and the annotated further reading. It is not my intention to provide a detailed and exhaustive account of the events which shaped these writings. Rather, in identifying key moments which inform and enable these texts, the aim is to create a coherent narrative against which to understand their impetus and their power. I have thus structured the introduction and indeed the volume itself in relation to particular struggles both inside and outside the USA which predominate in the writings themselves but which also reflect my own materialist interpretation of *why* this period offers us such a formidable body of anti-colonial analysis. Writing for these magazines were some of the most remarkable intellectuals of the age: including W. E. B. Du Bois (1868–1963), Hubert Harrison (1883–1927), Claude McKay (1889–1948) and George Padmore (1903–1959). Many of the essays collected here have never been re-published, and they are rarely anthologised together. Collectively they represent a sorely neglected resource in anti-colonial thought.

The collection spans the period 1917 to 1937 because this period saw a powerfully expressed black nationalism emerge through the rise of Garveyism and the formation of an important relationship between radical black politics and the Left. Jamaican born Marcus Garvey (1887–1940) founded the United Negro Improvement Association (UNIA) in New York in 1917 in order forge a sense of racial brotherhood sourced in a reclamation of African identity (Grant 2009: 54). The UNIA attracted millions of supporters in the African diaspora (see below) and challenged established black organisations in the USA and beyond. This historical period also saw a novel relationship between African American activists and the Left in the USA, a relationship which strongly informed the race politics of the time. This relationship did not only shape the radical Left and black activists of the Left, it informed a myriad of more moderate black organisations and individuals who were waging a struggle against racism in the USA and beyond. The interpretation of this relationship is a highly contested field of study, which for many years was dominated by a Cold War historiography which insisted that this relationship was characterised by manipulation of black activists by the white-led Left in the USA (Draper 1957; Klehr 1984). In the last 30 years this interpretation of the period has been challenged by a growing number of scholars who have pointed to the ways in which such a supposition must be predicated on a denial of agency to those black activists who shaped and drove the race-conscious internationalist anti-colonialism of the period (see Further Reading). The material in this collection is intended to show precisely the complexities and possibilities of the unique politics of resistance which these activists wrestled with in the pages of their publications.

This is not an uncomplicated story of breezy interracial solidarity or indeed transnational solidarity. The battles against racism both outside and inside the Left are integral to the formation of this anti-racist, anti-colonial, class-conscious politics. The tensions between African American born and Caribbean migrant activists inform the contours of these expressive polemics. The strains that emerge in the context of the race apathy, if not racist hostility, of the organised Left and the driving race consciousness of black activists are instrumental in shaping the form of the models of black internationalism which materialise in these writings. Indeed the palpable fervour in parts of this collection evidences a politics forged as much in the intricacies of local conflicts as in the powerfully imagined global solidarities.

Race Politics in the USA Post-World War I

Although the term 'New Negro' arose in the USA during the Reconstruction period following the Civil War, it has generally been deployed in relation to those black writers, artists and activists of the post-World War I period. As many recent critics have argued, the older understanding of the term as a purely *cultural* one is a misrepresentation of the politics of this extraordinary moment in African American politics (Foley 2008: 3–5). The post-war period saw a wave of black militancy in the USA where domestic anti-racism, international revolution and anti-colonial struggle gave impetus to the term 'New Negro' as explicitly active, anti-assimilationist, internationalist and scathing of the 'Old Negro'. The Old Negro was associated with accommodationist politics, particularly those of Booker T. Washington (1856–1915), where African Americans were encouraged to work within the structures of American racism and to recognise according to Washington that 'there is as much dignity in tilling a field as in writing a poem' (Grant 2009: 59). The New Negro would demand an end to US racism in all its forms. This meant challenging the 'Jim Crow' southern states where a strict segregation between black and white was backed up by legal and extra-legal violence and intimidation. It also meant challenging the institutionalised racism in the northern states where there was no legal segregation, but in reality African Americans suffered discrimination in every aspect of their lives. The New Negro thus was different to the Old Negro through a determination to confront the social structures of racism and in seeking new forms of solidarity. Accounting for the emergence of these politics within a purely domestic setting limits our understanding of the term. As Brent Hayes Edwards has argued, 'the "New Negro" movement is at the same time a "new" black internationalism' (Edwards 2003: 2). However, in the context of the material in this volume, material which precisely attempts to speak to both the local and the international within an anti-colonial framework, it is essential to understand the particular nature of race politics in the USA during this period.

In the five years between 1915 and 1920 over three-quarters of a million African Americans migrated from the Jim Crow south to the industrial north. In addition to fleeing the racist terror of the south, where lynching was rife as a means to control black populations, they were leaving a predominantly agricultural society to become part the growing working class of the large cities of the north. Although many African Americans worked in US industry, the American Federation of Labor, representing craft unions, was a thoroughly racist organisation which insisted on segregated unions. The Industrial Workers of the World (Wobblies) had a far more impressive reputation in organising black workers: even in the southern states they erected their banner of 'No Race, No Creed, No Color'. However, the numbers of black members they actually recruited is unknown (Foner 1974: 50). Significantly, the period saw an enormous swelling of the ranks of the black working class in the north, and the concept of the African American *as a worker* is one which dominates the radical black press of the period.

Over 380,000 African Americans had joined the army when the USA entered the war (Williams 2007: 349). Despite the nature of the Jim Crow army, many of these men experienced a life outside of the institutional racism of the USA and returned with a determination to fight against the racist structures which dominated every element of black life in the country. At the end of the war the returning black soldiers were banned from army parades, and the promises of equality made to them by President Wilson in return for their service were revealed to be illusory. Nineteen black soldiers of the 24th Infantry Regiment were summarily executed after a revolt in Houston in August 1917. Indeed the post-war period was dominated by so-called 'race riots' which in reality more clearly resembled pogroms against African American communities. The 'Red Summer' of 1919 saw an onslaught of racist violence across the USA, when between April and October there were at least 25 and up to 40 'race riots' (Tuttle 1996: 14). These attempts to terrorise the black population of the USA were met with a level of resistance which echoed the growing militancy of black communities in the period. For example the 'revolt' in Houston followed a mutiny by black soldiers in reaction to a violent assault by police officers on an African American woman. The soldiers marched on the city, where they had been variously and consistently racially abused for the preceding month. The resultant death of fourteen white civilians ensured the fate of the men who had fought back against the violent racism of the State (Hill 1987: xii). As the radical black magazine *The Crusader* (1918–1922) argued in relation to white terror:

> With us it will be a fight for life as well as for rights. And to the race fighting against mighty odds for its existence the use of any and every weapon at hand is not only permissible but compulsory. With the murderer clutching at our throats we cannot afford to choose our weapons, but must defend ourselves with what lies nearest, whether that be poison, fire or what. (*The Crusader*, January 1921: 1)

The Crusader's insistence here on an assertive politics of self-defence in the face of white supremacy was instrumental to its politics. In many ways it held American racism to account in a way which defamiliarised its apparent normality to insist upon its savage character. This ability was in no small part due to the way in which its mostly Caribbean-born editorial team precisely *experienced* American racism as profoundly novel and brutal.

Caribbean Migration

Essential to understanding the radical, black anti-colonial politics of this period is the influence of Afro-Caribbean migrants in the USA in the first decades of the twentieth century. Between 1906 and 1926 over 125,000 migrants from the Caribbean arrived in the USA, with nearly 60,000 of those settling in New York (W. James 1998: 358). Though a strict race/class hierarchy predominated in the black majority islands of the Caribbean, the area's complex pigmentocracy engendered a politics of race which was very different in form and structure to the USA's racial segregation. In the USA, Caribbean immigrants found themselves part of a despised minority. Moreover these men and women had grown up as subjects of European colonial rule and had a very particular relationship to the politics of anti-colonialism. Post-World War I America was a dangerous place for African Americans. Those who arrived from the Caribbean were greeted with a vicious racism, one which overwhelmed even the anti-immigrationist sentiment which prevailed in the period: this was a racism which was experienced in all of its variegated forms. According to the Jamaican poet and activist Claude McKay:

> It was the first time I had ever come face to face with such manifest, implacable hate of my race, and my feelings were indescribable . . . I had heard of prejudice in America but never dreamed of it being so intensely bitter. (*The Crisis*, November 1918: 22)

Many of these Caribbean migrants were drawn to both black radical and Socialist politics. Perhaps the most influential of the early arrivals was Hubert Harrison (1883–1927), who was born in St Croix in the Danish Caribbean, emigrated to New York in 1900, and joined the Socialist Party in 1911, resigning in 1918 (Perry 2001: xxiii). Harrison constantly argued within the Socialist Party for a commitment to race politics beyond the class reductionism of the traditional Left. In addition, he edited Marcus Garvey's *Negro World* for a time, wrote prolifically on questions of race and colonialism and was a compelling and charismatic speaker in the streets of Harlem. Harrison influenced many radicals in Harlem, not least those who would go on to form the African Blood Brotherhood (ABB) in 1919.

There has been a resurgence of interest in this organisation in recent years (Makalani 2011; Zumoff 2014), and the ABB magazine *The Crusader* features regularly in Part I of this collection. The ABB was a black radical organisation formed in 1919 which saw itself as the vanguard of an oppressed racial minority at the prey of a rapacious white supremacism. The organisation was particularly concerned with race pride and early editions of *The Crusader* are the site of a richly articulated Afro-centrism which constantly underlined the importance of black history, culture and achievement. Allied to this was a strong identification with the Bolshevik revolution and the Irish national struggle. The ABB read race in the US as intimately connected to the politics of empire and while it loudly proclaimed its race pride it also demanded a broader anti-colonial struggle:

> The Negro masses must get out of their minds the stupid idea that it is necessary for two groups to love each other before they can enter into an

alliance against their common enemy. Not love or hatred, but identity of interest at the moment dictates the tactics of practical people. (Cited in Hill 1987: lxviii)

The Crusader was edited by Cyril Briggs (1888–1966) who was born on the island of Nevis and emigrated to New York in 1905. He worked as a journalist in the USA, most famously for the *Amsterdam News*, from which he was fired due to his anti-war stance. His voice is ubiquitous in *The Crusader*, in which he writes under his own name but also that of C. Valentine and C. Lorenzo. Other important members of the organisation were Richard B. Moore (1893–1978) from Barbados, Claude McKay (1889–1948) and W. A. Domingo (1889–1968) from Jamaica, Otto Huiswoud (1893–1961) from Surinam, and Grace Campbell (1883–1943) who was born in Georgia of Caribbean parentage. Campbell was an important radical of the period yet she does not appear in the pages of *The Crusader*. This is not simply a question of the visibility of female activists in the public sphere in the 1920s and 1930s. African American women activists worked assiduously in their communities, especially Harlem. Throughout the various articulations of liberation in the pages of the black radical press, it is inevitably conceived of in gendered terms. The concept of 'black manhood' is pervasive in this period and indeed in the civil rights period which followed it. Although there are calls for women's suffrage dotted throughout the pages of many of the newspapers and magazines in this volume, the concept of liberation is generally imagined in relation to black men reclaiming traditional masculinity denied them by the pathologically fixated gendered racism of white supremacism. Racist ideologies and practices in the USA insisted on the danger that African American men posed through the myth of the black rapist. The historical reality of sexual violence enacted on black women by white men from slavery onwards was displaced onto the black male body which threatened both white female bodies and the body politic. Although there were important African American women activists during this period, including Grace Campbell, Maude White (1908–), Williana Burroughs (1882–1945) and Louise Thompson (1901–1999), their sporadic presence in these publications is somewhat glaring. Williana Burroughs wrote for the *Daily Worker* and *The [Harlem/Negro] Liberator*, she had a regular column 'Women's Department' in the latter publication in 1935. She covered issues from child labour, to the unemployment of domestic workers, to healthy eating. However these short articles do not fit with the wider themes of this volume, nor are they representative of her status as a committed and prominent Communist of the era (McDuffie 2011: 31–3). The relative paucity of black women's voices in the black radical press not only points to the dominant ideologies of gender of the period, even within radical circles, it also documents the complex, if common, gendering of race within the context of American racism.

The language of empire is similarly one which is constructed in relation to the gendered lexicon of European colonialism. As Michelle Stephens has argued 'empire's language of sovereignty specifically became a way for black intellectuals to imagine the future freedom of the race, in sovereignty and statehood' (Stephens 2005: 20). It is precisely this gendered language of sovereignty that the radicals of the period re-claimed and re-appropriated. For example, the clarion call of the New Negro was 'self-determination', a term that was particularly inflected by the black radicals in the USA in ways which informed the anti-colonial politics that emerged in the wake of World War I. As Barbara Foley has noted:

> Seizing on the rhetoric of self-determination infusing the entire spectrum of post-war politics, from Versailles to the Kremlin, advocates of Pan-Africanism moved this discourse to the left, not only proposing a global alliance of peoples in the African diaspora but also beginning to theorize African Americans as a colonized people. (Foley 2008: 14–15)

Thus, anti-racism at home, and anti-colonialism abroad were often imagined as not only connected struggles, but as indivisible ones. This meant not just that the radical press gave more space to struggles happening in Africa or the Caribbean, but the frameworks offered to imagine black liberation at home were intimately bound up with the struggles in the diaspora and, in certain cases (Ireland, India), anti-colonial struggles outside of those which affected those of African descent. In the more obviously Communist-inspired publications this framework was also to encompass 'white workers', but as the material here demonstrates this was often a more complex rhetorical negotiation. In the context of US racism the sometimes stated commitment to working-class unity did not and indeed could not find expression in any ideal form but in the politics of pragmatism, albeit often a pragmatism allied to a very particular vision of internationalism.

The ABB was an organisation which increasingly became allied to the politics of the Communist International (Comintern), the organisation set up in the aftermath of the Russian Revolution to further the cause of workers' revolution worldwide. The ABB was an independent organisation which sought theoretical and political dialogue with the Comintern as opposed to shared activities with the splintering Communist movement in the USA. The local politics of the shifting grounds of the Left in the early 1920s are an important context in which to understand the material in this volume, as the various allegiances of the writers here to either the Socialist or Communist Party, or to neither, account for some of the particular inflections which would later emerge as serious political divergences in understanding anti-colonialism.

Socialists, Communists and the Comintern

Following the Bolshevik revolution the Socialist Party in the USA went through a series of splits and factions. In 1922, two organisations which had split from the Socialist Party joined to become the Workers Party of America, which would eventually become the Communist Party of America (CPUSA). Thus in the period up until 1922, most of the publications in this volume supported voting for the Socialist Party. *The Messenger*, edited by African Americans A. Philip Randolph (1889–1979) and Chandler Owen (1889–1967), was officially the black newspaper of the Socialist Party and is *particularly* interested in election politics, but most of the radical and moderate newspapers and magazines saw the Socialist Party as an important alternative to the Republican and Democratic Parties. Traditionally the Socialist Party had an economic reductionist understanding of race in relation to the USA, famously summed up by the radical Socialist agitator Eugene V. Debs: 'We have nothing special to offer the Negro and we cannot make separate appeals to all the races. The Socialist Party is the Party of the working class, regardless of colour – the working class of the whole world' (Spero and Harris 1968: 405). Nevertheless, many of the Caribbean and African American writers and activists of the post-war period were drawn to the Socialist Party, particularly in Harlem where the local branch was black dominated and consistently demanded a foregrounding of race in Socialist Party politics. After the split, many of those activists around the ABB joined the Communist Party. Thus, for example, whilst early editions of *The Crusader* and Socialist Party publication *The Messenger* spoke approvingly of the other, and even offered joint subscription, a more antagonistic relationship emerges after the split.

What is more significant here, as many commentators on this period have emphasised, is that it was initially not to the *local* Socialist or Communist parties that black activists gave their allegiance during this period. It was to the Comintern, which seemed to be free of the passive, carping racism which dominated the Left in the USA itself. As Briggs recollected: 'My interest in Communism was inspired by the national policy of the Russian Bolsheviks and the anti-imperialist orientation of the Soviet State birthed by the October Revolution' (cited in Hill 1987: xxv).

At the second world congress of the Comintern in the summer of 1920, Lenin explicitly set out the anti-colonial conditions, which informed membership:

> In all their propaganda and agitation – both within parliament and outside it – the Communist parties must consistently expose that constant violation of the equality of nations and of the guaranteed rights of national minorities which is to be seen in all capitalist countries, despite their 'democratic' constitutions ... all Communist parties should render direct aid to the revolutionary movements among the dependent and underprivileged nations (for example, Ireland, the American Negroes, etc.) and in the colonies. (Lenin 1965: 145)

The Comintern seemed to offer a vision of liberation in which questions of national and racial oppression would be central. The fourth congress in 1922 was attended by two members of the ABB, Claude McKay and Otto Huiswoud, the latter being also by this time a member of the Communist Party. Both men addressed the congress; McKay ended his speech with his hope that 'we shall soon see a few Negro soldiers in the finest, bravest, and cleanest fighting forces in the world – the Red Army and Navy of Russia – fighting not only for their own emancipation, but also for the emancipation of all the working class of the whole world' (*Bulletin of the IV Congress of the Communist International*, December 1922: 11). As Makalani notes, 'early twentieth-century black radicals were witness to a world that they believed teetered between revolution and repression, self-determination and ever-expanding empires' (Makalani 2011: 3). However, the source of that repression, the meaning of that self-determination and of the relationship between revolution and empire, were the topic of intense debate, the contours of which are best understood in relation to the mass liberatory movement of Garveyism.

Garveyism

Garvey's UNIA was the largest and most powerful black nationalist movement in the USA in the early 1920s. At its peak it had over two million members in the USA, with a further two million in the Caribbean, Africa and Australia (W. James 1998: 136). Garvey was initially sympathetic to Bolshevism and identified strongly with anti-imperialist struggles including those of India and Ireland. However, he became increasingly conservative and often echoed the rhetoric of black self-help preached by Booker T. Washington. Whilst the UNIA publication, *Negro World* (1918–1933), features in this collection it does so mainly in terms of the black radicals who wrote for it who were initially critical friends, and then simply critics, of Garveyism. ABB members W. A. Domingo and Hubert Harrison were both some-time editors of *Negro World*. The relatively limited reproduction in this book of articles from the newspaper is not intended to skew the influence of this powerful black radical politics. Indeed as the articles about Garveyism attest it often dominated the attempt to forge an anti-colonial politics of resistance. However, Garveyism has been much written about and its publication frequently cited in the historiography of the period. In the context of this volume, it is the impact of the UNIA on competing forms of black radical thought that is significant. The vitriol against Garvey which seems to unite a wide range of black activists and writers of the period is driven in part by a recognition of the attraction that Garvey's emigrationist discourse held for many black subjects in the USA and the Caribbean.

At the centre of Garveyism was a concept of race solidarity which attracted and repelled both radical and moderate anti-racist and anti-colonial thinkers. Fired by a dream of a powerful black empire in Africa, Garvey set up the Black Star Line, a shipping company that would ferry those in the diaspora who wished to return 'home'. The UNIA wished to establish African American migration to Liberia, but also wished to ensure that Liberia would be an attractive prospect for those for whom the daily horrors of American racism were a cogent 'push factor':

> We must send our scientists, our mechanics and our artisans and let them build railroads, let them build the great educational and other institutions necessary, and when they are constructed the time will come for the commend to be given 'Come home' to Lennox Avenue, to 7th Avenue. (Cited in Grant 2009: 264)

For many of Garvey's critics this was a call for a black colonisation of Africa, and it provoked furious alternative visions of internationalism and anti-colonialism from a broad spectrum of writers. Elements of black opposition to Garveyism were often extremely hostile to the UNIA, especially though not exclusively on the Left. Garvey's earlier Bolshevik sympathies were little in evidence by 1925 when he proclaimed: 'the only convenient friend the Negro worker or laborer has, in America at the present time, is the white capitalist' (Garvey 1967: 69). Garvey's mass organisation provoked a variety of challenges to African

American politics, not least the attempt to articulate an alternative pan-Africanist vision of liberation.

The tensions between Caribbean-born and American-born black activists became heightened during this period and the black radical press of the time is a rich source of complex and contradictory assertions of an American politics attuned to anti-colonial struggles abroad. The hostility towards Garveyism from the black Left in particular, and Garvey's own distancing of the UNIA from the Left, open up an often extremely bad-tempered, but fascinating, space for polemical assertions of the meaning of black freedom both domestically and in the colonies. The sheer scale of the invective underlines the significance of Garveyism as an influence on anti-colonial politics, and the repudiation of Garveyism is a contradictory strategy of resistance to racial oppression at home and abroad. The extremely personal nature of the attacks does not render silent the political divergences around the status of Caribbean immigrants, the nature of the black bourgeoisie and the complexity of 'Africa' as an originary homeland and a geo-political reality.

Most unedifying in these debates was the spectacle of black radicals calling for Garvey's deportation and bringing his business dealings to the attention of the newly formed Bureau of Investigation, which under J. Edgar Hoover was waging a relentless war of 'intelligence' against the Left. The Bureau was particularly interested in the danger that black radicals posed in terms of desegregation and 'communism' and at one time investigated all of Garvey's major critics (Kornweibel 1999: 19–36). The impetus for the particular invective which emerged around Garvey was his meeting with the Ku Klux Klan in July 1922 which suggested for many that the UNIA could not be seen as a progressive force. Garvey's deportation in 1927 coincided with a new initiative which saw the formation of the League against Imperialism in that year and a congress in Frankfurt in 1929. There, African American and Afro-Caribbean Communists met with African radicals and the International Trade Union Committee for Negro Workers (ITUCNW) was formed. This organisation was to become very important in the 1930s because of its quest to place the black working class from Africa and the diaspora at the vanguard of an anti-imperialist politics.

Race Politics During The Depression: The Comintern and Grass-Roots Activism

The 1930s saw the emergence of an impressive, if complicated, set of interracial alliances in the mobilisation against fascism and racism in the

USA and beyond. This period saw the CPUSA become a serious pole of attraction to African American activists. This was a result of a variety of factors, not least the Party's championing of the case of the 'Scottsboro Boys', the attempted legal lynching of nine black teenagers between the ages of 13 and 19 years on a trumped-up rape charge in Alabama in 1931. Where more moderate organisations like the National Association for the Advancement of Colored People (NAACP) were initially hesitant in their defence of the young men, the CPUSA took charge of the defence, turned the case into a cause célèbre, and succeeded in keeping the defendants from the electric chair. (Though the ultimate fate of the young men, trapped in systems of incarceration and poverty, is a grim index of mid-century American racism.) If CPUSA *activities* around racism suggested the novelty of a predominantly white organisation which was committed to confronting the white supremacy, their *theoretical* zig zags also opened up a space for a reimagining of anti-colonial politics.

The Comintern of the 1930s was a very different organisation to that which was set up in the aftermath of the Russian Revolution that so fired the imagination of the early black radicals. The victory of the Stalinist bureaucracy in the late 1920s with its commitment to 'Socialism in one country' transformed the function of the Comintern (C. L. R. James 1937: 202). Less an instrument for world revolution than for defending Mother Russia, the international members frequently found themselves acting on directives which made little sense in relation to political imperatives in their own countries. Oddly, more by accident than design, these directives were important in terms of attracting African Americans to the Party in the USA. The so-called Third Period (1928–1935) was one in which the collapse of world capitalism was predicted and thus 'reformists' were the major enemy for prolonging the dying gasps of a system on its knees. The consequences of this in Europe were catastrophic as communist parties were instructed that the 'social fascists' of the social democratic parties were more of a threat than fascism itself (Rosenhaft 1983: 113). However, in the context of black politics in the USA, the ire heaped upon black moderates in this context has an earlier echo with the New Negro movement and the growing impatience amongst African Americans with their 'leaders'. During this period the Trinidadian-born writer and activist George Padmore (1903–1959) edited the *Negro Worker*; in its pages, alongside other radical publications of the period, a sophisticated vision of a black radicalism attuned to the legacies of colonial power emerges. Padmore broke bitterly with the Communist movement in 1934, for reasons that are still debated in the historiography (Adi 2013: xxiii; Weiss 2013: 378). But the timing is interesting. The Third

Period was superseded in 1935 by the period of the 'Popular Front' that moved away from the sectarianism of the preceding years to embrace broad alliances with anti-fascists in the wake of Hitler's rise to power in Germany. The anti-colonial politics of *this* period were not as centrally structured around radical black nationalism as in the 1920s but were rather a celebration of black struggles and black culture as inherently progressive, anti-fascist and internationalist. The period of the Popular Front saw the Communist Party at the height of its influence with black communities in the USA. One reason for this was that many black Communists had already been building alliances with a broad range of black activists in relation to the Italian invasion of Ethiopia in 1935.

Anti-Colonialism and Anti Fascism

The invasion of Ethiopia by Mussolini's Italy in 1935 proved a rallying call for African American anti-colonialists. The seeming, and actual, apathy of the white world to this fascist invasion of a sovereign and symbolically powerful African nation galvanised a powerful broad movement in support of Ethiopia. The radical press drew explicit links between the forces of fascism invading Ethiopia and the forces of white supremacism terrorising black people in the southern states. In Harlem over 20,000 protestors took to the streets, and Italian-run bars which displayed portraits of Mussolini were boycotted by African Americans, forcing many to shut up shop (Gilmore 2008: 183). Ethiopia, as one of only two states on the continent never to have been colonised, held a particular place in the hearts and minds of the African diaspora. As Cedric Robinson notes: '"Ethiopia", confluent with the notion of Africa, became a most ancient point of reference a term signifying historicity and racial dignity in ways the term "Negro" could not match'(Robinson 1983: 60). As the writings in this volume show, the invasion of Ethiopia by a *fascist* imperial aggressor enabled a very specific type of anti-colonial politics which suggested that the fight for Ethiopia's independence necessitated a fight against fascism, and a fight against fascism necessitated anti-colonial, class-conscious politics of resistance.

When Franco led his uprising against the democratically elected government of Spain in 1936, Mussolini sent 1,000 of his troops from Ethiopia to support the fascist struggle in Spain. Opponents of the Ethiopian invasion responded with similar 'solidarity'. In the radical black press the Spanish Civil War was configured as directly connected to the fascist invasion of Ethiopia, where the racial nature of fascism was consistently stressed. By the late 1930s *Crisis* journalist George Streator could claim that in Harlem 'Spanish freedom and Negro freedom were made to be synonymous' (Naison 1985: 197). The anti-colonial call which had been mobilised in the face of fascist aggression in Ethiopia was seized upon in the context of Franco's Spain. Nearly 100 African Americans joined the Lincoln Brigade to fight for Spanish Republicans, their commitment to the cause was summed up in a letter home from one of the men which became the subtitle of a book about their experiences, *'This ain't Ethiopia, but it'll do'* (Collum and Berch 1992). Langston Hughes went to Spain as a reporter stating that black people globally needed to 'fight the forces that have raped Ethiopia', and Paul Robeson visited Spain and sang to the volunteers, exhorting the readers of the *Daily Worker* to:

> rally to the side of Republican Spain every black man in the British Empire ... For the Liberation of Spain from oppression of fascist reactionaries is not a private matter of the Spaniards, but the common cause of all advanced and progressive humanity. (Cited in Foner 1998: 119)

Whilst it is possible to read this moment as an instance of purely *communist* internationalism, to do so is to sever the connection between the anti-fascist anti-colonialism in the 1930s and the anti-colonial anti-racism of the New Negro movement. What the writings in this volume demonstrate is the development of a black radical tradition, which is both influenced by and influences left-wing anti-colonial politics. The pioneers of these eclectic liberation politics were not merely acting on directives from the Communist movement, they were attracted to variants of Marxism and the traditions of Bolshevism and committed to reshaping those politics in relation to 'race'. Mobilising black agency was central to the reimagining of the world on a variety of race/class axes. It is that commitment to *connecting* with black workers and activists that drives the black radical press, and the language, imagery and tone of the writings presented here are key to this collection.

The Radical Press

In the early part of the twentieth century Caribbean migrants brought with them the tradition of 'stepladder speaking' in opposition to the official press (Makalani 2011: 33). Hubert Harrison was particularly impressive in this regard and was finely attuned to the importance of the press in the dissemination of racist stereotypes.

> The newspapers of this country have many crimes to answer for. They feature our criminals in bold headlines: our substantial men when noticed

at all are relegated to the agate type division. Their methods, whether they obtain through set purpose or through carelessness, constantly appeal to the putrid passion of race hatred. They cause rapine to break loose by nurturing rancor. They help create untold sorrow. They are week-kneed and apologizing when the hour is bloody ... But Truth in the Negro's case is not even unleashed. Truth, in fact, is chained up and well guarded, and it is this terrible task of setting Truth free that the Negro must essay in the very teeth of the American press. It is not an easy task to voice an adequate protest, for it needs the widest publicity. And since prejudice will oppose, it needs prestige also. Any such effort must feel itself feeble, and yet it must be made. (Hubert H. Harrison 1911, 'The Negro and the Newspapers', in Perry 2001)

Harrison's insistence on the 'task of setting Truth free' in the context of a seemingly monolithic and violent racism in early twentieth century America is an insistence on the importance of articulating a black radical protest which is adequate to the discursive wars of race. Harrison, there, is not only calling for a politics of resistance, but a politics which addresses those who were charged with the task of breaking the white monolith – African Americans themselves. The material in this volume is overwhelmingly taken from the black radical press, thus it is material which is directly agitational in form, attempting to carve an alternative public sphere in which to enunciate a very specific race/class anti-colonial politics.

There is a myriad of other sources in which to trace the emergence of this distinctive internationalist discourse – FBI files, internal Party bulletins, speeches, letters, memoirs – yet this volume is concerned almost exclusively with the newspapers and magazines of the period. This is not because the rich material in other sources is 'lesser' in investigating the unique anti-colonial politics of this period. Indeed, many recent important studies have mined all these sources to create a powerful intervention into the disputed relationship between black activists in the USA and the Left (see Works Cited and Further Reading). The focus in this instance is on the radical press of the period because here is located the attempt to rally a particular constituency, African Americans, to an internationalist, often class-based, vision of anti-colonial politics. Thus the newspapers and magazines speak on a variety of registers which are attuned to the materialities and lived experiences of black Americans and concurrently are attempting to forge a new race-conscious anti-colonial politics. This imbues these writings with a rich polemical and illustrative intent which is cognisant of reaching its intended audience in both familiar and unfamiliar ways.

This was a vital counter public sphere and the manner in which the readership was addressed is of huge importance to this collection. The NAACP's more 'respectable' *The Crisis* (1910–present), for example, is very different in tone to Garvey's *Negro World*, or indeed to Briggs's *The Crusader* and Owens and Randolph's *The Messenger*. In their explicit appeal to 'ordinary' African Americans the latter two publications' signature declamatory style ensured that the local experiences of racism are a constant referent in relation to wider struggles of anti-colonialism. The attempt here was actively to promote the model of a new black, political subject whose agency resides not in his status but in his willingness to fight.

On the face of it *The Crisis* was addressing a different readership, as the more 'scholarly' tone and the trumpeting of 'Negro successes' in the world of business suggests. However, as Barbara Foley has noted in relation to *The Crisis*, it 'also gave more than sporadic voice to radical perspectives' (Foley 2008: 25). Indeed, one could argue that the nature of American racism during this period demanded angry and immoderate responses; this is most obvious in *The Crisis* in relation to its central commitment to anti-lynching campaigns. There is a lot of cross-referencing in these publications, suggestive of a cross-readership or at the very least a favourably imagined cross-readership.

Not all of the texts here are written by African Americans, indeed the influence of Caribbean radicals on African American politics is key to this period. Rather these are texts written by black radicals living in the USA during this period and primarily addressing their work to an African American readership. There are two caveats here. Whilst *Negro Worker* was certainly read by African Americans it is addressing a wider black constituency. Yet, both Padmore and William Patterson's (1891–1980) membership of the CPUSA as their entry into the world of anti-colonial politics is significant, and any study interested in anti-colonial politics of the period could not neglect this important publication. There are also articles included here by black radicals who are addressing a Communist/Socialist audience which may or may not be of African descent. These are not included for 'contrast', the articles chosen for this collection are those which best give voice to the politics of these activists in the period and thus include some seminal essays that appeared in journals for which an anti-racist understanding of the world was paramount to its wider politics of liberation.

Hubert Harrison, Cyril Briggs, A. Philip Randolph, Louise Thompson, W. E. B. Du Bois, George Padmore, and the variety of other writers and activists who make up this collection have quite different styles of writing and often have quite divergent if not opposing responses to the events of the period. Some of these writers are Socialists, some Communists, some neither. Some of these writers remained within the Communist or Socialist movements and some broke bitterly from the organisations of the Left. The wider politics of the impact of Stalinist imperatives can be gleaned in some of this material, especially in relation to George Padmore's break with communism. That history however does not form the basis of this introduction precisely because the framework to understanding this form of anti-colonial politics has too often been one which reads these texts as naive examples of communist 'manipulation' of black politics. The historical trajectory of this volume is precisely one which insists on a framework in which black agency is central to these politics. The articles collected here demonstrate the forging of an internationalist anti-colonialism which emerges in very specific historical contexts and enjoys a complicated relationship with Communist and Socialist politics. Yet the genesis of these politics emerge outside of the organised local Left and are imbued with enthusiastic support for the world-changing revolution in Russia and the implications of that revolution for a new anti-imperialism. The defeat of that promise in the decades that followed should not delimit our readings of these texts. The aim here is to place them in their historical context and to revisit their eclectic and compelling arguments in the context of a commitment to anti-racist, anti-colonialism which sought to broaden the boundaries of an understanding of what black freedom could mean.

Works Cited

Adi, Hakim (2013), *Pan-Africanism and Communism: The Communist International, Africa and the Diaspora 1919–1939*, Trenton, NJ: Africa World Press.

Collum, Danny Duncan and Victor A. Berch (1992), *African Americans in the Spanish Civil War: 'This Ain't Ethiopia, but It'll Do'*, New York: Hall.

Draper, Theodore (1957), *The Roots of American Communism*, New York: Viking Press.

Edwards, Brent Hayes (2003), *The Practice of Diaspora: Literature, Translation, and the Rise of Black Internationalism*, Cambridge, MA: Harvard University Press.

Foley, Barbara (2008), *Spectres of 1919: Class and Nation in the Making of the New Negro*, Chicago: University of Illinois Press.

Foner, Philip (1974), *Organised Labour and the Black Worker*, New York: Praeger.

Foner, Philip (ed.) (1998), *Paul Robeson Speaks: Writings, Speeches, Interviews, 1918–74*, New York: Citadel Press

Gilmore, Glenda Elizabeth (2008), *Defying Dixie: The Radical Roots of Civil Rights (1919–1950)*, New York: W.W. Norton & Company.

Garvey, Amy Jacques (1967), *The Philosophy and Opinions of Marcus Garvey*, Volume 1, London: Frank Cass & Co.

Grant, Colin (2009), *The Negro with the Hat: Marcus Garvey*, London: Vintage.
Hill, Robert (1987), 'Racial and Radical: Cyril V. Briggs, *The Crusader Magazine* and the African Blood Brotherhood 1918–1922', in Robert Hill (ed.), *The Crusader*, New York: Garland.
James, C. L. R. (1937), *World Revolution 1917–1936: The Rise and Fall of the Communist International*, London: Martin Secker & Warburg.
James, Winston (1998), *Holding Aloft the Banner of Ethiopia: Caribbean Radicalism in Early Twentieth-Century America: 1900–1932*, London: Verso.
Klehr, Harvey (1984), *The Heyday of American Communism*, New York: Basic Books.
Kornweibel, Theodore (1999), *Seeing Red: Federal Campaigns Against Black Militancy, 1919–1925*, Bloomington, IN: Indiana University Press.
Lenin, V. I. (1965) *Collected Works*, Volume 31, Moscow: Progress Publishers.
Makalani, Minkah (2011), *In the Cause of Freedom: Radical Black Internationalism from Harlem to London, 1917–1939*, Chapel Hill, NC: University of North Carolina Press.
McDuffie, Erik S. (2011), *Sojourning For Freedom: Black Women, American Communism and the Making of Black Left Feminism*, Durham, NC, and London: Duke University Press.
Naison, Mark (1985), *Communists in Harlem during the Depression*, New York: Grove Press.
Perry, Jeffrey B. (ed.) (2001), *A Hubert Harrison Reader*, Middletown, CT: Wesleyan University Press.
Robinson, Cedric J. (1983) *Black Marxism*, London: Zed Books.
Rosenhaft, Eve (1983), *Beating the Fascists? The German Communists and Political Violence, 1929–1933*, Cambridge: Cambridge University Press.
Spero, Sterling and Harris, Abraham (1968), *The Black Worker*, New York: Atheneum.
Stephens, Michelle (2005), *The Black Empire: The Masculine Global Imaginary of Caribbean Intellectuals in the United States 1914–1962*, Durham, NC, and London: Duke University Press.
Tuttle, William M. (1996), *Race Riot: Chicago in the Red Summer of 1919*, Chicago and Urbana-Champaign: University of Illinois Press.
Weiss, Holger (2013), *Framing a Radical African Atlantic*, Leiden: Brill.
Williams, Chad L. (2007), 'Vanguards of the New Negro: African American Veterans and Post-World War I Racial Militancy', *The Journal of African American History*, 92 (3) (summer), 347–70.
Zumoff, Jacob (2014), *The Communist International and US Communism, 1919–1929*, Leiden: Brill.

Further Reading

Adi, Hakim (2013), *Pan-Africanism and Communism: The Communist International, Africa and the Diaspora 1919–1939*, Trenton, NJ: Africa World Press. A meticulous study of the International Trade Union Committee of Negro Workers (ITUCNW), with a particular focus on Comintern archival sources.
Dawhare, Anthony (2003), *Nationalism, Marxism, and African American Literature between the Wars*, Jackson, MS: University Press of Mississippi. A polemical and convincing reading of African American literature and its relationship to Marxism.
Derrick, Jonathan (2008), *Africa's Agitators: Militant Anti-Colonialism in Africa and the West, 1918–1939*, London: Hurst & Company. A study of both

anglophone and francophone anti-colonial writings which modulates the influence of communism on black internationalism of the period.

Edwards, Brent Hayes (2003), *The Practice of Diaspora: Literature, Translation, and the Rise of Black Internationalism*, Cambridge, MA: Harvard University Press. A transcontinental investigation of the internationalist consciousness of the African diaspora, with a particular engagement with literary and textual expressions of solidarity and difference.

Foley, Barbara (2008), *Spectres of 1919: Class and Nation in the Making of the New Negro*, Chicago: University of Illinois Press. A spirited rereading of the politics of the New Negro movement.

Gilmore, Glenda Elizabeth (2008), *Defying Dixie: The Radical Roots of Civil Rights: 1919–1950*, New York: W.W. Norton & Company. An important historical investigation of the 'long civil rights movement' which argues that African American activists of the earlier period laid the ground for the movements of the 1960s.

James, Winston (1998), *Holding Aloft the Banner of Ethiopia: Caribbean Radicalism in Early Twentieth-Century America: 1900–1932*, London: Verso. A seminal historical investigation of the impact of Caribbean migrants on black radical politics in the USA. James provides essential detail of the lives and politics of a variety of pan-Africanist, Communist and Socialist migrants.

Kelley, Robin (1990), *Hammer and Hoe: Alabama Communists during the Great Depression*, Chapel Hill, NC: University of North Carolina Press. Seminal historical text in which African Americans understood Socialist politics through the prism of their own cultural experiences.

McDuffie, Erik S. (2011), *Sojourning For Freedom: Black Women, American Communism and the Making of Black Left Feminism*, Durham, NC, and London: Duke University Press. A rich excavation of the contributions of an impressive number of female African American Communists and their negotiations with class, race and gender in the USA from the radical early 1920s to the start of the Cold War.

Makalani, Minkah (2011), *In the Cause of Freedom: Radical Black Internationalism from Harlem to London, 1917–1939*, Chapel Hill, NC: University of North Carolina Press. A highly readable and engaging study of the interconnections between African diasporic, Asian and European radicals and how these relationships shaped a transnational politics of dizzying imagination.

Naison, Mark (1985), *Communists in Harlem during the Depression*, New York: Grove Press. A passionate account of Communist activity in Harlem with a particular interest in the cultural sphere.

Solomon, Mark (1998), *The Cry was Unity: Communists and African Americans, 1917–1936*, Jackson, MS: University Press of Mississippi. Meticulous historical investigation of the period which utilises documents from the Russian Center for Preservation and Study of Documents of Recent History (RTsKhIDNI).

Stephens, Michelle (2005), *The Black Empire: The Masculine Global Imaginary of Caribbean Intellectuals in the United States 1914–1962*, Durham, NC: Duke University Press. An extremely engaging interdisciplinary critique of the gendered politics at the centre of the newly imagined transnational subject of the period.

Weiss, Holger (2013), *Framing A Radical African Atlantic*, Leiden: Brill. Maintaining a particular focus on the ITUCNW this book concentrates on black activists within the Communist movements of the period.

Part I
Red, Black and Green: The Emergence of Left Black Radicalism 1917–1929

Chapter 1
Bolshevism

Bolshevism was particularly attractive to many African American activists for a variety of reasons. First and foremost was Lenin's thesis of self-determination for oppressed nations (1916) but also the reputation of the Bolsheviks for defending minorities. As Claude McKay stated in 1921 'Bolshevism . . . has made Russia safe for the Jew . . . It might make these United States safe for the Negro' (*Negro World*, 20 September 1919). The documents presented here articulate a bond between red Russia and black America. Cyril Briggs's article 'Bolshevism's Menace: To Whom and to What?' (1920) encapsulates this sense of solidarity with the Bolsheviks, while Hubert Harrison's 'A New International' (1920) acidly critiques the African American middle class for bearing 'the white man's burden'. The impact of the Bolshevik revolution, understood as an anti-colonial one, is writ large in these writings.

Bolshevism and World Democracy
(Editorial, *The Messenger*, July 1918)

Bolshevism is the Banquo's ghost to Macbeth capitalists of the world whether they inhabit Germany, England, America or Japan. It is a forward of a true world democracy. The Soviets represent the needs and aims of the masses.

Bolshevism has already defied the imperialist vultures to lay their cards of secret diplomacy on the table of justice before the High Court of World Opinion. It has lead the world in making a concrete application of the principle of self-determination of smaller nationalities.

Ukrania, Finland and Persia have been permitted to achieve their own destiny.

A sound and just economic, political and social programme of reconstruction is gradually being adopted.

Bolshevism is not yet one year old in Russia. Russia is still at war with a great nation and is virtually without help from her former allies. One hundred and eighty seven millions of peoples have been delivered from the autocracy of the Czar – a people 85 per cent of whom are illiterate.

Bolshevism has given these peoples a new hope, a new promise, a new ideal – economic and political freedom!

Will Bolshevism succeed? The Tories of England and America asked the same question about the American people after the revolution of 1776. The Bourbons of France doubted the power of the aristocracy – after the revolution of 1789. Governments are living organisms which have structure and function and are governed by the laws of growth. Hence the Russian people must be helped; not hindered, they are still young.

Get out of Russia
(Editorial, *The Messenger*, March 1919)

This is the cry of every lover of liberty and democracy. 'But why,' the doubting Thomases ask, 'should the allied armies come out of Russia?' Have not the financial rulers in the various allied countries loaned millions of dollars to the Russian Czar, that was? Have not the allies 'made the world safe for democracy,' and do not the French, English and American bankers, who are the underwriters of the Russian loans, represent democracy? Besides what right have a people – 180 millions of Russian peasants, oppressed and exploited, for whom the Czar, their erstwhile benefactor, borrowed money in good faith, to repudiate such well approved and accepted capitalist ethical arrangements – debts? Villians! Culprits! Thieves! 'They will reap what they have sown,' says the 'Good Book,' which we capitalists so dearly love.

Again these Russians have no respect whatever for law and order. They preach the doctrines of Bolshevism – the doctrine of human and property destruction. Hence they must be taught a lesson. We must shoot Bolshevism out of them and shoot capitalist democracy into them.

But, happily, none of these things move the Russian people. They have come to learn that most times the very man who cries 'Stop Thief' usually has the loot under his own arm. They have found out that those who have been preaching about democracy the loudest are the most unwilling to extend it to others. They have learnt that the bourgeois democrats neither wanted the Kaiser to rule nor do they want the people of Germany, of Russia or of any other country to rule; and when a severe economic interpretation of the history of the motives of the allied countries, in this war, is made it will be found that the allies consider the rule of Kaiser as the lesser of the two evils.

But even if the allied governments do not defer to the judgment of international justice and immediately withdraw their armies from Russia, it is not improbable that when the armies are withdrawn they will be most effective instruments in the propagation of Bolshevism. And this portentous nightmare of eventually withdrawing armies thoroughly saturated with the virus of real democracy, is the only grounds upon which the allies will entertain any plea of withdrawing the armies from Russia. Self-interest is the only motive which rules the actions of the ruling nations, and it should be the only motive which should rule the actions of the working classes. The international proletariat should concertedly call an international labor strike unless the allied governments immediately withdraw their armies from Russia and also accord the Soviet government a voice at the peace table.

An international strike is the only weapon in the hands of the working people which can force Great Britain, France, America, Italy and Japan to give a seat in the peace conference to the accredited representatives of the Russian people.

Now as after every war in human history, the spirit of reaction gains the ascendency in the victorious countries. The victors are always intoxicated with their power. But just as the Kaiser spoke imperiously, as his fate was being written by the invisible hand of the German revolution, so are the masters – the diplomats of the ruling governments today, thoughtlessly treading upon the crater of an international social volcano, whose molten lava of class passions threaten to drench the land in blood: to wash away the dikes of our false civilization; to sweep on its course the derelict and hypocritical kings of capitalism, and to erect upon the ruins thereof a new civilization, a new social order, a true international peoples' republic – a 'world Soviet.'

It will be the blackest of all international crimes in the history of mankind if the world condones any 'black hand' movement to blackjack the Russian revolution by military occupation and denying the Soviet government a voice in the peace conference. It was Russia who stayed the red and reeking hand of German militarism with her millions of men, while the allies were mobilizing their man power and munition power.

The vast problem of reorganizing the social machinery of 180 millions of peoples just released from the clutches of the worst despotism in history, scattered over an area comprising one sixth of the known land of the world, is no child's play. Order cannot be secured within the short period of a year in Russia any more than it was secured in American after the revolt of 1776 or in France after the revolution of 1789. America was even torn by a Civil War for four years after she was supposed to have attained national unity. No-one interfered then in the internal affairs of America. Why, then, do the so-called liberals and bourgeois democrats desire to interfere in the internal affairs of Russia now? This is the most significant experiment in the international laboratory of world politics, sociology and economics. If allowed to pursue its natural course unhindered, the science of government will be immeasurably enriched by the legislative and administrative invention which shall emerge out of the process. Again we demand that the allies get out of Russia!

The Bolsheviki
(*The Crusader*, May 1919)

'They have turned earth upside down,'
    Says the foe;
They have come to bring our town
    Wreck and woe.'
To this never ending cry
Boldly hear we make reply;
    Yea and no.

Upside down the world has lain
    Many a year;
We to turn it back again
    Now appear.
Will ye, nill ye, ye will do
What at last no man shall rue;
Have no fear.
    Anonymous

We Want More Bolshevik Patriotism
(Editorial, *The Messenger*, May/June 1919)

We want more Bolshevik patriotism in this country. We want a patriotism which springs from the breast of the people. We want a patriotism to attract rather than coerce. We want a patriotism where the people are more articulate and the profiteers less articulate. We want a patriotism which is proclaimed by the teeming millions and not by the scheming few who would make millions of dollars. We want a patriotism which thinks more of the children than of the fathers: which loves posterity more than ancestry. We want a simple patriotism which spontaneously emanates from the bosom of the masses because they love the country, and not a "hat waving" patriotism, based upon fear of punishment. We want more patriotism which recognized the substance of justice, fair play and public service, and not a sullen, reluctant form of patriotism which proclaims its love under the lash of pressure. We need more patriotism which loves the country because the country accords to all a chance – the humble and the high, the lowly and the lordly, the nobility and the poor ability, the strong and the weak, the rich and the poor. We want more patriotism which gives unselfish service – popular service and not profiteering service.

We want no landless patriots in a country of almost unlimited lands. We want no patriot talking about "my country," not a foot of whose land he owns. We want a patriotism which practices that "Any man who protects the country's flag shall be protected by that flag." We want a patriotism not streaked with race, color, or sex lines.

We want a patriotism represented by a flag so red that it symbolizes truly the oneness of blood running through each one of our veins.

We want more patriotism which surges with turbulent unrest while men – black or white – are lynched in this land. We want more patriotism which makes us hungry while our fellowmen are without food. We want more patriotism which produces chills while our fellowmen are cold. We want no black and white patriotism which demands separate camps, separate ships and separate oceans to travel on.

What we really need is a patriotism of liberty, justice and joy. That is Bolshevik patriotism and we want more of that brand in the United States.

Make their Cause your Own
(Editorial, *The Crusader*, July 1919)

The Soviet Government of Russia is the only government outside of our own Africa and democratic South America in which a Negro occupies a high and responsible position. And Soviet Russia has neither Negro population nor Negro 'colonies'.

The New York Call, a Socialist news-paper, is the only daily paper in New York City which is perpetually and honestly concerned about the Negro and which nearly every day comments upon his wrongs and calls the nation to task for their existence.

The Socialist Party is the only Party in the United States that dared to place an anti-lynching plank in its national platform: the only party that demanded honest self-determination for the African peoples and the end of disfranchisement in the southern states of the United States.

No race has less of the idle non-producing rich than the Negro race.

No race would be more greatly benefited proletariat than the Negro race, which is essentially a race of workers and producers.

With no race are the interests of Labor so clearly identified with racial interests as in the case of the Negro race.

No race would be more greatly benefitted by the triumph of Labor and the destruction of parasitic Capital Civilization with its Imperialism incubus that is squeezing the life-blood out of millions of our race in Africa and the islands of the sea, than the Negro race.

Is the lesson clear?

We need not fight alone if we breast the sea upon the irresistible tide of liberalism that is at present shaping the world.

Socialism the Negro's Hope
by W. A. Domingo[1] *Editor of the Negro World*
(*The Messenger*, July 1919)

It is a regrettable and disconcerting anomaly that, despite their situation as the economic, political and social door mat of the world, Negroes do not embrace the philosophy of socialism, and in greater numbers than they now do. It is an anomaly because it is reasonable to expect those who are lowest down to be the ones who would most quickly comprehend the need for a change in their status and welcome any doctrine which holds forth any hope of human elevation. In matters of religion they respond and react logically and naturally enough, for to them, the religion of Christ, the lowly Nazarene, brings definite assurance of surcease from earthly pains and the hope of celestial readjustment of mundane equalities. Their acceptance of the Christian religion with its present day emphasis upon an after-life enjoyment of the good things denied them on the earth is conclusive proof of their dissatisfaction with their present lot, and is an earnest of their susceptibility to Socialism,

---

[1] W. A. Domingo emigrated to the USA from Jamaica in 1910. He had worked with Garvey in Jamaica, and was the first editor of *Negro World* which he edited from August 1918–July 1919. Domingo turned away from Garveyism due to his left-wing politics, and associated himself with the Socialist Party and then the ABB.

which intends to do for human beings what Christianity promises to do for them in less material regions.

That they and all oppressed dark peoples will be the greatest beneficiaries in a socialist world has not been sufficiently emphasized by Socialist propaganda among Negroes.

Perhaps this is not clearly understood, but a little examination of the facts will prove this to be the case.

Throughout the world Negroes occupy a position of absolute inferiority to the white race. This is true whether they are black Frenchmen, black Englishmen, black Belgians or black Americans.

As between themselves and the masses of white proletarians their lives are more circumscribed, their ambition is more limited and their opportunities for the enjoyment of liberty and happiness more restricted. White workingmen of England who are Socialists are immeasurably the political and social superiors of the average Negro in the West Indies or Africa; white workingmen of France, who are Socialists are unquestionably the political and social superiors of Senegalese and Madagascan Negroes; white workingmen of the United States who are Socialists are indisputably the social and political superiors of the millions of Negroes below the Mason and Dixon line; yet despite their relative and absolute superiority these white workers are fighting for a world freed from oppression and exploitation, whilst Negroes who are oppressed cling to past and present economic ideals with the desperation of a drowning man.

Socialism as an economic doctrine is merely the pure Christianity preached by Jesus, and practiced by the early Christians adapted to the more complex conditions of modern life. It makes no distinction as to race, nationality or creed, but like Jesus it says "Come unto me all ye who are weary and heavy laden and I will give you rest." It is to procure that rest that millions of oppressed peoples are flocking to the scarlet banner of international Socialism.

So far, although having greater need for its equalizing principles than white workingmen, Negroes have been slow to realize what has already dawned upon nearly every other oppressed people: That Socialism is their only hope.

The 384,000,000 natives of India groaning under the exploitation of the handful of English manufacturers, merchants and officials who profit out of their labor are turning from Lloyd George and the capitalistic Liberal Party to Robert Smillie, the Socialist and the Independent Labor Party. The 4,000,000 Irish who suffer national strangulation at the hands of British industrialists and militarists have turned to the

Socialists of England for relief besides becoming Socialists themselves. The Egyptians who are of Negro admixture being convinced that their only hope for freedom from British exploitation is in international Socialism are uniting forces with British Socialists and organized labor. In fact, every oppressed group of the world is today turning from Clemenceau, Lloyd George and Wilson to the citadel of Socialism, Moscow. In this they are all in advance of Western Negroes with the exception of little groups in the United States and a relatively well organized group in the Island of Trinidad, British West Indies.

Because of ignorant and unscrupulous leadership, Negroes are influenced to give their support to those institutions which oppress them, but if they would only do a little independent thinking without the aid of preacher, politician or press they would quickly realize that the very men like Thomas Dixon, author of "The Clansman," Senators Hoke Smith of Georgia and Overman of North Carolina, who are fighting Socialism or as they maliciously call it Bolshevism are the same men who exhaust every unfair means to vilify, oppress and oppose Negroes. If anything should commend Socialism to Negroes, nothing can do so more eloquently than the attitude and opinions of its most influential opponents toward people who are not white.

On the other hand, the foremost exponents of Socialism in Europe and America are characterized by the broadness of their vision towards all oppressed humanity. It was the Socialist Vandervelde of Belgium, who protested against the Congo atrocities practiced upon Negroes; it was the late Keir Hardie and Philip Snowdon of England, who condemned British rule in Egypt; and in the United States it was the Socialist, Eugene V. Debs,[2] who refused to speak in Southern halls from which Negroes were excluded. Today, it is the revolutionary Socialist, Lenin, who analyzed the infamous League of Nations and exposed its true character; it is he as leader of the Communist Congress at Moscow, who sent out the proclamation: "Slaves of the colonies in Africa and Asia! The hour of proletarian dictatorship in Europe will he the hour of your release!"

---

[2] Eugene V. Debs (1855–1926) Radical Socialist, one of the founding members of the Industrial Workers of the World (Wobblies) and later leader of the Socialist Party.

Did Bolshevism Stop Race Riots in Russia
(By W. A. Domingo, *The Messenger*, September 1919)

But for the fact that Pushkin,[3] Russia's greatest poet, was of Negro descent and the further fact that his descendants are part of the now deposed royalty of that great country, the majority of Negroes have little knowledge of and still less interest in Russia. Because of its rigorous climate and its removal from close and easy contact with the rest of the world, particularly the tropics, few Negroes have emigrated to or travelled in Russia. Those who have gone there, went as sailors, body servants or theatrical performers.

The great war did more to familiarize the minds of the outside world with Russian affairs than all the lectures, histories and geographies had ever accomplished. This is also true of Negroes. They, like the rest of mankind, viewed with astonishment the bewildering military successes and reverses of Russia in the war which finally terminated in the destruction of the mightiest autocracy in world and the rise of the proletariat – the common working people – into power. To the average Negro these various historical events have no greater significance than as passing phases of human conduct. Few of them are able to discover any connection between themselves – their future – and the new society that is slowly but surely emerging from the alleged chaotic social and industrial conditions of Russia. To them and naturally so, it is a very far cry from Alabama to Turkestan, from the West Indies to Archangel and from Sierra Leone to Moscow.

The distances are too great and the connections seemingly nebulous. But despite this there is a great connection between the future of the Negro race the world over and the success of the theories – now under trial in Russia – which are collectively known as Bolshevism.

Comparing Old Russia with the countries bent on the destruction of Soviet Russia it will be noticed that they stood for many things in common – things that befitted doing harm to "backward peoples" and subject races.

England, France, Portugal, Belgium and the United States are countries with large Negro and other subject races under their control who are varyingly exploited economically, ostracized socially and powerless

---

[3] The Russian writer Alexander Pushkin (1799–1837) is of particular interest to African Americans in this period owing to his slave ancestry; his great-grandfather was brought as a slave to Russia from Cameroon as a gift to Peter the Great.

politically. Czarist Russia resembled those countries in that the Empire was a congeries of various subject races, such as Jews, Tartars, Kalmuks, Poles, Armenians and Lithuanians, who were disenfranchised, oppressed and murdered. When Czardom was overthrown and Bolshevism was established the first thing done by the new government was to proclaim the absolute equality of all races that occupied that vast territory. This equality was not theoretical, but was made practical from the very start. As a result Trotsky, a Jew, became Minister of War and Karl Peters, a Lett,[4] was made a Commissar.

So completely devoted to their ideals of human equality and justice were the Bolsheviki that they immediately renounced sovereignty over the portion of Persia, a dark-skinned country, that had been occupied by Russia in agreement with Great Britain in 1906. Be it noted that Great Britain, although ostensibly fighting for democracy and the rights of small nations, continued to occupy its portion of Persia and vigorously protested against the noble act of national restitution done by Soviet Russia.

As if to show the Negro race that justice and equality are only possible under Bolshevism, an American Negro named Gordon, who had gone to Russia with the American Ambassador to occupy the dignified position of doorkeeper, became converted to Bolshevism and was elected to a high official position in one of the Russian Committees. This was reported in the *World's Work* Magazine for October, 1918, and later confirmed by the testimony given by the Rev. George Simons of Petrograd before the Overman Congressional committee investigating Bolshevism in America. A cynic has said that perhaps the deposition of Gordon from his exalted position is the real reason why President Wilson, a Southerner, is waging war on Russia without a formal declaration of war by Congress.

Perhaps the greatest analogy between Russia and the United States can be found in the former's treatment of Jews and in the latter's treatment of Negroes. Under the autocratic Czar Jews were treated in very much the same manner as Negroes are treated in the democratic United States. They had no political rights, they were segregated within the Pale, and the avenues of opportunity were closed to them. Life to them was merely a cycle of sorrow, oppression and despair. Just as American Negroes have had their Atlanta, East St. Louis, Washington and Chicago, so had the Jews of Russia their Kishineff and other pogroms.[5] Just as Negro

---

[4] Lett – a member of a Baltic people constituting the main population of Latvia.

[5] In 1903 and 1905 anti-Semitic pogroms occurred in Kishinev where up to seventy Jews were killed.

loyalty in wars has proven futile as a deterrent or preventative of lynch law and oppression so did Jewish fealty to Russia prove non-effective in abating their persecution and suffering.

However, the great revolution came and the Czar and the newspapers that lied about Jews, priests who condoned the persecution of a weaker race and military officers who inflamed the blood lust of the common soldiers, were swept out of power.

In their place was established a government led by men who had suffered the scorn of the high and the abuse of the lowly, men who could understand and appreciate the real causes of Jewish oppression. One of the first things that the new government did was sternly to suppress and punish those of the old regime who retained the old psychology of race hatred if caught inciting the people to start pogroms – race riots – against Jews. After a few executions of lynchers and race-rioters the Bolshevik government succeeded in making Soviet Russia unsafe for mobocrats, but safe for Jews and other oppressed racial minorities.

According to latest, reliable reports, such as those of Isaac Don Levine of the *New York Evening Globe*, Moscow and Petrograd are safer for all their population – Jew, Gentile, and Infidel – than Chicago and Washington have recently been for their black inhabitants. On the other hand, in Poland, where Bolshevism does not hold sway, an American Commission is at present investigating the recent massacre of Jews in that recently reconstructed and freed country. In Siberia, under Kolchack,[6] the Jewish population see their daughters raped and men slain by brutal soldiers who are egged on by corrupt and fanatical priests and anti-Bolshevists. In Southern Russia, the soldiers of General Gregorieff, who, with the support of the Allies, is redeeming Holy Russia (?) from "barbarism," have treated Odessa to a saturnalia of Jewish blood while the following clipping speaks for itself as to conditions in the Ukraine.[7]

"The anti-Bolshevik Yiddish 'Day' of New York, has the following cablegram from its European correspondent, N. Shifrin, under date of July 11th: "Persons who have arrived in Copenhagen tell about the cruelties of Petlura's[8] soldiers of which they have been eye-witnesses. At the station Tchudnovolinsk, 36 Jews were killed in one car. In Dubno,

---

[6] Alexander Kolchak (1874–1920) was one of the main military leaders of the counter-revolutionary White Russian forces during the civil war of 1917–1921.

[7] General Gregorieff (DOB unknown–1919) of the White Army presided over a massacre of the Jewish quarter in Odessa in 1919.

[8] Symon Petliura (1879–1926), Ukranian nationalist who was ascribed responsibility for a series of pogroms in Ukraine between 1918–1920.

they saw 18 Jews executed in the market place. In Rovno and Lutnik they find daily two or three Jews murdered in their houses. Under the Ukrainian Soviet government no pogroms have occurred anywhere."

The lesson to be gained from these numerous examples is that racial oppression in its various forms of disfranchisement, lynching and mob murder prevails in non-Bolshevik Russia but has been abolished in the territory dominated by Lenin and his followers. The Allies who are today fighting Soviet Russia in the name of freedom, have colonies which they exploit and sections of their own countries in which they at times permit the unrestrained passions of white majorities to run riot upon Negro minorities. In contrast to this racial failure on the part of the self-righteous Allies and non-Bolshevik governments to protect small racial groups it is noticeable that all minorities are successfully protected in Soviet Russia.

The question naturally arises: Will Bolshevism accomplish the full freedom of Africa, colonies in which Negroes are in the majority, and promote human tolerance and happiness in the United States by the eradication of the causes of such disgraceful occurrences as the Washington and Chicago race riots? The answer is deducible from the analogy of Soviet Russia, a country in which dozens of racial and lingual types have settled their many differences and found a common meeting ground, a country, which no longer oppresses colonies, a country from which the lynch rope is banished and in which racial tolerance and peace now exist.

Bolshevist!!!
(Editorial, *The Crusader*, October 1919)

Bolshevist is an epithet that present-day reactionaries delight to fling around loosely against those who insist on thinking for themselves and on agitating for their rights. We do not know exactly what the reactionaries desire to convey by the term – we do not think they know themselves. However, if as appears by its frequent use against those who are agitating in the people's interests and for justice for the oppressed, the term is intended to cover those "bad agitators," who are not content that the people shall forever be enslaved in the clutches of the cut-throat child-exploiting, capitalist-imperialist crew, than assuredly we are Bolshevists. This epithet nor any other holds any terrors for us. If to fight for one's rights is to be Bolshevists then we are Bolshevists and let them make the most of it!

And for the further information of the asses who use the term so loosely we will make the statement that we would not for a moment hesitate to ally ourselves with any group, if by such an alliance we could compass the liberation of our race and redemption of our fatherland. A man pressed to earth by another with murderous intent is not under any obligation to choose his weapons. He would be a fool if he did not use any or whatever weapon was within his reach. Self preservation is the first law of human nature.

Bolshevism and Race Prejudice
(Editorial, *The Crusader*, December 1919)

Many of our editors and cartoonists are showing an inclination to couple Bolshevism with race prejudice.

On a basis of hard, cold facts nothing could be farther from the truth. The only pogroms against the Jewish race being committed in Russia today are occurring outside of Soviet Russia, in the territories jointly controlled by Denikin[9] and the Holy Allies and by Kolchak and the Holy Allies and by the said Holy Allies and their minor tools. In Soviet Russia pogroms are no more because, for one thing, there are no reactionary capitalist influences at work to pit worker against worker and race against race. In America where these influences are still in operation race riots and pogroms are the rule rather than the exception. In Soviet Russia all men are equal, of whatever race, and nearly all races are represented in high offices, the principle of merit ruling rather than color of skin or racial origin and the Negro race, too, although almost nil in point of population, comes in for such representation as was related by a disgusted citizen of these *truly y'know* democratic United States, who threw up his hands in holy terror at the spectacle of a Negro in high office and rushed back to this land of the *truly y'know* brave and the free to relate with hot resentment to his almost as hotly resenting white fellow citizens the shocking heresy on the part of Russia in that she recognized the Negro as a Man.

That Negro editors and cartoonists should fall for the lies about Soviet Russia put out by the white capitalist press is all the more surprising when it is considered that these same Negro cartoonists and editors are members of a race even more viciously lied about by the same white capitalist press. Surely with our own experience in mind, we should be

---
[9] Anton Denikin (1872–1947) leading general in the White Army.

wary about swallowing, hook, sinker and all, all they say about others to whom they are also opposed.

Bolshevism's Menace: To Whom and To What?
(By Cyril Briggs, *The Crusader*, February 1920)

Of a truth, Bolshevism is a menace. That much is conceded alike by friend, foe and neutral. That is the chief motif of the tune that is constantly dinned into the ears of the Negro and the world in general.

But just whom and what does Bolshevism menace? Is it not vital that we should know exactly against whom and what is directed this alleged threat of Bolshevism? Against the Negro and rest of the workers, or against those who are exploiting the workers of the world and robbing the Negro group of both its labor and of its fatherland? If against us, should we not fight it, and if against the imperialist thieves of Europe, who are our foes, should we not be glad of its spread?

England and France and the rest of the piratical crew claim that Bolshevism is a menace to "democracy." What is "democracy"? The "democracy" in which an autocratic minority living in France and England rule and oppress "subject peoples" against their known wishes and legitimate aspirations and solely for the benefit of home industries and manufacturers? The "democracy" which imposes its will upon weaker peoples by force and murders them when this alien superimposed will is questioned, as "democratic" England is doing today in Egypt, India, Persia, Mesopotamia, the West Indies and many other unfortunate countries, as "democratic" France is now doing in Morocco, West Africa and Indo-China? The "democracy" which exploits, under the murderous capitalist system, its own people, its weak women and young children? Is this the "democracy" to which the spread of Bolshevism is a menace? Then may God advance the spread of Bolshevism throughout Europe, Asia and Africa and in every country where oppression stalks!

On the other hand what is Bolshevism? Regarding it there are myriad lies, tales and rumors, but from what one can deduct from the testimony of impartial witnesses like Col. Robins and Mr. Bullitt[10] it appears to be a system of government of the people by the people and for the people,

---

[10] Raymond Robins (1873–1954) headed the American Red Cross expedition to Russia in 1917 and published his co-written pamphlet *On Behalf of Russia: An Open Letter to America* in 1918. William C. Bullitt (1891–1967) was a diplomat and journalist

and under which the resources of the country, like the mines, the coal fields and water power, are owned and operated as they ought to be, by the State. Under Bolshevism all persons are producers. There are no classes. All are workers. We are told that Bolshevism's success in forcing the parasites to work lies in the fact that preference in rationing is given, and rightly, to those who produce, after, of course, the wants of the mothers, children and sick have been attended to. But this is the domestic side of Bolshevism and while a study of this side will do much to explain the phenomena now taking place in Russia, it is in the international side in which we are especially interested. What is Russian Bolshevism's attitude toward the people of other countries, especially oppressed people like the Africans, Indians, and Irish?

Bolshevism in its international phase is feared by the capitalist-imperialist powers even more than they fear Bolshevism in its domestic operations.

Bolshevism, from the international stand-point is totally different from, and wholly opposed to imperialism. In fact, one of the first acts of Soviet Russia was the renunciation of the imperialist claims of Czarist Russia on the territory and destiny of the people of Persia, thus repudiating the part played by old Russia and Great Britain in the strangling of Persia. Soviet Russia has gladly and promptly recognized the right of self-determination of the peoples of Finland, Poland, the Ukraine and other parts of the former Russian Empire. The right to self-determination of even certain weak and so called "backward" peoples in Asiatic Russia has been recognized by the Bolshevists.

Bolshevism so far, then, is in direct opposition and contradiction of the "principles" of "democracy" as those principles are applied by England and India, Africa, Ireland, and elsewhere, and by France in Africa and Indo-China. And it is to these "principles" to this "democracy," that Bolshevism is a menace. Like Wilson's mistake in talking about the rights of "peoples great and small," Bolshevism is setting a bad example to the enslaved populations under British and French rule. It is putting ideas extremely injurious to the masters in the heads of the African, Indian and Irish peoples. That Bolshevism is a direct menace (and is seen as such) to the lying wickedness of *European eminent domain* under guise of carrying "the white man's burden," is demonstrated by the flowing statement from a capitalist source:

"and the triumph of Russian Bolshevism, as now constituted, means

---

who went on a mission to Soviet Russia to negotiate diplomatic relations with the USA and reported positively on Bolshevik Russia in 1919.

the victory of the doctrine and their allies, the I.W.W. in America, and the destruction of Great Britain's power in India, in all other parts of Asia and in the Dark Continent."

If Bolshevism will free the "subject races," what should be the attitude of these races towards Bolshevism?

The New York Sun, in an editorial comment on the overwhelming defeat of Kolchak, Denikin and other anti-Bolshevists, also lets the cat out of the bag in these two paragraphs:

"And now so Lenin and his disciples are turning their faces eastword as to the land of promise. Mohammedan hostility against the European rulers that hold so much of Islam in bondage is to be the great means of spreading Bolshevism throughout Asia.

"Already Great Britain becomes anxious. She realizes that the new Russia offers a menace to her power in the East not less than that of the former Czar. But what means she will take to prevent the threatened overflow of radicalism form the north into Persia and India remains to be seen. That she must act at once, however is becoming evident to all."

And in these confessions and indiscreet comments of the capitalist press, in this anxiety of the chief enslaving powers, we have the answer and the truth as to who and what Bolshevism means.

Bolshevism in Barbados
(By Hubert Harrison,[11] from *When Africa Awakes*, 1920[12])

Among the newspapers in Barbados there is a charming old lady by the name of the *Barbados Standard*. From time to time this faded creature gets worried about the signs of awakening observable in those Negroes who happen to be living in the twentieth century. Then she shakes and shivers, throws a few fits, froths at the mouth, and, spasmodically flapping her arms, yells to all and sundry that there is "Bolshevism among Negroes."

Recently this stupid old thing and its congeners have discovered evidences of a Bolshevist R-r-r-revolution in Trinidad, and, presumptively,

---

[11] Hubert Harrison (1883–1927), came to New York from St Croix in 1900. He was an extremely influential early black Socialist who as both an orator and a writer consistently pointed to the necessity of placing race at the centre of class politics. As well as an intermittent member of the Socialist Party he was also an activist within the Industrial Workers of The World (Wobblies).

[12] *When Africa Awakes* (1920) is a collection of Harrison's speeches and articles.

all over the British West Indies. Now the specter which these fools fear is nothing but the shadow cast by the dark body of their own system of stiff-necked pride, stark stupidity and stubborn injustice whenever the sun of civic righteousness rises above the horizon of sloth and ignorance. But, like fools afraid of their own shadows, they point at the thing for which they alone are responsible and shriek for salvation.

We shouldn't care to suggest to them that to lie down and die would be one good way to avoid these fearful shadows, because we see the possibility of another way. Let them resolve that they will cease making a lie of every promise of liberty, democracy and self determination that they frantically made for 1914–19. Let the white Englishman learn that justice exists not only for white Englishmen, but for all men. Let him get off the black man's back, stand out of the black man's light, play the game as it should be played, and he will find very little need for wasting tons of print paper and thousands of pounds in a crusade against the specter of Bolshevism.

Everywhere Bolshevism Brings Terror to the Heart of Imperialism
(By W. A. Domingo, *The Emancipator*, 13 March 1920)

Everywhere Bolshevism brings terror to the heart of Imperialism, secret diplomacy, hypocrisy and oppression, and yet, the chieftains of this liberating doctrine are afraid of some of the very races whom they would free.

This is the great paradox – the great tragedy, some of the very Indians and negroes are the potential hangmen of their only disinterested friend – Soviet Russia.

It is not idle fear that Trotsky voices. It is easy for propaganda to reach a literate people; but it is a tremendously more difficult task for it to reach an illiterate people. Poland and Romania illustrate this.

However, there are signs of negro awakening. All over the West Indies there are strikes and unrest; in South Africa, benighted and oppressed land, 40,000 natives are on strike, and two colored delegates to a labor conference in Johannesburg have been hailed as comrades and brothers. One of them even seconded a motion to support Soviet Russia to the limit. Social equality was also recognized as a prerequisite to industrial unity and racial harmony. The dawn is breaking in Negrodom.

Black soldiers from the West Indies, South Africa and a certain self-righteous republic, imbued with the spirit of the New Negro will not be willing tools of those who now rule Egypt, India, the West Indies, Africa and Arkansas with machine guns in the destruction of the people's non-imperialist government of Russia.

We appreciate Trotsky's fear, but feel that it is a little overdrawn. The war has opened the eyes of the darker races a little, they will no longer be their own enslavers. On the Comrades of Trotsky in other lands devolves the duty of paying attention to the 'needs' of the black masses whom the Russian war minister sees as the only possible material in the hands of the imperialists of the world.

A New International
(By Hubert Harrison, *Negro World*, 15 May 1920)

In the eyes of our overlords internationalism is a thing of varying value. When Mr. Morgan wants to float a French or British loan in the United States' when Messrs. Wilson, Clemenceau, Lloyd George and Orlando want to stabilize their joint credit and commerce; when areas like the Belgian Congo are to be handed over to certain rulers without the consent of their inhabitants – then the paeans of praise go up to the god of "internationalism" in the temple of "civilization." But when any portion of the world's disinherited (whether white or black) seeks to join hands with other groups in the same condition, then the lords of misrule denounce the idea of internationalism as anarchy, sedition, Bolshevism and disruptive propaganda.

Why the difference? It is because the international linking up of those peoples is a source of strength to those who are linked up. Naturally, the overlords want to strengthen themselves. And, quite as naturally, they wish to keep their subject masses from strengthening themselves in the same way. Today the great world-majority, made up of black, brown and yellow peoples. Are stretching out their hands to each other and developing a "consciousness of kind" – as Professor Giddings would call it. They are seeking to establish their own centers of diffusion for their own internationalism, and this fact is giving nightmares to Downing street, the Quai d'Orsay and other centers of white capitalist internationalism.

The object of the capitalist international is to unify and standardize the exploitation of black, brown and yellow peoples in such a way that the danger to the exploiting groups of cutting each other's throats over the spoils may be reduced to a minimum. Hence the various agreements, mandates and spheres of influence. Hence the League of Nations, which is notoriously not a league of the white masses, but of their gold-braided governors. Faced by such a tendency on the part of those who bear the white man's burden for what they can get out of it, the darker peoples of the world have begun to realize that their first duty is to themselves. A similarity of suffering is producing in them a similarity of sentiment and the temper of that sentiment is not to be mistaken.

To the white statesmen "civilization" is identical with their own overlordship, with their right and power to dictate to the darker millions what their way of life and of allegiance shall be. To this the aroused sentiment of the world's darker majority demurs. They want to be as free as England, America or France. They do not wish to be "wards of the nations" of Europe any longer. And the problem for the white statement of the future will be to square democracy with the subjection of this dark majority. Can they achieve either horn of this dilemma? Can they effect a junction of the two?

Frankly, we doubt it. Continued suppression may be fraught with consequences disastrous to white overlordship. In any case the tendency toward an international of the darker races cannot be set back. Increasing enlightenment, the spread of technical science, and the recently acquired knowledge of the weak points of white "civilization" gained by the darker peoples during the recent World War, are enough to negative such a supposition. The darker peoples will strive increasingly for their share of sunlight, and if this is what white "civilization" opposes, then white "civilization" is likely to have a hard time of it.

The Negro and Radical Thought
(By W. E. B. Du Bois,[13] *The Crisis*, July 1921)

Mr. Claude McKay, one of the editors of *The Liberator* and a Negro poet of distinction, writes us as follows:

"I am surprised and sorry that in your editorial, "The Drive", published in THE CRISIS for May, you should leap out of your sphere to sneer at the Russian Revolution, the greatest event in the history of humanity; much greater than the French Revolution, which is held up as a wonderful achievement to Negro children and students in white and black schools. For American Negroes the indisputable and outstanding fact of the Russian Revolution is that a mere handful of Jews, much less in ration to the number of Negroes in the American population, have

---

[13] W. E. B. Du Bois (1868–1963) historian, writer, activist and leading pan-Africanist. Du Bois was a towering figure in African American politics, he was the founder of the NAACP journal *The Crisis* in 1910 and its editor until 1933.

attained, through the Revolution, all the political and social rights that were denied to them under the regime of the Czar.

"Although no thinking Negro can deny the great work that the N.A.A.C.P. is doing, it must be admitted that from its platform and personnel the Association cannot function as a revolutionary working class organization. And the overwhelming majority of American Negroes belong by birth, condition, and repression to the working class. Your aim is to get for the American Negro, the political and social rights that are his by virtue of the Constitution, the rights which are denied him by the southern oligarchy with the active cooperation of the state governments and the tacit support of northern business interests. And you aim is a noble one, which deserves the support of all progressive Negroes.

"But the Negro in politics and social life is ostracized only technically by the distinction of color; in reality the Negro is discriminated against because he is of the lowest type of worker.

"Obviously, this economic difference between the white and black workers manifests itself in various forms, in color prejudice, race hatred, political and social boycotting and lynching of Negroes. And all the entrenched institutions of white America,– law courts, churches, schools, the fighting forces and the Press, – condone these iniquities perpetrated upon black men; inequities that are dismissed indifferently as the inevitable result of the social system. Still, whenever it suits the business interests controlling these institutions to mitigate the persecutions against Negroes, they do so with impunity. When organized white workers quit their jobs, Negroes, who are discouraged by the whites to organize, are sought to take their places. And these strike-breaking Negroes work under the protection of the military and the police. But as ordinary citizens and workers, Negroes are not protected by the military and police from the mob. The ruling classes will not grant Negroes those rights which, on a lesser scale and more plausibly, are withheld from the white proletariat. The concession of these rights would immediately cause a Revolution in the economic life of this country."

We are aware that some of our friends have been disappointed with THE CRISIS during and since the war. Some have assumed that we aimed chiefly at mounting the band wagon with our cause during the madness of the war; others thought that we were playing safe so as to avoid the Department of Justice; and still a third class found us curiously stupid in our attitude toward the broader matters of human reform. Such critics, and Mr. McKay is among them, must give us credit for standing to our guns in the past at no little cost in many influential quarters, and they must also remember that we have one chief cause, – the emancipation of the Negro, and to this all else must be subordinated – not because other questions are not important but because to our mind the most important social question today is recognition of the darker races.

Turning now to the that marvelous set of phenomena known as the Russian Revolution, Mr. McKay is wrong in thinking that we have ever intentionally sneered at it. On the contrary time may prove, as he believes, that the Russian Revolution is the greatest event of the nineteenth and twentieth centuries, and its leaders the most unselfish prophets. At the same time THE CRISIS does not know this to be true. Russia is incredibly vast, and the happenings there in the last five years have been intricate to a degree that must make any student pause. We sit, therefore, with waiting hands and listening ears, seeing some splendid results from Russia, like the cartoons for public education recently exhibited in America, and hearing of other things which frighten us.

We are moved neither by the superficial omniscience of Wells nor the reports in the *New York Times*, but this alone we do know: that the immediate work for the American Negro lies in America and not in Russia, and this, too, in spite of the fact that the Third Internationale has made a pronouncement which cannot but have our entire sympathy:

"The Communist Internationale once forever breaks with the traditions of the Second Internationale which in reality only recognized the white race. The Communist Internationale makes its task to emancipate the workers of the entire world. The ranks of the Communist Internationale fraternally unites men of all colors; white, yellow and black – the toilers of the world."

Despite this there comes to us black men two insistent questions: What is today the right program of socialism? The editor of THE CRISIS considers himself a Socialist but he does not believe that German State Socialism or the dictatorship of the proletariat are perfect panaceas. He believes with most thinking men that the present method of creating, controlling and distributing wealth is desperately wrong; that there must come and is coming a social control of wealth; but he does not know just what form that control is going to take and he is not prepared to dogmatize with Marx or Lenin. Further than that, and more fundamental to the duty and outlook of THE CRISIS is this question: How far can the colored people of the world, and particularly the Negroes of the United States, trust the working classes?"

Many honest thinking Negroes assume, and Mr. McKay seems to be one of these, that we have only to embrace the working class program to have the working class embrace ours; that we have only to join trade Unionism and Socialism or even Communism, as they are today expounded, to have

Union Labor and Socialists and Communists believe and act on the equality of mankind and the abolition of the color line. THE CRISIS wishes that this were true, but it is forced to the conclusion that it is not.

The American Federation of Labor, as representing the trade unions in America, has been grossly unfair and discriminatory towards Negroes and still is. American Socialism has discriminated against black folk and before the war was prepared to go further with this discrimination. European Socialism has openly discriminated against Asiatics. Nor is this surprising. Why should we assume on the part of unlettered and suppressed masses of white workers, a clearness of thought, a sense of human brotherhood, that is sadly lacking in the most educated classes?

Our task, therefore, as it seems to THE CRISIS is clear. We have to convince the working classes of the world that black men, brown men, and yellow men are human beings and suffer the same discrimination that white workers suffer. We have in addition to this to espouse the cause of the white workers, only being careful that we not in this way allow them to jeopardize our cause. We must, for instance, have bread. If our white fellow workers drive us out of decent jobs, we are compelled to accept indecent wages even at the price of "scabbing." It is a hard choice, but whose is the blame? Finally despite public prejudice and clamor, we should examine with open mind in literature, debate and in real life the great programs of social reform that are day by day being put forward.

This was the true thought and meaning back of our May editorial. We have an immediate program for Negro emancipation laid down and thought out by the N.A.A.C.P. It is foolish for us to up this practical program for a mirage in Africa or by seeking to join a revolution which we do not at present understand. On the other hand, as Mr. McKay says, it would be just as foolish for us to sneer or even seem to sneer at the blood-entwined writhing of hundreds of millions of our white human brothers.

Reds Seek Negro Recruits to Help Start Revolution
(*Negro World*, 9 July 1921)

Pamphlets Urging Force Discovered by Police

NEW YORK, June 30 – The police today began inquiry into what they think may prove to be a nation-wide propaganda intended to stir up Negro discontent throughout America and further the cause of "a Soviet Republic of America."

Morris Sorner, forty-two, white, of 124 Ludlow street, arrested last night while distributing, it is alleged, circulars of an incendiary nature, admitted today, the police say, the he had been hired to scatter an appeal headed "The Tulsa Massacre,"[14] urging organized force as the only remedy to apply against "mobs of business men who outrage the Negroes and workers." He declined to say who hired him.

The police also continued a search of the neighborhood of Second avenue Fifteenth and Sixteenth, where the incendiary leaflets, signed by the "Executive Committee, Communist Party of America," were being distributed.

Tulsa Rising

"By the time this leaflet is in hand," the circular read, "the whole world will have learned of the horrible massacre of Negroes in Tulsa.

"No words are vivid enough to describe the actions of the well-dressed and armed mob of business men who, with automobiles and airplanes, surrounded the Negro quarter of Tulsa on June 1, killed ninety persons and injured more than 200 and made more than 10,000 Negroes homeless.

"There is only one appeal to stop these fiendish and bloody outrages – the appeal to organized force. The only language that the bloodthirsty capitalists of America can understand is the language of organized power.

"Only by reprisals, by answering force with force will business men and their white guards, the Ku Klux Klan, etc., be restrained from their assaults on the Negroes and the working people."

Labor was criticized for its attitude towards the Negro as follows:

Wants Revolution

"We've failed to organize the Negro and refused to treat him as our equal brother. We are to blame. Break down the barriers in the union. Wipe out the color lines. There is only one line we can draw, and that is the class line."

---

[14] The 'Tulsa Riot' of May 1921 was a sustained attack on the African American community of Tulsa resulting in the death of up to 300 African Americans and the destruction of the black businesses and properties. The riot was initially blamed on the ABB who according *The New York Times* were 'seeking to foment unrest among the Negroes'.

Part of the poster dealt with sovietism. It read:

"Under the Russian czar the Jews were the victims of race riots and pogroms. Workers and peasants overthrew the capitalist government and established a workers' government – the soviet republic of Russia. Only by following our Russian comrades' heroic example and establishing here the soviet republic of America will the workers, white and black, be able to work in peace and enjoy the fruits of their labor.

"Down with the capitalist system! Long live the Workers' Republic of America!"

Negroes in Soviet Russia
(Editorial, *The Messenger*, April 1923)

News dispatches tell of Claude McKay, the Negro poet, author of *Harlem Shadows*, as one of the two Negroes who addressed the Fourth Communist Internationale in Moscow. He plead for his race. It is reported that resolutions were adopted in the interest of Negro emancipation. While it is too early to estimate the significance of such resolutions, the mere presence of Negroes, either as spectators or members, in the great deliberative bodies of the world, radical, liberal and conservative, is an interesting instance of the monistic behaviors of races, mentally, morally and physically.

It is a cogent argument in favor of a basic egalitarianism. If modern anthropology and sociology have established anything it is that races have similar vices and virtues, similar instincts and habits, that their reactions to physical, economic, political and social stimuli, are similar. Thus, that Negroes, like whites, elect to study the new social phenomena of a workers republic, should not strike us as strange at all.

Soviet Russia and the Negro
(By Claude McKay,[15] *The Crisis*, December 1923)

The label of propaganda will be affixed to what I say here. I shall not mind; propaganda has now come into its respectable rights and I am

---

[15] Claude McKay (1889–1948) was a prolific Jamaican-born poet and writer. He attended the 1922 Congress in Moscow and contributed to a range of radical magazines of the period. Co-editor of *The Liberator* for a time, McKay was best known for his powerful poetic response to the 1919 'race riots', *If We Must Die*; he was an influential and erudite writer of the period.

proud of being a propagandist. The difference between propaganda and art was impressed on my boyhood mind by a literary mentor, Milton's poetry and his political prose set side by side as the supreme examples. So too, my teacher,–splendid and broadminded though he was, yet unconsciously biased against what he felt was propaganda–thought that that gilt-washed artificiality, "The Picture of Dorian Gray", would outlive "Arms and the Man" and "John Bull's Other Island". But inevitably as I grew older I had perforce to revise and change my mind about propaganda. I lighted on one of Milton's greatest sonnets that was pure propaganda and a widening horizon revealed that some of the finest spirits of modern literature–Voltaire, Hugo, Heine, Swift, Shelly, Byron, Tolstoy, Ibsen–had carried the taint of propaganda. The broader view did not merely include propaganda literature in my literary outlook; it also swung me away from the childish age of the enjoyment of creative work for pleasurable curiosity to another extreme where I have always sought for the motivating force or propaganda intent that underlies all literature of interest. My birthright, and the historical background of the race that gave it to me, made me very respectful and receptive of propaganda and world events since the year 1914 have proved that it is no mean science of convincing information.

American Negroes are not as yet deeply permeated with the mass movement spirit and so fail to realize the importance of organized propaganda. It was Marcus Garvey's greatest contribution to the Negro movement; his pioneer work in that field is a feat that the men of broader understanding and sounder ideas who will follow him must continue. It was not until I first came to Europe in 1919 that I came to a full realization and understanding of the effectiveness of the insidious propaganda in general that is maintained against the Negro race. And it was not by the occasional affront of the minority of civilized fiends–mainly those Europeans who had been abroad, engaged in the business of robbing colored peoples in their native land–that I gained my knowledge, but rather through the questions about the Negro that were put to me by genuinely sympathetic and cultured persons.

The average Europeans who read the newspapers, the popular books and journals, and go to see the average play and a Mary Pickford movie, are very dense about the problem of the Negro; and they are the most important section of the general public that the Negro propagandists would reach. For them the tragedy of the American Negro ended with "Uncle Tom's Cabin" and Emancipation. And since then they have been aware only of the comedy–the Negro minstrel and vaudevillian, the boxer, the black mammy and butler of the cinematograph, the caricatures of the romances and the lynched savage who has violated a beautiful white girl.

A very few ask if Booker T. Washington is doing well or if the "Black Star Line" is running; perhaps some one less discreet than sagacious will wonder how colored men can hanker so much after white women in face of the lynching penalty. Misinformation, indifference and levity sum up the attitude of western Europe towards the Negro. There is the superior but very fractional intellectual minority that knows better, but whose influence on public opinion is infinitesimal, and so it may be comparatively easy for white American propagandists–whose interests behoove them to misrepresent the Negro–to turn the general indifference into hostile antagonism if American Negroes who have the intellectual guardianship of racial interests do not organize effectively, and on a world scale, to combat their white exploiters and traducers.

The world war has fundamentally altered the status of Negroes in Europe. It brought thousands of them from America and the British and French colonies to participate in the struggle against the Central Powers. Since then serious clashes have come about in England between the blacks that later settled down in the seaport towns and the natives. France has brought in her black troops to do police duty in the occupied districts in Germany. The color of these troops, and their customs too, are different and strange and the nature of their work would naturally make their presence irritating and unbearable to the inhabitants whose previous knowledge of Negroes has been based, perhaps, on their prowess as cannibals. And besides, the presence of these troops provides rare food for the chauvinists of a once proud and overbearing race, now beaten down and drinking the dirtiest dregs of humiliation under the bayonets of the victor.

However splendid the gesture of Republican France towards colored people, her use of black troops in Germany to further her imperial purpose should meet with nothing less than condemnation from the advanced section of Negroes. The propaganda that Negroes need to put over in Germany is not black troops with bayonets in that unhappy country. As conscript-slave soldiers of Imperial France they can in no wise help the movement of Negroes nor gain the sympathy of the broad-visioned international white groups whose international opponents are also the intransigent enemies of Negro progress. In considering the situation of the black troops in Germany, intelligent Negroes should compare it with that of the white troops in India, San Domingo and Haiti. What might not the Haitian propagandists have done with the marines if they had been black instead of white Americans! The world upheaval having brought the three greatest European nations–England, France and Germany–into closer relationship with Negroes, colored Americans should seize the opportunity to promote finer inter-racial understanding. As white Americans in Europe are taking advantage of the situation to intensify their propaganda against the blacks, so must Negroes meet that with a strong counter-movement. Negroes should realize that the supremacy of American capital today proportionately increases American influence in the politics and social life of the world. Every American official abroad, every smug tourist, is a protagonist of dollar culture and a propagandist against the Negro. Besides brandishing the Rooseveltian stick in the face of the lesser new world natives, America holds an economic club over the heads of all the great European nations, excepting Russia, and so those bold individuals in Western Europe who formerly sneered at dollar culture may yet find it necessary and worthwhile to be discreetly silent. As American influence increases in the world, and especially in Europe, through the extension of American capital, the more necessary it becomes for all struggling minorities of the United States to organize extensively for the world wide propagation of their grievances. Such propaganda efforts, besides strengthening the cause at home, will certainly enlist the sympathy and help of those foreign groups that are carrying on a life and death struggle to escape the octuple arms of American business interests.

And the Negro, as the most suppressed and persecuted minority, should use this period of ferment in international affairs to lift his cause out of his national obscurity and force it forward as a prime international issue.

Though Western Europe can be reported as being quite ignorant and apathetic of the Negro in world affairs, there is one great nation with an arm in Europe that is thinking intelligently on the Negro as it does about all international problems. When the Russian workers overturned their infamous government in 1917, one of the first acts of the new Premier, Lenin, was a proclamation greeting all the oppressed peoples throughout the world, exhorting them to organize and unite against the common international oppressor–Private Capitalism. Later on in Moscow, Lenin himself grappled with the question of the American Negroes and spoke on the subject before the Second Congress of the Third International. He consulted with John Reed,[16] the American journalist, and dwelt on the urgent necessity of propaganda and organizational work among the

---

[16] John Reed (1887–1920), radical American writer and Communist who penned the classic account of the Bolshevik Revolution, *Ten Days That Shook The World* (1919).

Negroes of the South. The subject was not allowed to drop. When Sen Katayama[17] of Japan, the veteran revolutionist, went from the United States to Russia in 1921 he placed the American Negro problem first upon his full agenda. And ever since he has been working unceasingly and unselfishly to promote the cause of the exploited American Negro among the Soviet councils of Russia.

With the mammoth country securely under their control, and despite the great energy and thought that are being poured into the revival of the national industry, the vanguard of the Russian workers and the national minorities, now set free from imperial oppression, are thinking seriously about the fate of the oppressed classes, the suppressed national and racial minorities in the rest of Europe, Asia, Africa and America. They feel themselves kin in spirit to these people. They want to help make them free. And not the least of the oppressed that fill the thoughts of the new Russia are the Negroes of America and Africa. If we look back two decades to recall how the Czarist persecution of the Russian Jews agitated Democratic America, we will get some idea of the mind of Liberated Russia towards the Negroes of America. The Russian people are reading the terrible history of their own recent past in the tragic position of the American Negro to-day. Indeed, the Southern States can well serve the purpose of showing what has happened in Russia. For if the exploited poor whites of the South could ever transform themselves into making common cause with the persecuted and plundered Negroes, overcome the oppressive oligarchy–the political crackers and robber landlords–and deprive it of all political privileges, the situation would be very similar to that of Soviet Russia to-day.

In Moscow I met an old Jewish revolutionist who had done time in Siberia, now young again and filled with the spirit of the triumphant Revolution. We talked about American affairs and touched naturally on the subject of the Negro. I told him of the difficulties of the problem, that the best of the liberal white elements were also working for a better status for the Negro, and he remarked: "When the democratic bourgeoisie of the United States were execrating Czardom for the Jewish pogroms they were meting out to your people a treatment more savage and barbarous than the Jews ever experienced in the old Russia. America", he said religiously, "had to make some sort of expiatory gesture for her sins. There is no surfeited bourgeoisie here in Russia to make a hobby of ugly

---

[17] Sen Katayama (1859–1933), Japanese-born early member of the American Communist Party who was well known to ABB members and took a keen interest in race politics in the USA.

social problems, but the Russian workers, who have won through the ordeal of persecution and revolution, extend the hand of international brotherhood to all the suppressed Negro millions of America."

I met with this spirit of sympathetic appreciation and response prevailing in all circles in Moscow and Petrograd. I never guessed what was awaiting me in Russia. I had left America in September of 1922 determined to get there, to see into the new revolutionary life of the people and report on it. I was not a little dismayed when, congenitally averse to notoriety as I am, I found that on stepping upon Russian soil I forthwith became a notorious character. And strangely enough there was nothing unpleasant about my being swept into the surge of revolutionary Russia. For better or for worse every person in Russia is vitally affected by the revolution. No one but a soulless body can live there without being stirred to the depths by it.

I reached Russia in November–the month of the Fourth Congress of the Communist International and the Fifth Anniversary of the Russian Revolution. The whole revolutionary nation was mobilized to honor the occasion, Petrograd was magnificent in red flags and streamers. Red flags fluttered against the snow from all the great granite buildings. Railroad trains, street cars, factories, stores, hotels, schools–all wore decorations. It was a festive month of celebration in which I, as a member of the Negro race, was a very active participant. I was received as though the people had been apprised of, and were prepared for, my coming. When Max Eastman[18] and I tried to bore our way through the dense crowds, that jammed the Tverskaya Street in Moscow on the 7th of November, I was caught, tossed up into the air, and passed along by dozens of stalwart youths.

"How warmly excited they get over a strange face!" said Eastman. A young Russian Communist remarked: "But where is the difference? Some of the Indians are as dark as you." To which another replied: "The lines of the face are different. The Indians have been with us long. And so people instinctively see the difference." And so always the conversation revolved around me until my face flamed. The Moscow press printed long articles about the Negroes in America, a poet was inspired to rhyme about the Africans looking to Socialist Russia and soon I was in demand everywhere–at the lectures of poets and journalists, the meetings of soldiers and factory workers. Slowly I began losing self-consciousness with the realization that I was welcomed thus as a symbol, as a member

---

[18] Max Eastman (1883–1969) was an influential Socialist writer and editor who co-founded *The Liberator*.

of the great American Negro group–kin to the unhappy black slaves of European Imperialism in Africa–that the workers in Soviet Russia, rejoicing in their freedom, were greeting through me.

Russia, in broad terms, is a country where all the races of Europe and of Asia meet and mix. The fact is that under the repressive power of the Czarist bureaucracy the different races preserved a degree of kindly tolerance towards each other. The fierce racial hatreds that time in the Balkans never existed in Russia. Where in the South no Negro might approach a "cracker" as a man for friendly offices, a Jewish pilgrim in old Russia could find rest and sustenance in the home of an orthodox peasant. It is a problem to define the Russian type by features. The Hindu, the Mongolian, the Persian, the Arab, the West European–all these types may be traced woven into the distinctive polyglot population of Moscow. And so, to the Russian, I was merely another type, but stranger, with which they were not yet familiar. They were curious with me, all and sundry, young and old, in a friendly, refreshing manner. Their curiosity had none of the intolerable impertinence and often downright affront that any very dark colored man, be he Negro, Indian or Arab, would experience in Germany and England.

In 1920, while I was trying to get out a volume of my poems in London, I had a visit with Bernard Shaw who remarked that it must be tragic for a sensitive Negro to be an artist. Shaw was right. Some of the English reviews of my book touched the very bottom of journalistic muck. The English reviewer outdid his American cousin (except the South, of course, which could not surprise any white person much less a black) in sprinkling criticism with racial prejudice. The sedate, copperhead "Spectator" as much as said: no "cultured" white man could read a Negro's poetry without prejudice, that instinctively he must search for that "something" that must make him antagonistic to it. But fortunately Mr. McKay did not offend our susceptibilities! The English people from the lowest to the highest, cannot think of a black man as being anything but an entertainer, boxer, a Baptist preacher or a menial. The Germans are just a little worse. Any healthy looking black coon of an adventurous streak can have a wonderful time palming himself off as another Siki or a buck dancer. When an American writer introduced me as a poet to a very cultured German, a lover of all the arts, he could not believe it, and I don't think he does yet. An American student tells his middle class landlady that he is having a black friend to lunch: "But are you sure that he is not a cannibal?" she asks without a flicker of a humorous smile!

But in Petrograd and Moscow, I could not detect a trace of this ignorant snobbishness among the educated classes, and the attitude of the common workers, the soldiers and sailors was still more remarkable. It was so beautifully naive; for them I was only a black member of the world of humanity. It may be urged that the fine feelings of the Russians towards a Negro was the effect of Bolshevist pressure and propaganda. The fact is that I spent most of my leisure time in non-partisan and anti-bolshevist circles. In Moscow I found the Luxe Hotel where I put up extremely depressing, the dining room was anathema to me and I grew tired to death of meeting the proletarian ambassadors from foreign lands some of whom bore themselves as if they were the holy messengers of Jesus, Prince of Heaven, instead of working class representatives. And so I spent many of my free evenings at the Domino Café, a notorious den of the dilettante poets and writers. There came the young anarchists and menshevists and all the young aspirant fry to read and discuss their poetry and prose. Sometimes a group of the older men came too. One evening I noticed Pilnyal the novelist, Okonoff the critic, Feodor the translator of Poe, an editor, a theatre manager and their young disciples, beer-drinking through a very interesting literary discussion. There was always music, good folk-singing and bad fiddling, the place was more like a second rate cabaret than a poets' club, but nevertheless much to be enjoyed, with amiable chats and light banter through which the evening wore pleasantly away. This was the meeting place of the frivolous set with whom I eased my mind after writing all day.

The evenings of the proletarian poets held in the Arbot were much more serious affairs. The leadership was communist, the audience working class and attentive like diligent, elementary school children. To these meetings also came some of the keener intellects from the Domino Café. One of these young women told me that she wanted to keep in touch with all the phases of the new culture. In Petrograd the meetings of the intelligentsia seemed more formal and inclusive. There were such notable men there as Chukovsky the critic, Eugene Zamiatan the celebrated novelist and Maishack the poet and translator of Kipling. The artist and theatre world were also represented. There was no communist spirit in evidence at these intelligentsia gatherings. Frankly there was an undercurrent of hostility to the bolshevists. But I was invited to speak and read my poems whenever I appeared at any of them and treated with every courtesy and consideration as a writer. Among those sophisticated and cultured Russians, many of them speaking from two to four languages, there was no overdoing of the correct thing, no vulgar wonderment and bounderish superiority over a Negro's being a poet. I was a poet, that was all, and their keen questions showed that they were much more interested in the technique of my poetry, my views on and my position regarding the modern literary movements than in the difference of my color. Although I will not presume that there was no attraction at all in that little difference!

On my last visit to Petrograd I stayed in the Palace of the Grand Duke Vladimir Alexander, the brother of Czar Nicholas the Second. His old, kindly steward who looked after my comfort wanders round like a ghost through the great rooms. The house is now the headquarters of the Petrograd intellectuals. A fine painting of the Duke stands curtained in the dining room. I was told that he was liberal minded, a patron of the arts, and much liked by the Russian intelligentsia. The atmosphere of the house was theoretically non-political, but I quickly scented a strong hostility to bolshevist authority. But even here I had only pleasant encounters and illuminating conversations with the inmates and visitors, who freely expressed their views against the Soviet Government, although they knew me to be very sympathetic to it.

During the first days of my visit I felt that the great demonstration of friendliness was somehow expressive of the enthusiastic spirit of the glad anniversary days, that after the month was ended I could calmly settle down to finish the book about the American Negro that the State Publishing Department of Moscow had commissioned me to write, and in the meantime quietly go about making interesting contacts. But my days in Russia were a progression of affectionate enthusiasm of the people towards me. Among the factory workers, the red-starred and chevroned soldiers and sailors, the proletarian students and children, I could not get off as lightly as I did with the intelligentsia. At every meeting I was received with boisterous acclaim, mobbed with friendly demonstration. The women workers of the great bank in Moscow insisted on hearing about the working conditions of the colored women of America and after a brief outline I was asked the most exacting questions concerning the positions that were most available to colored women, their wages and general relationship with the white women workers. The details I could not give; but when I got through, the Russian women passed a resolution sending greetings to the colored women workers of America, exhorting them to organize their forces and send a woman representative to Russia. I received a similar message from the Propaganda Department of the Petrograd Soviet which is managed by Nicoleva, a very energetic woman. There I was shown the new status of the Russian women gained through the revolution of 1917. Capable women can fit themselves for any position; equal pay with men for equal work; full pay during the period of pregnancy and no work for the mother two months before and two months after the confinement. Getting a divorce is comparatively easy and not influenced by money power, detective chicanery and wire pulling. A special department looks into the problems of joint personal property and the guardianship and support of the children. There is no penalty for legal abortion and no legal stigma of illegitimacy attaching to children born out of wedlock.

There were no problems of the submerged lower classes and the suppressed national minorities of the old Russia that could not bear comparison with the grievous position of the millions of Negroes in the United States to-day. Just as Negroes are barred from the American Navy and the higher ranks of the Army, so were the Jews and the sons of the peasantry and proletariat discriminated against in the Russian Empire. It is needless repetition of the obvious to say that Soviet Russia does not tolerate such discriminations, for the actual government of the country is now in the hands of the combined national minorities, the peasantry and the proletarian. By the permission of Leon Trotsky, Commissar-in-chief of the military and naval forces of Soviet Russia, I visited the highest military schools in the Kremlin and environs of Moscow. And there I saw the new material, the sons of the working people in training as cadets by the old officers of the upper classes. For two weeks I was a guest of the Red navy in Petrograd with the same eager proletarian youth of new Russia, who conducted me through the intricate machinery of submarines, took me over aeroplanes captured from the British during the counter-revolutionary war around Petrograd and showed me the making of a warship ready for action. And even of greater interest was the life of the men and the officers, the simplified discipline that was strictly enforced, the food that was served for each and all alike, the extra political educational classes and the extreme tactfulness and elasticity of the political commissars, all communists, who act as advisers and arbitrators between the men and students and the officers. Twice or thrice I was given some of the kasha which is sometimes served with the meals. In Moscow I grew to like this food very much, but it was always difficult to get. I had always imagined that it was quite unwholesome and unpalatable and eaten by the Russian peasant only on account of extreme poverty. But on the contrary I found it very rare and sustaining when cooked right with a bit of meat and served with butter—a grain food very much like the common but very delicious West Indian rice-and-peas.

The red cadets are seen in the best light at their gymnasium exercises and at the political assemblies when discipline is set aside. Especially at the latter where a visitor feels that he is in the midst of early revolutionary days, so hortatory the speeches, so intense the enthusiasm of the men. At all these meetings I had to speak and the students asked me general questions about the Negro in the American Army and Navy, and when I gave them common information known to all American Negroes, students, officers and commissars were unanimous in wishing this group of young American Negroes would take up training to become officers in Army and Navy of Soviet Russia. The proletarian students of Moscow were eager to learn of the life and work of Negro students. They sent messages of encouragement and good will to the Negro students of America and, with a fine gesture of fellowship, elected the Negro delegation of the American Communist Party and myself to honorary membership in the Moscow Soviet.

Those Russian days remain the most memorable of my life. The intellectual Communists and the intelligentsia were interested to know that America had produced a formidable body of Negro intelligentsia and professionals, possessing a distinctive literature and cultural and business interests alien to the white man's. And they think naturally, that the militant leaders of the intelligentsia must feel and express the spirit of revolt that is slumbering in the inarticulate Negro masses, precisely the emancipation movement of the Russian masses had passed through similar phases. Russia is prepared and waiting to receive couriers and heralds of good will and interracial understanding from the Negro race. Her demonstration of friendliness and equity for Negroes may not conduce to produce healthy relations between Soviet Russia and democratic America, the anthropologists 100 per cent pure white Americanism will soon invoke Science to prove that the Russians are not at all God's white people I even caught a little of American anti-Negro propaganda in Russia. A friend of mine, a member of the Moscow intelligentsia, repeated to me the remarks of the lady respondent of a Danish newspaper: that I should not be taken as a representative Negro for she had lived in America and found all Negroes lazy, bad and vicious, a terror to white women. In Petrograd I got a like story from Chukovsky, the critic, who was on intimate terms with a high worker of the American Relief Administration and his southern wife. Chukovsky is himself an intellectual "Westerner", the term applied to those Russians who put Western-European civilization before Russian culture and believe that Russia's salvation lies in becoming completely westernized. He had spent an impressionable part of his youth in London and adores all things English, and during the world war was very pro-English. For the American democracy, also, he expresses unfeigned admiration. He has more Anglo-American books than Russian in his fine library and considers the literary section of the *New York Times* a journal of a very high standard. He is really a maniac of Anglo-Saxon American culture. Chukovsky was quite incredulous when I gave him the facts of the Negro's status in American civilization.

"The Americans are a people of such great energy and ability," he said, "how could they act so petty towards a racial minority?" And then he related an experience of his in London that bore a strong smell of *cracker* breath. However, I record it here in the belief that it is authentic for Chukovsky is a man of integrity: About the beginning of the century, he was sent to England as correspondent of a newspaper in Odessa, but in London he was more given to poetic dreaming and studying English literature in the British museum and rarely sent any news home. So he lost his job and had to find cheap, furnished rooms. A few weeks later, after he had taken up his residence in new quarters, a black guest arrived, an American gentleman of the cloth. The preacher procured a room on the top floor and used the dining and sitting room with the other guests, among whom was a white American family. The latter protested the presence of the Negro in the house and especially in the guest room. The landlady was in a dilemma, she could not lose her American boarders and the clergyman's money was not to be despised. At last she compromised by getting the white Americans to agree to the Negro's staying without being allowed the privilege of the guest room, and Chukovsky was asked to tell the Negro the truth. Chukovsky strode upstairs to give the unpleasant facts to the preacher and to offer a little consolation, but the black man was not unduly offended:

"The white guests have the right to object to me," he explained, anticipating Garvey, "they belong to a superior race."

"But," said Chukovsky, "I do not object to you, I don't feel any difference; we don't understand color prejudice in Russia."

"Well," philosophized the preacher, "you are very kind, but taking the scriptures as authority, I don't consider the Russians to be white people."

Chapter 2
Irish Anti-Colonial Struggle and Black Radical Politics

The impact of Bolshevism worked in parallel with a powerfully articulated black nationalism, and support for the Irish Republican struggle which is the focus of the documents in this section. Most obviously, the connection to the Irish struggle in part reflects the Caribbean constituency of many of these radicals who had grown up under British rule, and so a blow against the empire was close to home. But more than this, the championing of the Irish struggle is indicative here of a politics of 'race', class and nation as a powerfully articulated commitment to an internationalist anti-racism which insists on the primacy of race, but does so in order to broaden the boundaries of race politics. Claude McKay's 'How Black Sees Red and Green' (1921) captures the ambiguities of romantic identification with the Irish national liberation struggle and the reality of black experience of Irish American racism. His relocating of the Irish struggle into an international workers struggle is an attempt to reimagine international solidarity in terms of class and oppression. *The Crusader*'s championing of the Irish struggle in the documents presented names the enemy as the 'Anglo-Saxon race' thus forging a bond between Irish and African American resistance. It is notable that American-born black radicals are more ambiguous about the Irish due to their experiences of Irish racism towards African Americans in the USA. Both *The Crisis* and *The Messenger* are often less heady in their reports on Irish freedom.

Friends of Irish Freedom
(Editorial, The Messenger, November 1917)

Here is a new problem that has come to the fore in our American life.

The Irish in America are making a militant fight for the freedom of Ireland. They are giving forceful and determined utterance to the ideals of Casement and O'Connell, those martyrs of the Sinn Fein revolution.[1]

The Irish are calling for Great Britain to make good her claim of "fighting for the smaller nationalities" by lifting her imperial heel from off the tired neck of Ireland. For 800 years Great Britain has withheld "Home Rule" from Ireland. Irishmen remember the bitter days of the potato famine. And the Friends of Irish Freedom are calling for an accounting. They have Great Britain on the hip and they are going to feed fat the grudge they bear her.

The radicals must thank these brave souls for their founding firm for free-speech. They are doing their "bit" in keeping what democracy we have in the world.

England
(Editorial, *The Crusader*, June 1919)

How do we love her! Why shouldn't we? Does not her 'benevolent rule' preserve British 'law and order' in black men's countries from Cairo to the Cape and from the Indian Ocean eastwards to the Atlantic swell? Is she not civilizing – off the face of the earth – millions of Black and Brown men in different parts of the world? Has she not offered the Andaman and Maltese Islands as a 'refuge' for brown and black men who are so impertinent as to object to her benevolent (malevolent) rule? Has she not brought poverty and division and the foolish caste system to the West Indians driving them into strange lands to seek a livelihood? Has she not, with France, robbed and plundered the black man in Africa and handicapped his efforts in the Black Republic of Liberia? Is she not now shooting down Egyptians for the crime of asking for their country? Has she not bombed undefended towns of India from the air – something it was very barbarous for German Zeppelins to do to English towns but which, of course, it is quite proper and cultured for the English to do to Indian towns?

And are we not faithful dogs and servile slaves, licking and fawning over the hand that strikes us?

England! How we love you!

---

[1] Roger Casement (1864–1916), Irish Republican and human rights activist who was executed for his part in the 1916 Easter Rising. Daniel O'Connell (1775–1847), extremely influential Irish politician and MP who campaigned for Catholic emancipation in Ireland.

Internationalism
(*The Messenger*, August 1919)

We wish to extend a welcome to De Valera, President to the Irish Republic.[2] We have admired during the war the stamina, the independence and courage of the Irish people in insisting upon their rights without regard to other temporary circumstances. De Valera has been well received here and we regard it as good democracy for him to be so received. The Irish have also shown signal intelligence in making their problem international, in carrying it to outside of Ireland for solution. The ignorant Negro leaders of the country might take a tip from De Valera in the presentation of their problems. Carry the Negro problem out of the United States, at the same time that you present it in the United States. There mere fact that the country does not want the Negro problem carried to Europe is strong evidence that it ought to be carried there. William Monroe Trotter[3] has caught the point and gone to Europe to embarrass the President of the United States, who has been making hypocritical professions about a democracy in the United States which has not existed and does not exist. On the pretense of this being "a land of the free and home of the brave" President Wilson has held a certain moral leadership in Europe which any old school statesman there was better fit to hold, from honesty of purpose and the undemocratic position of his country. If Du Bois and Moton[4] had not been handpicked Negroes who were carrying out orders of their bosses, they would have done just what Trotter attempted and thereby could have performed some useful service for the Negro.

The international method of dealing with problems is the method of the future. Almost all democratic problems have been settled through force of international opinion. Our Revolutionary War of 1776 was made possible through the assistance of French troops under Lafayette, who responded to assistance because of the revolutionary opinion of the

---

[2] Éamon de Valera (1882–1975) was a Irish Republican who toured the USA in 1919 as the President of Ireland in exile. Sinn Féin had won the 1918 election and were seeking recognition for the new Irish Parliament which was not recognised by Britain.

[3] William Monroe Trotter (1872–1934) was a prominent African American civil rights activist and one of the founding members, with W. E. B. Du Bois, in 1905 of the Niagara Movement which sought to challenge the conservative politics of Booker T. Washington.

[4] Robert Moton (1867–1940) was an African American educator who succeeded Booker T. Washington as the principal of the Tuskegee Institute. Seen as a conservative by left-wing black activists of the period.

Frenchmen. Our Civil War was won by the North, because Karl Marx, the founder of Socialism, Frederick Douglass who had more character and intelligence than any of our present day old crowd leaders and other persons interested in universal democracy, appealed to the public opinion of England to oppose the system of chattel slavery which still obtained in the United States. Douglass was able to get a hearing in England when the United States would not grant a hearing. It was possible to get a hearing in the North where slavery was abolished while a hearing in the South was not possible. The beneficiary of a system cannot be relied upon to change that system from which he receives his benefits. England cannot be relied upon to relieve the Irish people of their oppression because the landed estates of Ireland are yielding great profits to the absentee landlords of Great Britain. The Negro in the United States cannot expect much assistance from those who control this government because the manufacturers and capitalists whom President Wilson says are the government of this country, are making huge profits out the cheap labor of Negroes. Great Britain would not consider the independence of the American colonies, because she was drawing huge taxes on tea, clothing, machinery and other articles and instruments. The United States grows eloquent over the pogroms committed against Jews in Poland, but the burning of a Negro every day or so in Texas or Georgia or Mississippi (which by the way are in the United States) does not disturb our good President Wilson, who calmly states to the Senate "America shall lead the way!" Is there any wonder that Leon Trotsky of Russia should regard our President as "the arch hypocrite in Christendom?"

Another reason why international opinion is so important is that every country is ready to pose as being democratic to some other country and most ready to take up the persecutions of other peoples as a means of directing attention from its own mismanagement and abuse and tyranny. It is a species of international hypocrisy – international deception, which is a mark of advancing civilization. The more enlightened people become, the more necessary it is to make use of psychological forces rather than physical forces. They can be deceived more easily than they can be coerced. Ideas move the world, but those ideas must be sound ideas. As Lester F. Ward says, "Opinions beget desires and desires beget actions." The action, however will be sound or unsound, in proportion as the opinion is intelligent and informed. Enlightened international opinion is the most powerful opinion in the world. It should be propagated for numerous reasons, but we must let it suffice to close with the above citation. Long live Internationalism!

Approaching Irish Success
(Editorial, *The Crusader*, August 1919)

There is little doubt that the Irish principle of "when you fight, FIGHT" is soon to be vindicated and Irish sacrifices for liberty crowned with great and important if not complete, success.

By strikes, riots, rebellions and other forceful means the Irish people have forced the world to take cognizance of British misrule and oppression of Ireland, and world public opinion is today exerting a potent influence to bring the English around to a recognition of the fact that the Irish people have rights which the English are bound to respect.

One of two things seems bound to happen very soon. Announcement by England of a Dominion form of government within the "Bloody Empire" for Ireland, or an embarrassing recognition for England of the "Irish Republic" by other nations, led by the United States. Whichever way it goes, the Irish people are bound to benefit greatly in the near future from their heroic cause of Irish freedom. And the maxim remains true: "When you fight, FIGHT!" and "he who would be free himself must strike the blow." There is no middle course when dealing with the oppressor.

Negro Police Captains
(Editorial, *The Messenger*, July 1919)

There is a growing feeling of unrest and uneasiness among Negroes in the United States. They have been so generally deceived and lied to by police officials that now they don't believe anything they hear such officials say. Every nine out of ten Negroes (probably the percentage is *greater*) firmly believes that no white man can be trusted – that all are hypocritical on the Negro problem. We, of course, know better, but the facts have convinced the average Negro to the contrary. One of the things which has produced this deep seated distrust is the ruthless brutality and the inexcusable beating up of Negroes by policemen. Our intimate contact with all the large Negro centers enables us to know how tense and bitter is the feeling between whites and blacks. All such big Negro communities are *Magazines of Race Prejudice Dynamite*, ready to explode at any moment upon putting the flame to the fuse. Riots are imminent – real race riots – in all such large cities as New York, Philadelphia, Baltimore, Washington, Chicago, Pittsburgh and St Louis. The arrest of a Negro in such large settlements of Negroes immediately suggests to the other

Negroes that the man arrested is being imposed upon by the white officers. Again, most of the police in the above named centers are Irishmen, the race which Negroes as a whole, dislike most.

All of this is unfortunate, but undoubtedly true. It is the product of America's chief commodity – race prejudice. What you ask is the immediate program to adopt in warding off this impending race conflict?

First the problem of policing needs to be radically changed and reconstructed. In the Negro settlements of New York, Philadelphia, etc., the bulk of the policemen should be Negroes and the police captains should be – not Irish heavyweights – but Negroes. IT IS A PROBLEM OF SOCIAL PSYCHOLOGY. The Negro population has only a normal reaction to seeing a Negro policemen arrest a Negro. But when it is a case of whites who are generally hostile to men of color – the feeling is entirely different.

We would also recommend to the Mayors of big cities with large Negro population that they appoint as police captains intelligent, cool, sober men of the Negro race – men who have a common sympathy with their race and yet a high sense of regard for duty. No Negro stool-pigeon editors and politicians should be placed in this position, because it requires tact, intelligence and poise. There are numbers of discharged colored officers who could creditably fill these places. We would heartily support such men as Captain Napoleon B. Marshall of the old New York Fifteenth Regiment or Lieutenant William N Colson of the 367th Infantry. These are men of intelligence tact, character and broad sympathy. The first named is not of our political faith either. Such men should be found in all the large cities and there would be nothing amiss about any Mayor's getting the men from any city to hold such a responsible position.

We invite a serious consideration of our proposals on this question. We wonder what Mayor will have the brains, courage and foresight to take the lead. Intelligent police captains will undoubtedly serve them well in the coming race conflicts which bid fair to sweep the country.[5]

---

[5] There was an angry response to this article in the 19 October issue. A letter from an Irishman, P. O. Huaithne, exhorted the writers to 'also remember that thousands of good Irishmen found a grave while battling for your emancipation from slavery. Their natural love of liberty made them leap to the task, and in conclusion I hope that colored men will wean themselves of the alleged dislike of the Irish. Yours in the Gaelic.'

Forward
(By W. E. B. Du Bois, *The Crisis*, September 1919)

WE black folk easily drift into intellectual provincialism. We know our problem and tend to radical thought in its solution, but do we strive to know the problems of other forward forging groups whose difficulties are inevitably intertwined with ours? Here, for instance, is the question of the ownership of public utilities – the railroads, the telegraph and telephone and the street cars – utilities used largely, if not primarily, by the working class, and businesses which have yielded immense fortunes to private owners in the past. What do we think of these questions – are we studying them? Are we intelligent on the facts? Do we know that the United States is almost the only civilized country that does not own its railroads and wires, and that the municipal ownership of street transportation is widespread?

Or take the battle of North Dakota under the Non-Partisan League; are we swallowing easily the gossip of a prejudiced press, or do we realize that these western farmers are resolutely grappling with the mightiest problem of present-day life – how to prevent the necessities of the poor from being simply the opportunity of predatory wealth to amass dangerous fortunes? North Dakota is putting her government into the business of banking and publishing, running grain elevators and stockyards, packing-houses and flour mills and overseeing mines. Will she fail?

Perhaps, but her efforts are worth watching, and failure never yet proved wrong right. Beyond these questions lie the Suffering Groups – Ireland, India, Russia. From long tradition – since the draft riots of the Civil War – Negroes have had no sympathy with the Irish. But they must not rest in this unreason. Let every colored man read this month a history of Ireland.

If he does not rise from it bitter with English cruelty and hypocrisy, he is callous indeed. The cry of oppressed India sounds right in our own land in the persistent attempts of England to secure the transportation of Hindus accused of the treason of trying to make their country free.

And, finally, the one new Idea of the World War – the idea which may well stand in future years as the one thing that made the slaughter worthwhile – is an Idea which we are like to fail to know because it is today hidden under the maledictions hurled at Bolshevism.

It is not the murder, the anarchy, the hate, which for years under Czar and Revolution have drenched this weary land, but it is the vision of great dreamers that only those who work shall vote and rule.

England, Again
(By W. E. B. Du Bois, *The Crisis*, March 1920)

Two criticisms have been made of the editorial on England in the January number of THE CRISIS. One writer reminds us of the great work of emancipation and the suppression of the slave trade, started by England early in the nineteenth century. The other, would not have us forget the hostile attitude of Irish Americans towards Negroes.

Of none of these facts are we a moment forgetful. In the Emancipation of Negroes, Englishmen, like Clarkson, Wilberforce, and Sharpe, were splendid pioneers; and the riots against Negroes in Cincinnati, Philadelphia, and New York, during the nineteenth century, in nearly all cases, were instigated and led by Irishmen. More than this: Today, the decisive influence in the American Catholic Church, which keeps black priests out of her pulpits, is the Irish influence, – for the mother Catholic Church is not, and never was, anti-Negro. Her black priests and bishops have for a thousand years sat in her counsels, and the first Catholic bishop, of North America, was a full-blooded Negro.

Again, it was liberal, far-sighted Englishmen who gave to the world the democratic parliamentary ideal, which all races and colors receive today as civilization's rightful heritage.

Nevertheless, two things are sure: One cannot indict a whole nation, nor can one excuse a national wrong, because of individual right, or past desert.

Ireland today deserves freedom. She has suffered, and suffered horribly at the hands of Englishmen. In Ireland and Russia, have arisen the greatest spiritual movements of the twentieth century. And we who suffer in slavery and degradation, – shall we hesitate to extend a hand of sympathy to the Irish, simply because their descendants in America are so largely the followers of American snobbery? We must not forget that Irish-Americans, like John Boyle O'Reilly and Archbishop John Ireland, and Irishmen like Daniel O'Connell, have always recognized Negroes as fellow-men.[6]

The great services of England to the world and to the Negro race must not for a moment blind us to the fact that today the dominant powers

---

[6] John Boyle O'Reilly (1844–1890), Irish member of the Irish Republican Brotherhood who settled in Boston and was an anti-slavery advocate in his newspaper, *The Pilot*. John Ireland (1838–1918) was the Irish-born Archbishop of Saint Paul Minnesota who was known for his strong anti-slavery stance during and after the Civil War.

in England are moving heaven and hell to keep black and brown men in economic and political slavery to minister to British power and luxury . . .

Heroic Ireland: Irish Fight for Liberty the Greatest Epic of Modern Times and a Sight to Inspire to Emulation all Oppressed Groups (By Cyril Briggs, *The Crusader*, February 1921)

The spectacle of a Little People intrepidly and tirelessly opposing the might of the world's greatest Empire and Oppressor, is one that must thrill all lovers of liberty and give birth to aspirations of freedom and emulation of daring deeds in the breasts of all the oppressed peoples of the world.

The Irish fight for liberty is the greatest Epic of Modern History. It is a struggle that should have the sympathy and active support of every lover of liberty – of every member of an oppressed group. The Negro in particular should be interested in the Irish struggle, for while it is patent that Ireland can never escape from the menace of "the overshadowing empire" so long as England is able to maintain her grip on the riches and manpower of India and Africa it is also clear that those suffering together under the heel of British imperialism must learn to CO-ORDINATE THEIR EFFORTS before they can HOPE TO BE FREE. The mighty tyrant is not to be toppled over by an unaided Ireland, however courageously her valiant sons may fight; nor yet by an Africa or India unaided. England menaced in ONLY ONE QUARTER AT THE SAME TIME can successfully defend her ill-gotten spoils and her bleeding conquests – can easily maintain her grave-yard peace – her boasted *pax Britannica*. But England menaced on many quarters AT THE SAME TIME, faced by the determined bayonets of ALL her "subject peoples" would be an England AT THE END OF ROPE. And until England is brought to the end of her rope there will be no freedom for Ireland, India or Africa.

Co-ordination of efforts will win the day, but preceding co-ordination there must be understanding and appreciation of the aims and aspirations of each other. The British are now trying to embarrass the Irish fight for freedom as well as to justify their own Hunnishness in Ireland by the belated publication of papers pertaining to prove Irish collusion with "the enemy" during the recent war. There is so little proof of this given in the British "papers" that their publication has failed to raise a ripple of interest even in England. But suppose there had been collusion between the Irish and the Germans. Who, from the Irish standpoint, was the enemy?

The Germans who, not having had the opportunity, even though possible possessed of the inclination, had not murdered Irish men, women and children, burned Irish cities to the ground, destroyed Irish creameries and factories, and in a thousand and one atrocious ways made war upon the Irish people – or the English who having both the opportunity and the inclination have done (and are still doing) these things?

In shocked tones they tell us of "wanton Sinn Fein attacks on constituted authority" in the shape of British soldiers and officials in Ireland. But by what right are British soldiers and officials maintained on Irish soil in direct violation of the plebiscite by which more than nine-tenths of the Irish people declared themselves in favour of an independent republic and elected their own constituted authorities? When Englishmen complain of attacks on their mercenaries stationed in Ireland and brand such attacks as "murderous" and speaks of their casualties in battle as "murders," it is time to ask by what divine decree is British rule established in Ireland that it is to be considered as inviolate and unchangeable.

It should be easily possible for Negroes to sympathize with the Irish Fight against tyranny and oppression, and vice-versa, since both are in the same boat and both the victims of the same Anglo-Saxon race – albeit the Negro suffers in the New World as well as in the Old World, in Africa as well as in the United States.

Irish Boycott on British Goods
(Editorial, *The Crusader*, March 1921)

The Irish people and the Negro people have much in common. To begin with, they are both oppressed by stronger groups. Secondly the oppressors, in the main, of both Celt and Negro, are identified with the Anglo-Saxon race. Thirdly, the great enemy of the Irish people is also the greatest enemy of the Negro people. Not only does Great Britain tyrannize it over more Negroes and other colored races than are ruled by any other nation in the world, but Great Britain is also the bulwark of the Anglo-Saxon White Guards and of all the reactionary things for which they stand.

But how differently do Irish and Negroes meet the common foe! That is, the members of the two races in America. The difference is not so marked in Africa and Ireland, where both races are engaged in deadly war against the Anglo-Saxon – the war in Egypt and other parts of Africa being none the less deadly for its apparent spasmodic qualities.

But how different in America! While the Irish in America persist in carrying the war to the enemy's pocket book in a determined boycott that is giving John Bull many a sleepless night, the while giving hope and moral support to the warriors in Ireland, the Negro, on the other hand, goes blindly on unintelligently supporting, by buying their goods, the great enemy of his race – the English.

How long will we Negroes of America remain indifferent to the sufferings of our kindred under "British" rule, and blind to the vast power of the economic boycott to chastise our enemy and effect reprisals for the wrongs and insults heaped upon us by the supercilious Anglo-Saxons.

A Negro boycott of British goods, loyally carried out, would at any time be effective. But at this time, more than ever, since it would have the co-operation of the Irish whose boycott the British are already beginning to feel.

And why not now? Should not two groups fighting the same enemy act in unison and move in co-operation? Let every Negro purchaser, whether buying for himself or an employer, agree to boycott all goods of British manufacture or British handling and the self-styled "ruler of the subject races" would soon have to lay aside her proud and cruel ambition to boss the darker millions of the earth. On with the boycott! Press home the war for liberation! Strike for a free Africa and a redeemed race! Hit them where it will hurt most – in their pocketbooks! Aim at the bulwark of Anglo-Saxon domination! On with the boycott!

Bleeding Ireland
(Editorial, *The Crisis*, March 1921)

No people can more exactly interpret the inmost meaning of the present situation in Ireland than the American Negro. The scheme is simple. You knock a man down and then have him arrested for assault. You kill a man and then hang the corpse for murder. We black folk are only too familiar with this procedure. In a given city, a mob attacks us unprepared, unsuspecting, and kills innocent and harmless black workingmen in cold blood. The bewildered Negroes rush together and begin to defend themselves. Immediately by swift legerdemain the mob becomes the militia or a gang of "deputy sheriffs". They search, harry and kill the Negroes. They disarm them and loot their homes, and when the city awakes after the "race riot", the jail is filled with Negroes charged with rioting and fomenting crime!

So In Ireland! The Irish resist they have resisted for hundreds of years, various and exasperating forms of English Oppression. Their resistance is called crime and under ordinary conditions would be crime; In retaliation not only the "guilty" but the Innocent among them are murdered and robbed and public property is burned by English guardians of the Peace!

All this must bring mingled feelings of dismay to Irishmen. No people in the world have in the past gone with blither spirit to "kill niggers" from Kingston to Delhi and from Kumassi to Fiji. In the United States, Irish influence not only stood behind the mob in Cincinnati, Philadelphia and New York, but it still stands in the American Federation of Labor to keep out Negro workingmen. All this contains no word of argument against the ultimate freedom of Ireland – which God speedily grant! – but it does make us remember how in this world it is the Oppressed who have continually been used to cow and kill the Oppressed in the interest of the Universal Oppressor.

How Black Sees Green and Red
(By Claude McKay, *The Liberator*, 4 June 1921)

LAST summer I went to a big Sinn Fein demonstration in Trafalgar Square. The place was densely packed, the huge crowd spreading out into the Strand and up to the steps of the National Gallery. I was there selling the *Workers' Dreadnought*, Sylvia Pankhurst's pamphlet, *Rebel Ireland*, and Herman *Gorter's Ireland: The Achilles Heel of England*; I sold out completely. All Ireland was there. As I passed round eagerly in friendly rivalry with other sellers of my group, I remarked aged men and women in frayed, old fashioned clothes, middle aged couples, young stalwarts, beautiful girls and little children, all wearing the shamrock or some green symbol. I also wore a green necktie and was greeted from different quarters as "Black Murphy" or "Black Irish." With both hands and my bag full of literature I had to find time and a way for hearty handshakes and brief chats with Sinn Fein Communists and regular Sinn Feiners. I caught a glimpse also of proud representatives of the Sinn Fein bourgeoisie. For that day at least I was filled with the spirit of Irish nationalism–although I am black!

Members of the bourgeoisie among the Sinn Feiners, like Constance Markievicz and Erskine Childers, always stress the fact that Ireland is the only "white" nation left under the yoke of foreign imperialism.[7]

---

[7] Constance Markievicz (1868–1927) was an Irish Republican Socialist and leading member of the Irish Citizen Army who became the first woman to be elected to the House

There are other nations in bondage, but they are not of the breed; they are colored, some are even Negro. It is comforting to think that bourgeois nationalists and patriots of whatever race or nation are all alike in outlook. They chafe under the foreign bit because it prevents them from using to the full their native talent for exploiting their own people. However, a black worker may be sensitive to every injustice felt by a white person. And I, for one, cannot but feel a certain sympathy with these Irish rebels of the bourgeoisie.

But it is with the proletarian revolutionists of the world that my whole spirit revolts. It matters not that I am pitied, even by my white fellow-workers who are conscious of the fact that besides being an economic slave as they, I am what they are not–a social leper, of a race outcast from an outcast class. Theirs is a class, which though circumscribed in its sphere, yet has a freedom of movement-a right to satisfy the Simple cravings of the body–which is denied to me. Yet I see no other way of upward struggle for colored peoples, but the way of the working-class movement, ugly and harsh though some of its phases may be. None can be uglier and harsher than the routine existence of the average modern worker. The yearning of the American Negro especially, can only find expression and realization in the class struggle. Therein lies his hope.

For the Negro is in a peculiar position in America. In spite of a professional here and a business man there, the maintenance of an all-white supremacy in the industrial and social life, as well as the governing bodies of the nation, places the entire Negro race alongside the lowest section of the white working class. They are struggling for identical things. They fight along different lines simply because they are not as class-conscious and intelligent as the ruling classes they are fighting. Both need to be awakened. When a Negro is proscribed on account of his color, when the lynching fever seizes the South and begins to break out even in the North, the black race feels and thinks as a unit. But it has no sense of its unity as a class—or as a part, rather, of the American working-class, and so it is powerless.

The Negro must acquire class-consciousness. And the white workers must accept him and work with him, whether they object to his color and morals or not. For his presence is to them a menacing reality. American Negroes hold some sort of a grudge against the Irish. They have asserted that Irishmen have been their bitterest enemies, that the social and

---

of Commons in 1918, though she did not take her seat in line with Sinn Fein policy. Erskine Childers (1870–1922) was an Irish Republican and novelist, author of *The Riddle of the Sands* (1903).

economic boycott against Negroes was begun by the Irish in the North during the Civil War and has, in the main, been fostered by them ever since. The Irish groups in America are, indeed, like the Anglo-Saxons, quite lacking in all the qualities that make living among the Latins tolerable for one of a conspicuously alien race. However I react more to the emotions of the Irish than to those of any other whites, they are so passionately primitive in their loves and hates. They are quite free of the disease which is known in bourgeois phraseology as Anglo-Saxon hypocrisy. I suffer with the Irish. I think I understand the Irish. My belonging to a subject race entitles me to some understanding of them. And then I was born and reared a peasant; the peasant's passion for the soil possesses me, and it is one of the strongest passions in the Irish revolution.

The English, naturally, do not understand the Irish, and the English will not understand unless they are forced to. Their imperialists will use the military in Ireland to shoot, destroy and loot. Their bourgeoisie will religiously try to, make this harmonize with British morality. And their revolutionists – I would almost say that the English revolutionists, anarchists, socialists and communists, understand Ireland less than any other political group. It appears that they would like to link up the Irish national revolution to the English class struggle with the general headquarters in England.

And as Sinn Fein does not give lip-service to communism, the English revolutionists are apparently satisfied in thinking that their sympathy lies with the Irish workers, but that they must back the red flag against the green. And the Irish workers hate the English. It may not sound nice in the ears of an "infantile left" communist to hear that the workers of one country hate the workers of another. It isn't beautiful propaganda. Nevertheless, such a hatred does exist. In the past the Irish revolutionists always regarded the Royal Irish Constabulary as their greatest enemy. Until quite recently its members were recruited chiefly from the Irish workers themselves; but the soldiers of the Irish Republican Army shot down these uniformed men like dogs, and when at last thousands of them deserted to Sinn Fein, either from fear of their fighting countrymen, or by their finer instinct asserting itself, they were received as comradeship, fed, clothed and provided with jobs. I saw one of the official Sinn Fein bulletins which called upon the population to give succor to the deserting policemen. They were enemies only while they wore the uniform and carried out the orders of Dublin Castle. Now they are friends, and the British have turned to England and Scotland for recruits. And so all the hatred of the Irish workers is turned against the English. They think, as do all subject peoples with foreign soldiers and their officers lording it over them, that even the exploited English proletariat are their oppressors.

And it is true at least that the English organized workers merrily ship munitions and men across the channel for the shooting of their Irish brothers. Last Spring, following on a little propaganda and agitation, some London railmen refused to haul munitions that were going to Ireland. They had acted on the orders of Cramp, the strong man of their union.[8] But the railroad directors made threats and appealed to Lloyd George, who grew truculent. J. H. Thomas, the secretary of the Railwaymen's union, intervened and the order was gracefully rescinded. As usual, Thomas found the way out that was satisfactory to the moral conscience of the nation. It was not so much the hauling of munitions, he said, but the making of them that was wrong. The railroad workers should not be asked to shoulder the greatest burden of the workers' fight merely because they hold the key to the situation!

It is not the English alone, but also the anglicized Irish who persist in mis-understanding Ireland. Liberals and reactionary socialists vie with each other in quoting Bernard Shaw's famous "Ireland has a Grievance." Shaw was nice enough to let me visit him during my stay in London. He talked lovingly and eloquently of the beauty of medieval cathedrals. I was charmed with his clear, fine language, and his genial manner. Between remarking that Hyndman was typical of the popular idea of God, and asking me why I did not go in for pugilism instead of poetry – the only light thought that he indulged in – he told of a cultured Chinaman who came all the way from China to pay homage to him as the patriarch of English letters. And just imagine what the Chinaman wanted to talk about? Ireland! It was amusingly puzzling to Shaw! Yet it was easy for me to understand why a Chinaman whose country had been exploited, whose culture had been belittled and degraded by aggressive imperial nations, should want to speak to a representative Irishman about Ireland.

Whilst the eyes of the subject peoples of the world are fixed on Ireland, and Sinn Fein stands in embattled defiance against the government of the British Empire; whilst England proclaims martial law in Ireland, letting her Black and Tans[9] run wild through the country, and Irish men and

---

[8] Charlie Cramp (1876–1933), British trade unionist and president of the National Union of Railworkers.

[9] Black and Tans were mostly British ex-soldiers drafted into Ireland by the British Government during the War of Independence (1919–1921) who became infamous for their human rights' abuses.

women are giving their lives daily for the idea of freedom, Bernard Shaw dismisses the revolutionary phenomenon as a "grievance." Yet the Irish revolutionists love Shaw. An Irish rebel will say that Shaw is a British socialist who does not understand Ireland. But like Wilde he is an individual Irishman who has conquered England with his plays. There the fierce Irish pride asserts itself. Shaw belongs to Ireland.

I marvel that Shaw's attitude towards his native land should be similar to that of any English bourgeois reformist, but I suppose that anyone who has no faith, no real vision of International Communism, will agree with him. To the internationalist, it seems evident that the dissolution of the British Empire and the ushering in of an era of proletarian states, will give England her proper proportional place in the political affairs of the world. The greatest tradition of England's glory flourishes, however, in quite unexpected places. Some English communists play with the idea of England becoming the center of International Communism just as she is the center of International Capitalism. I read recently an article by a prominent English communist on city soviets. It contained a glowing picture of the great slums transformed into beautiful dwellings and splendid suburbs. When one talks to a Welsh revolutionist, a Scotch communist, or an Irish rebel, one hears the yearning hunger of the people for the land in his voice.

One sees it in his eyes. When one listens to an earnest Welsh miner, one gets the impression that he is sometimes seized with a desire to destroy the mine in which his life is buried. The English proletarian strikes one as being more matter-of-fact. He likes his factories and cities of convenient makeshifts. And when he talks of controlling and operating the works for the workers, there burns no poetry in his eyes, no passion in his voice. English landlordism and capitalism have effectively and efficiently killed the natural hunger of the proletariat for the land. In England the land issue is raised only by the liberal-radicals, and finds no response in the heart of the proletariat. That is a further reason why England cannot understand the Irish revolution.

For my part I love to think of communism liberating millions of city folk to go back to the land. The English will not let go of Ireland. The militarists are hoping that the Irish people, persecuted beyond endurance, will rise protesting and demonstrating in a helpless and defenseless mass. Then they can be shot down as were the natives of Armitsar in India. But against a big background of experience the generals of the Irish Army are cautious. The population is kept under strict discipline. The systematic destruction of native industries by the English army of occupation forces them to adopt some communist measures for self-preservation. They are imbibing the atmosphere and learning the art of revolution.

I heard from an Irish communist in London that some Indian students had been in Dublin to study that art where it is in practical operation. It is impossible not to feel that the Irish revolution – nationalistic though it is – is an entering wedge directed straight to the heart of British capitalism.

Hon. Marcus Garvey, as Spokesman for 400,000,000 Negroes, Telegraphs Arthur Griffith and Premier Lloyd George on the Settlement of The Irish Question and Creation of a Self-Governing Irish Free State
(*Negro World*, 17 December 1921)

Liberty Hall, New York, Saturday evening, Dec 11 1921.

Before one of the largest audiences that has packed Liberty Hall since the opening days of the last convention of Negro peoples of the world, the Hon. Marcus Garvey read telegrams of congratulation that was sent by him in the name of four hundred million Negroes to Arthur Griffith, Vice-President of the Provisional Republic of Ireland, and to David Lloyd George upon their signing the document that gives to Ireland her partial freedom.[10] These telegrams breathed the spirit of rejoicing that Ireland after a most bitter struggle, had won such a notable victory, and that her success was cause for inspiration to Negroes the world over and to have greater hopes than heretofore for the final redemption of Africa, their motherland.

To Arthur Griffith Mr. Garvey said, in part, in his message of congratulation, that "the stage is set for a greater day for Ireland," while in his telegram to the British Premier he said that "the step is a laudable one, and we hope you will continue to listen to the cry of the oppressed multitude of your great empire and thus save humanity from the conflicts of war."

The President-General then read another telegram, this one being addressed to Mr. H. G. Wells, the celebrated English novelist and writer,

---

[10] Following Civil War in Ireland in 1922 a treaty was signed between the British Government and the Irish negotiating committee which granted twenty-six counties of Ireland the status of 'Free State' while six counties in the north-east of the country remained a part of Britain.

who is engaged by the *New York World* to write special articles on the disarmament conference now sitting at Washington D.C.

Mr. Wells had written an article on Africa and the Negro that appeared in today's Sunday issue of *The World*, the headline to the article being that Africa is growing in importance as a possible cause for war unless the powers take certain steps to govern its development. He was taken to serious task for his views as expressed in the article, which, Mr. Garvey said, indicated they were based upon information received by Mr. Wells from the "Uncle Tom" class of Negro. Mr. Wells, however, has to learn that there is today a New Negro, and a new statesmanship of the Negro, that does not beg or plead, but demands that the Negro be given his just rights. He invited the British novelist to come to Liberty Hall, and there see the New Negro as he is, and thus have corrected his erroneous impressions of the colored people.

Continuing his comment upon Ireland receiving her partial freedom, Mr. Garvey said that the policy of the Englishman for centuries had been to rob and exploit other people's countries, some times under the guise of religion, and at other times in shamefaced boldness Africa was one of those countries she had exploited, and whose people she had robbed of what is theirs.

America, the Negro has been told is the white man's country, and Europe, it is said, is for the Europeans; then surely there must be some place on the earth that belongs to him, and that place is Africa. There can be no settlement of the question of world peace, he said, until the 400,000,000 Negroes of the world receive their just rights, for the new manhood of the Negro race is not going to yield up those rights.

Mr. Wells in his article remarked that the Europeans should go to Africa and take the oil and fats and other natural products there, and use them for their own needs, since they are of no great value to the native population. This statement Mr. Garvey ridiculed with the bitterest scorn and sarcasm, and said that if Wells and his ilk think that they will have an easy time getting these rich products in Africa, as in the past – that is, by the policy of exercising force and theft – they are entirely mistaken. They may do so for a year or two, or five years longer, but ultimately there will be an awakening, and when once the Negro is awakened to the wrongs that are done him, and the rights and possessions that are his, he is a dangerous thing.

Sir Wm. H. Ferris, Assistant President-General, in making the opening speech, spoke of the fact that the Negro today is now being taken notice of by the press, this in contrast to the fact that but four years previous, whenever a conference of the A. M. E. Zion Church, for instance, was held anywhere, but small space was devoted to its doings in any of the white papers. This, he said, is because the world is beginning to realize that the Negro has a brain and will of his own, and is now exercising it for his development and advancement.

He referred to the bravery and valor of black soldiers, and said the possibilities for achievement today, under improved environment and better condition, should enable the Negro to achieve greater things in the world than ever before. His demands for an equal chance, for equal justice, for the protection of his rights, are only reasonable, and these the white man is beginning to learn, he will insist upon with stronger and stronger power as he advances in education, wealth and industrial accomplishment. In the past the black man waited for the Caucasian to give him a lift and a push upward, but today the new Negro is giving himself a life and a push, Independent of any one else.

This he was glad to see, for it is the very thing that the U.N.I.A. is striving to encourage the Negro to do, that he may become self-reliant and possess the things, physical, intellectual and material, necessary to sustain himself, as no nation and no race can hope to be a dominant race or people who do not reach this state of self-reliance and independence, in the economic, the intellectual and the physical world.

The addresses were received with enthusiastic appreciation by the vast audience, and the sallies and gibes made by Mr. Garvey against Mr. Wells (who, perhaps, will be a little more careful hereafter when writing upon the Negro and Africa) gave them great delight, and caused much uproarious laughter. The English writer's articles in *The New York World* may, perhaps, in the future lose much of their popularity, particularly those that may appear on this question, in view of Mr. Garvey's brilliant and withering ridicule and sarcasm.

A grand musical concert formed the first part of the program, in which Madam Fraser Robinson, Madam Houston and Miss Ruth Green took part, the contribution by the choir and the band being up to the high standard, heretofore set, and now so well known among Liberty Hall attendants.

HON. MARCUS GARVEY'S SPEECH

Hon. Marcus Garvey spoke as follows: I have a dual subject for tonight – Ireland and Africa. I will say a few words touching on the new Irish Free State. For 700 years the Irish race has been waging a relentless campaign for the purpose of freeing their country from the domination of an alien race. The time seems long – 700 years. But very few races would have stuck to one program – to one cause for such a lengthened period of time. Nevertheless the Irish stuck, and for 700years they fought. Hundreds and thousands of Irishmen have died as martyrs to the cause of Irish freedom. Coming down the centuries we have had Irish patriots as Robert Emmett,[11] O'Connell, Roger Casement and McSweeney. At a certain time the world laughed at them, the world mocked them, the world jeered them for their cause; nevertheless they continued their agitation until within recent years they forced the world's recognition. They compelled the attention of the world and I believe the death of McSweeney did more for the freedom of Ireland today than probably anything they did for 600 years prior to his death.[12]

Negroes' Cause Similar to Irish

We have a cause similar to the cause of Ireland. We have just started out three years ago. I wonder if we will keep it up for 700 years? Those of us who understand what liberty means: those of us who understand what the freedom of a people mean will keep it up for eternity. (Cries of Yea! Yea!) In the struggle upward many an Irishman fell by the wayside – fell out of line. In the struggle upward to a free and redeemed Africa many a Negro will fall out on the wayside, but nevertheless the mighty contingent, the great everlasting battalion will march on even to eternity. (Applause)

Glad Ireland Has Won Self-Government

I am glad that Ireland has won some modicum of self-government. I am not thoroughly pleased with the sort of freedom that is given to them, but nevertheless I believe that they have received enough upon which they can improve, because I hardly believe that it will take too long a period from the time that the Free State is given to them for a collapse in Europe that will bring about a compulsory freeing of all oppressed peoples by those who have held them in bondage for hundreds of years. So I am not with my friend De Valera at this minute; I am with my friend Arthur Griffith.[13] I believe his is a wise statesman in signing the pact and accepting a sort of Irish Free State, and I trust the Irish Parliament when called on Wednesday will ratify the understanding and agreement he has

---

[11] Robert Emmett (1778–1803), Irish Republican executed for his part in a failed uprising in 1803.
[12] Terence McSwiney (1879–1920). Sinn Fein Mayor of Cork who died on hunger strike in Brixton prison.
[13] De Valera opposed the treaty and led opposition to it. The pro- and anti-treaty forces mobilised and a civil war in Ireland followed (1922–1923).

come to and made with David Lloyd George (the bulldog of Europe). (Laughter)

Sends Cable of Congratulations to Arthur Griffith

I am about to send this cable to Arthur Griffith. He is the Vice-President of the Irish Republic. He has fought continuously; he has fought long; he has made great sacrifices for the cause of Ireland, and I think all oppressed peoples, all well-thinking peoples, all liberal-minded people should encourage such a man at this hour; and on behalf of four hundred million Negroes of the world who are looking toward freedom, but outside of that, who are always liberal-minded enough to appreciate the rights of all men, I am about to send this cable to Arthur Griffith in Dublin, Ireland:

"Arthur Griffith, Dublin, Ireland.

"Six thousand of us assembled in Liberty Hall, New York, representing the four hundred million Negroes of the world, send you congratulations on your masterly achievement of partial independence for Ireland. The stage is set for a greater day for Ireland. Long live the new Irish Free State.

"MARCUS GARVEY,

"Provisional President of Africa."

Cablegram to Lloyd George

And this cable goes to David Lloyd George:

"David Lloyd George, London – The Negro peoples of the world congratulate you for the splendid statesmanship you have demonstrated in granting to Ireland her internal freedom. The step is a laudable one and we hope you will continue to listen to the cry of the oppressed multitude of your great empire and thus save humanity from the conflicts of war.

"MARCUS GARVEY,

"Provisional President of Africa."

Irish Free State
(Editorial, The Messenger, February 1922)

After seven or more centuries of struggle with one of the bloodiest and cruelest tyrants of Christendom – Great Britain – the Irish people have finally achieved a slight measure of freedom in the form of the Irish Free State. No people have suffered, sacrificed, bled and died more willingly and freely for the right of self-determination than they. Be it said to the undying honor and credit of the Irish patriots that they never faltered, never equivocated, never retreated a single step before one of the most merciless foes that ever unsheathed a sword. But through veritable rivers of blood and tears; devastated cities and smoking villages, the Sinn Feiners carried on until "perfidious albion" was forced to consider terms of peace and the conditions of an Irish independent state.

Of course, all is not well at this hour. De Valera suspects that the Irish Free State is a Trojan Horse So accustomed is he to the wiles and trickery of the Welsh Premier Lloyd George that he cannot understand the British bearing gifts. On the other hand, Arthur Griffith and Michael Collins are willing to worry along with the present makeshift until the hour to strike for absolute independence from the British Empire.[14]

Meanwhile Sir James Craig is working with might and main to maintain Ulster free from the Irish Free Sate. But this is not all. The railway workers are on strike.

The Irish Free State, like the Soviet Government, is facing serious times. As to what will be the ultimate issue of these cross currents in Ireland, is too early to predict. Undoubtedly, Ireland will erelong achieve freedom. We hail the victorious march of the Irish people toward complete nationalism as a signal contribution to the cause of human liberty. We bid them onward, upward, forward! Now that Irish nationalism is flowering forth into self-determination the Irish workers are free to fight for a true worker's republic.

The Irish and the Negro
(By J. A. Rogers,[15] *The Messenger*, November 1924)

What has been said of the Jews also applies to the Irish. The Irish have long had the reputation of being the most vindictive haters of Negroes on the American continent. D. G. Croly, writing in 1863, attributed it to the fact that Negroes and Irishmen were so much alike in disposition. You may take his explanation or leave it, but the fact that some of the bitterest foes of Negroes are Irish, holds true. In the Chicago riot Irish youths from the so-called athletic clubs in the Irish neighborhood were

---

[14] Michael Collins (1890–1922), director of intelligence for Republican forces during the War of Independence and a signature to the treaty.
[15] Joel Augustus Rogers (1880–1966) was a Jamaican-American writer and historian.

the most bloodthirsty of all. A Catholic priest, a very good friend of mine, who used to work among the Negroes in New York City told me that when he went to Chicago soon after the riot he was surprised at the great hate the Irish there manifested for Negroes.

Yet it was not so many years ago that the Irish in America were in precisely the same position as the Negro now is. They were liable to be set upon and mobbed anywhere in America for no reason than being Irish. English sentiment then prevailed more strongly in America than it did now. Between 1830 and the outbreak of the Civil War there were several organizations like the Know Nothing Party,[16] who thought it a crime to be Irish, and one can fancy an American newspaper of those days apologizing to a Mrs Harris for saying she had Irish blood.

Here are some of the things that happened to the Irish, which one may verify by reading any history of the Know Nothing Party:

In 1834 the Ursuline convent at Charlestown, Boston, was burned by mobs and many killed. On Sunday, June 11, 1837, the Irish quarter was burned in Boston in what was known as the Broad Street riots. An Irish funeral and a fire engine, going to a fire, got in collision, and of course, the Irish, right or wrong, got the blame for it, with the result that the populace inflamed by the reading of the book "Maria Monk" killed many Irish.[17]

In May, 1834, there was an anti-Irish riot in Philadelphia that lasted three days. The Irish quarter was set afire, twenty-nine houses, two churches and one convent being burned. Many were killed. In July, 1844, there was another serious riot in the city when it was rumored that the Irish had hidden arms in the church of St Philip Neri. Among other places that had anti-Irish riots were Bath, Maine: Manchester, N.H.; St. Louis, Baltimore, Louisville, New York City and Brooklyn.

"Sixty years ago" says Dr. E. F. McSweeney, noted Irish-American scholar, "the bigoted slogan was: 'No Irish need apply.'" When the Civil War broke out, however, he says, the slogan was dropped, precisely as the Negro was reminded that he was an American citizen when it came to fighting and buying so-called Liberty bonds.

Above all, the Irish has the terrible background of oppression in his own country. What has happened may happen again. Let the Ku Klux, the modern Know Nothings, have their way and history would repeat

---

[16] Nickname for the Native American Party – an anti-immigration party of the mid-nineteenth century.

[17] *Awful Disclosures of Maria Monk, or, The Hidden Secrets of a Nun's Life in a Convent Exposed* (1836).

itself for the Irish. As to the Jews they might wish they were back in Russia, for while the Russians would shoot them down, the crackers would fry them alive. As long as there is any oppression around no minority group can call itself safe. The dragon having eaten the weakest victim reaches out for the next.

Chapter 3
The New Negro: Anti-Colonialism/Anti-Capitalism

The influence of the Russian Revolution and Irish Republicanism were instrumental to the emergence of an anti-colonial politics with a radical black subject at its core. The texts in this section push at the limits of 'The New Negro', to insist on the centrality of black achievement in the forming of a new revolutionary transnational black political subject. The concept of the 'New Negro' in these texts is cast in opposition to the 'Old Negro' who is presented within plantation tropes of acquiescence and assimilation. Many of the articles below also articulate the relationship between capitalism and colonial oppression in addition to imagining international struggles for African independence.

Africa for the Africans
(By Cyril Briggs, *The Crusader*, September 1918)

Victory for the Allies must usher in Democracy for all the people – regardless of race, creed or color. First because all races are engaged under the flag of the Allies in the war on Germany, Kaiserism and autocracy. Secondly, because the leaders of the Allied nations have specifically declared that they are fighting for World Democracy and the President of the United States has declared that "henceforth security of life, worship, industrial and social development should be guaranteed to all peoples who have lived hitherto under the power of governments devoted to a faith and purpose hostile to their own;" preceding this declaration with the remark that "No peace can last which does not recognize and accept the principle that governments derive all their just powers from the consent of the governed."

The President is plain and explicit, and we are not aware that he has issued any foot-notes with his notes and speeches to the effect that the principles he has declared are not applicable to all the branches of the human family. We therefore look for a free Africa, as well as a free Poland, Serbia and Belgium as one of the guaranteed results of an Allied victory – emphatically promised by the Chief Executive of a great people and the man who is also the recognized leader of Allied diplomacy.

A free Africa will mean that Africa will no longer be exploited by a ruling caste of European overlords, that the natives no longer will be crushed under the heel of alien rule superimposed by unrighteous force; that the civilization of Africa by machine guns and bad gin will cease and that "government of the people and by the people and for the people" shall be the rule in African as in European affairs as the truly democratic nations recognize and accept the principle inlaid in the American Declaration of Independence, and once more emphasized at the hands of President Wilson, that, "governments derive all their just powers from the consent of all the governed."

In that principle lies one of the chief reasons why we are in the war today. The Hun must be driven out of Belgium and Northern France, out of Serbia and Russia. The Kaiser must be taught that it is wrong for him to enforce or superimpose his rule upon others, simply because they are too weak to resist his organized force. He must be taught, so say our American leaders and newspapers, that Might does not constitute Right, and, of course if it is wrong for a nation in Europe to superimpose its government upon another nation in Europe, it is also wrong for a nation in Europe to superimpose its government upon a nation outside of Europe. Liberty and Democracy cannot be denied peoples upon mere geographical lines. There can be neither geographical nor racial lines where Democracy is concerned. It is for all or for none.

Nor can self-government be longer denied certain peoples upon the fantastic pretext that there are "superior" and "inferior" peoples. Reduced to its last analysis the pretense that "superiors" have the moral right to superimpose their authority upon "inferior" peoples is a mere euphemism for the vicious proposition that the stronger have the moral right to subjugate the weaker.

Is it not this very proposition that we are fighting in Europe? What difference is there in Germany trying to superimpose her authority upon the Serbians, Poles and Belgians, and other nations trying to superimpose their rule upon those Asiatics and Africans who have not yet learned Europe's dominant philosophy of FORCE. Wrong for one, it cannot be right for others.

Again, if "superior" peoples have the right to superimpose their will upon "inferior" peoples would it not follow that "superior" individuals have the right to rule "inferior" individuals? And in the one case as in the other, the test of superiority must be superiority of physical power. And if the right of the physically superior to govern is recognized would not this mean universal monarchy, since there must be in the world at any given time a man superior in physical strength to all other individuals? Would the apostles of the "superiority doctrine" stomach Jack Johnson as such a king?

And is the rule of the so-called "superior" best? Is it not true, as the *Outlook* some time ago pointed out, that even the mistakes a people make in governing themselves are more to be desired than the perfectly correct decisions that may be made for the people by the ruling caste.

And are the decisions of the "superior" always correct? Is the government of a ruling caste or a ruling nation better than government of the people by the people and for the people? That the European Powers can hardly claim success in their "government" of Africa is amply attested by the following quotations chosen at random from a mass of documentary evidence . . .

The Crusader intends to save the African people before they are exterminated. Will you help? The task is long and hard. And mighty the forces of sin and imperialism. But on our side are the eternal moral rights. The stars in their courses fight for us and the right. The victory of right over seemingly irresistible might is thus assured. The battle will be sharp, but the victory is assured. Ethiopia shall yet stretch forth her hand to Freedom and to God! And not Ethiopia alone, but ALL the oppressed of the earth. This is promised by the Stars in their courses fighting on the side of moral right. And promised too by the leaders of the great Allied Nations that fight against the German ideal of Might triumphant over Right. Now, then, this is our opportunity. The present our Salvation. We are fighting for Democracy. We must see to it that it is applied to African as well as to European, to the Negro as well as to the white man.

The Call
(By W. Francis Jr., *The Crusader*, September 1918)

Out from the clamor of war and strife
Comes forth an echo clear and bright,
Bidding all Afric's sons unite
Their strength to aid a common fight.
A call is issued unrestrained,
Throughout the land – in each domain,
To every soul, to every frame

That Negro blood flows through the veins.
Let every Negro in the land
Remove his cloak and take his stand:
And pledge to give a helping hand
To aid the cause of Afric's band.
To you – the shirker in our fold:
Can nothing spur you to enrol
Your help – your very heart and soul,
To aid a cause so manifold?
Let every tongue that strives to teach,
Let every man that loves to "preach,"
Insert the message in their speech
That every Negro's soul be reached.
To learn the word "unite" again,
To know its meaning clear and plain;
Ere long and evermore the same.
In every clime – on land and sea
May all the race in "Unity"
Help this grand universe to be
A truly great democracy.

Would Freedom Make Us "Village Cut-Ups"
(By Cyril Briggs, *The Crusader*, February 1919)

The Chicago Defender,[1] the only powerful Negro publication that is not voicing the overwhelming sentiment of the race for a free Africa, in its issue of December 28 revealed its reason for its silence on a matter so greatly affecting the future of the race. *The Defender* naively believes that for the Negro to have a country of his own where the inhabitants could exercise the functions of self-government and to which the New World Negro, tired of oppression, could migrate, would mean simply that we could "build a black 'white house' enact 'Jim Crow' laws against invading whites, carry razors, guns and knives to our hearts' content and if fact be regular village cut-ups without let or hindrance from the 'superior race.'"

Is the razor carrying village cut-ups the highest development to which the Negro free of the "superior race," could attain? Does *The Defender* know nothing of ancient Ethiopia and Meroe; of mediaeval

---

[1] *The Chicago Defender* (1905–present) a widely read and influential African American newspaper which campaigned consistently against racism.

Nupe, Benin and the Songhaii? Is the truth of the splendid progress of Liberia, hindered and hampered as she has been by imperialistic Britain and France and robbed by their concession-seekers, unknown to *The Chicago Defender?*

One of the main arguments used to "prove" the Negro's inferiority is the claim that the Negro is incapable of self-government. Incapable of governing himself what right has he to participate in the government of another people, even though he be also part of the nation? Is *The Defender* not aware of the falsity of this argument? Does it not know that both Liberia and Haiti have produced great administrators and diplomats who can favorably be compared with the leading European statesmen? Certainly it has only been through the ability of her statesmen that Liberia has so long been able to escape the clutching hands of thieving Europe.

Those of us who have advocated a free Africa have done so in recognition of the fact that the status of one section of race surely affects the status of all other sections, no matter what ocean rolls between. In a world of fast transportation and rapid thought communication we cannot be slaves in one part and expect to be recognized as free men in another part. Those of us who have spoken of returning to Africa, should a substantial part of that continent be set aside for the Negro, have considered such a return from the standpoint of escaping the oppressive and degrading conditions in this country and in the prospects of a free enjoyment of "security of life" and property, equal opportunities and the freest development along the lines of our own race genius. But *The Defender* can only see in the New Negro's natural and human desire to escape from galling and menacing conditions a wish to escape to some spot where we would be surrounded by ourselves and wants to know "how long it would be possible to keep a white face from their midst" satisfying its own curiosity to the effect that it would be impossible to do so for long and concluding its inquiry with the advice that "there is no use in moving away to get rid of that evil."

We would that the American Race Problem were as simple as *The Defender* believes or would have its readers believe. But unfortunately the almost daily lynchings, the recent revival of the Ku Klux Klan, the evident determination of the white South to keep the Black South in the mire, the government's apparent helplessness in the matter, its sanction of jim-crowism on the railroads it now controls, its qualifying statement in help advertisements that "Negroes and aliens" are not wanted, are only a few of the stern signs of the times warning us that the future of our children will not be safe in such a land. And we are afraid that all of the smart and bombastic sayings such as *The Defender's* that "if there is any moving to be done it's up to the other fellow" won't help or alter the situation in which 90,000,000 whites are determined to uphold "white supremacy" in what, in times of peace, they consider a "white man's country," against 10,000,000 Negroes who are becoming increasingly restive under weight of their wrongs.

But since *The Defender* has such aims on the African question it is a matter that really does not interest *The Defender*.

The Negro who opposes an African State because he is a Colored American – a half-a-man citizen of the United States – and intends to remain so, is attacking something that doesn't concern him. No-one is going to forcibly remove him. But if his fellow Negroes – the men who want a man's rights, equal opportunities, free development, security of life and property want to leave the United States it will be a good thing for them to have a free Africa to go to, where they can exult in an independent nationality and enjoyment of security of life and property and all the other rights of men, at the same time demonstrating afresh to the world the Negro's ability to govern himself.

Africa Speaks!
(Editorial, *The Crusader*, May 1919)

To the despoilers who would have the world believe that African men are delighted with European super-imposed "benevolent" (hypocritical!) rule and that African women live only to raise slaves for British, French and other European tyrants Africa gives the lie.

Nyasaland in 1914! *Morocco and Nigeria in* 1918–19! *Egypt in* 1919! These are a few of the more audible answers to the unspeakable lie that the peoples of Africa have less than the average human instincts for liberty and no aspirations for a political future free of the evils of alien rule.

Egypt, Morocco, Nigeria, Nyasaland! These are but the louder tones of an answer that is swelling from every African heart and square inch of African territory. So far some of the tones have been stifled and the facts censored and concealed by the despoilers. But concealment cannot change facts and sooner or later the mighty chorus will be heard the world over giving hope and encouragement and the signal for concerted effort to Negroes everywhere and sending fear and terror into the heart of the white oppressor.

Will the white man heed the warning and rid Africa of is loathsome presence or will it come to pass that the same land that gave Europe the gift of its first civilizations shall be the destroyer of the putrid, capitalistic imitation of the glorious Egyptian-Ethiopian-Greco civilizations!

Capitalism the Basis of Colonialism
(By W. A. Domingo, *The Messenger*, August 1919)

The various colonial empires of the world are maintained by force and trickery and are devoid of altruism in any shape or form. The motivating influence that brought them into existence was the intention of a better armed race or nation to reduce weaker races and nations to the point where they would be compelled to directly or indirectly produce wealth for the benefit of the dominant class of the "Mother Country." The true basis of all empires is economic in spite of the fact that apologists for colonial expansion exhaust all their ingenuity to assign moral intent to countries whose imperial rule is based upon openly exercised or slightly veiled force. This is as much true of the frank and brutal imperialism of Rome, Germany, France, Spain, Japan and Great Britain as it is of the less visible imperialism of the United States. The former countries more ingenuous than the latter, in acquiring new territory rarely, if ever attempted to cover up their intentions with hypocritical cant or resort to the outward forms of a "purchase"; they usually took whatever they had the power to seize and explained the conquest afterwards.

A very natural question to ask is; "Why do countries have colonies?" This is easily explained. In the first place, because of the capitalistic development of most "civilized" countries the vast majority of the population have been expropriated from the land and live in cities in ever increasing numbers. In the cities, because of the wonderful productivity of modern machines more goods are produced than can be bought up by the population of the producing country, hence the need for outlets in foreign countries. This condition makes foreign markets necessary. The only markets that can absorb any appreciable portion of manufactured goods are located in such countries as cannot or ARE NOT PERMITTED to develop industrially. To safeguard and insure a market against other industrially developed and exploiting countries, political control of the market is essential. Hence the imposing of the rule of the industrially developed exporting country upon the industrially undeveloped and importing country. However, sometimes the prospective colony may have infant industries of its own – enough to supply its own needs – or it may have ambitions to become self-sufficient. In such cases the "Mother" or exploiting country ordinarily effectuates the death of the existing industries or renders the ambition to create new industries, stillborn. This is illustrated by the manner in which the weaving and other industries of India were killed in the interest of English manufacturers and by the way in which the Jamaican government (which is dominated by English officials appointed by Downing Street, London) strangled the soap factory in Kingston some years ago.

The first reason for colonies is to provide safe markets for the surplus commodities of the "Mother Country."

Secondly, because of the needs of modern industry and the inability of manufacturing countries located in temperate regions to produce them, tropical products such as copra, rubber, coffee, cocoa, balata, pissava and hides have to be imported. In order that the supply will be steady and uninterrupted, political control of the source is necessary. This control manifests itself in the form of preferential tariffs between the colony and the "Mother Country." It explains the insistent demands of the Unionists of Great Britain for a preferential tariff with the colonies and the reason why Cuban imports into America are given a substantial rebate of Customs duties.

The second reason for the colonies is, therefore, to insure the mother country a safe and regular source of supply and raw materials.

Thirdly, because of the contradiction of modern capitalist civilization, instead of machines being a boon to the workers they have proven to be a curse. In all industrialized countries vast armies of unemployed exist who have been created by the man being displaced by his creature – the machine. These unemployed men and women serve two purposes. One, by their pressure on the factory gate to reduce wages to the lowest point of subsistence; two, by their ever-increasing numbers enlarge the proletarian population, thereby making of it a portentous menace to the system that created it. So as to avoid the latter phase from becoming too dangerous, the mother country, that is, the class that controls it, needs some place to which the "surplus" population can be conveniently exported. Hence, the various efforts to send unemployed Europeans to Australia, Canada, South Africa, New Zealand and other temperate countries. Germany, who came on the colonial field late, had to yield to this imperative economic law even though political control of her exported subjects was lost when they went to colonies of other exporting countries or to sparsely populated sovereign countries like Brazil. This in a measure explains the dual citizenship laws of Germany.

The third reason for colonies is to find congenial territory to which to export the "surplus" population of the mother country.

The fourth and last important reason for colonies is the intention to create sinecures for impecunious sons of the mother country, who by virtue of lineage and tradition belong to the class from which bureaucrats are largely recruited. This last reason which is the visible manifestation of actual political control of colonies serves a dual purpose. First, it serves as a guarantee that the colonial government, dominated by sons of the mother country will not be diverted into economic and political activities and alliances inimical to the interests of the land of their birth; and next by paying huge salaries and enormous pensions to these officials, substantial amounts are yearly extracted from the colonies and exported to enrich the Mother Country. To sum up: All Empires, no matter how seemingly benevolent, are based upon force and maintain the structural form of a central manufacturing, exporting and exploiting "Mother" country, whose influence radiates to the "colonies" through her possession of a merchant marine, political control and expropriation of the natives. These bases of influence in their turn have behind them power in the form of an army and navy.

Colonialism, therefore, is a product of Capitalism which may be defined as that system of wealth production and distribution that is based upon a favoured few living off and at the expense of the oppressed many. With the death of capitalism in the Mother or central country, will come the collapse of imperialism and its train [of] murder, high taxes, poverty, oppression and exploitation in the Colonies.

Loaded Dice
(By C. Valentine (Briggs), *The Crusader*, February 1920)

In a country whose government and resources are completely controlled by the white man, the Negro pays the game of life against a rival whose every cast is with loaded dice.

From his birth the Negro fights, bravely but hopelessly, against this game of loaded dice. As a child he is denied an equal opportunity with the white child of parents of the same class and means as his own parents. His environment is usually of an immoral and degraded nature. His parents are forced to live by the law of segregation (legal, unwritten or economic) in districts apart from the whites, said districts being generally adjacent to red light sections and usually forgotten by God and man. At school, if he is in the North, he is pestered and insulted by other children and his teachers, as well. If he is in the South he is forced to attend a jim-crow institution of ramshackle appearance, insanitary conditions, and poorly paid inefficient teachers. And in all parts of the country the schools deny him the racial backbone which comes from instruction in the history and achievements of one's race. History, like most of the other departments, is taught with the needs in view of the white child only. That white children may acquire race pride and the confidence, ambition and inspiration which spring from such pride, the history courses are full of the achievements of their own race, plus many achievements of the Black race claimed as of their own. White America goes for inspiration even to the sources of kindred European peoples, but omits mention of the part played by Negroes in the building up of this country and in its several wars. History is compiled and taught solely with the requirement of the white child in view. No thought is wasted upon the needs and psychology of the Negro child. He can take it or leave it.

But not only is the Negro child's special racial and psychological requirements neglected, but his race is also vilified and misrepresented as being inherently inferior to the white race and producing in all its existence no civilization higher than that of the cannibalistic age. Absolutely ignored is the fact, accepted by the leading scientists, that the Black man gave birth to civilization in Meroe, on the Upper Nile, and later gave the impetus to human progress which has resulted in the splendid material achievements of the present day by the discovery of the art of smelting iron, thus giving to mankind the sharp-edged tools without which the railroad, and the steamship, the skyscraper and the aeroplane, would all be impossible.

Of Moshesh, the great warrior-statesman of the Basutos;[2] of Crispus Attucks,[3] the first martyr of the American Revolution; of Toussaint L'Ouverture,[4] whom Wendel Phillips,[5] an Anglo-Saxon, designated as higher in all the attributes of greatness than Napoleon, Washington, or any of the other products of the white race, the Negro child is taught absolutely nothing.

In Business

Graduated, and lacking the essential racial background because of his deficient education, the Negro finds on every side the door of opportunity

---

[2] Moshoeshoe I (1786–1870) the ruler of the Basotho kingdom (present day Lesotho).

[3] Crispus Attucks (1723–1770), African American icon of the anti-slavery movement in the eighteenth century, he was the first casualty of the American revolution.

[4] Toussaint Louverture (1743–1803), leader of the Haitian Revolution of 1791–1804 which liberated the slaves of Haiti.

[5] Wendell Phillips (1811–1884), prominent American abolitionist.

closed to him for no other reason than that of racial identity. Should he apply for a clerical position he is instantly made aware of his alleged inferiority and the resultant impossibility of obtaining work on a basis of equality with white workers. In fact, his mere temerity in applying for such a position is taken as a sign of impudence that necessitates a "calling down." Nothing is asked of his possible qualifications for the position. That he may be more efficient than the white applicant is not a factor in the case. Or if he is more fortunate than the average of his race, he may find an opportunity for service along the lines of his training with one of the few large business enterprises of his race. Or he may be able to eke out a mere living in a small-scale business of his own among his people. But whether he is in law, real estate, commerce or even in the ministry he is continually at the mercy of the white who plays the game with a loaded dice.

In the great majority of cases he must rent his store or office from a white owner. And in every case he is forced to pay a much higher rental than the white tenants in the same or in adjoining buildings. (In several cases of recent investigations colored men were found paying double the rentals paid by white men in adjoining stores. In one instance where a colored man was paying $75 a month and his white neighbor only $35, the agent refused an offer of ten dollars additional on the white man's rent but was quite willing to accept one of five dollars additional on the colored man's rent.)

If he is operating a grocery or a dry goods or other retail business he must buy his stock from the white man. If he is operating a factory he must obtain his raw material from the white man. And in every instance he has to pay more for identical goods than his white retail competitor. And should there happen to be any special or sacrifice sale of certain goods, the opportunity to effect a big reduction on wholesale purchases is first offered the white retailer, and only brought to the attention of the colored retailer if it is found impossible to dispose of the stock among white customers of the firm making the sacrifice. The Negro thus makes a smaller profit on his sales, since he has to pay more for his goods on one hand, and on the other has to sell them at the existing level of prices to retain his customers.

And, now, to cap the climax, there is in several of his own segregated districts, and notoriously in the Harlem district, a concerted effort upon the part of white owners and agents (and even of Negro agents acting for white owners) to keep him out of the stores and thus out of the business life of his own sections. Upon one pretext and another the line is being drawn against the Negro business man who is doing or is desirous of doing business in his own segregated districts.

And should he attempt to operate outside of his own districts, say, to open a store in an Italian or other white district he will starve for patronage. If he goes into the financial and commercial districts and tries to enter into competition with Big white Business he will find the same toss of loaded dice against him. In fact, the bigger his attempt, the greater his ambition, the fiercer and more crooked is the game against him. Entering the "Charmed Circle of Big Biz," he finds that every white hand is turned against him, either openly or sneakingly. And that, not in ordinary business competition, but deliberately and with malicious intent. He will find that to maintain his rights, and even make collections of moneys to which he may be justly entitled for services rendered he must fight – litigate, litigate, litigate! And here, too, he discovers that the big law firms – usually possessed of the best legal talent – will not take a case for a Negro against a white man. And as he must take what talent he can get, he is generally beaten at the outset, since in the realm of American law, Might (of skill and experience) is right. Or if not beaten legally he is sold out by one white skin to another white skin. Ninety-nine times out of a hundred his white lawyer, hired to represent his interest, will give him the double-cross. But why not retain a Negro lawyer, you ask? Well, because for one thing, the average Negro lawyer has not had enough practice in big cases to enable him to handle them efficiently. And, in the second place, (also explaining why the average Negro lawyer lacks such practice) to pit a Negro lawyer against a white would be to insult the sensibilities and challenge the race pride of the judge, who in all cases is white. And to insult the sensibilities and challenge the pride of race of a white judge, even if only normally prejudiced against the Negro, is to throw one's case away.

Such is the brief and incomplete review of the odds against the Negro in the "Game of Loaded Dice." There are many other phases and numerous other inequalities in the fame, as each reader knows from personal experience, whether as an applicant for a "position," the possessor of a job, or as a unit in the advance guard of Negro business and commerce.

The New Negro – What is He?
(Chandler Owen and A. Philip Randolph, *The Messenger*,
August 1920)

Our title was the subject of an editorial in the *New York Age* which formed the basis of an extensive symposium. Most of the replies, however, have been vague and nebulous. THE MESSENGER, therefore, undertakes to supply the *New York Age* and the general public with a definite and clear portrayal of the New Negro.

It is well nigh axiomatic that the most accurate test of what a man or institution or a movement is, is first, what its aims are; second what its methods are, or how it expects to achieve its aims; and third, its general relations to current movements. Now, what are the aims of the New Negro? The answer to this question will fall under three general heads, namely, political, economic and social.

In politics, the New Negro, unlike the Old Negro, cannot be lulled into a false sense of security with political spoils and patronage. A job is not the price of his vote. He will not continue to accept political promissory notes from a political debtor, who has already had the power, but who has refused to satisfy his political obligations. The New Negro demands political equality. He recognizes the necessity of selective as well as elective representation. He realizes that so long as the Negro votes for the Republican or Democratic party, he will have only the right and privilege to elect but not to select his representatives. And he who selects the representatives controls the representative. The New Negro stands for universal suffrage.

A word here about the economic aims of the New Negro. Here, as a worker, he demands the full product of his toil. His immediate aim is more wages, shorter hours and better working conditions. As a consumer, he seeks to buy in the market, commodities at the lowest possible price.

The social aims of the New Negro are decidedly different from those of the Old Negro. Here he stands for absolute and unequivocal *"social equality."* He realizes that there cannot be any qualified equality. He insists that a society which is based upon justice can only be a society composed of *social equals*. He insists upon identity of social treatment. With respect to intermarriage, he maintains that it is the only logical, sound and correct aim for the Negro to entertain. He realizes that the acceptance of laws against intermarriage is tantamount to the acceptance of the stigma of inferiority. Besides, laws against intermarriage expose Negro women to sexual exploitation, and deprive their offspring, by white men, of the right to inherit the property of their father. Statistics show that there are nearly four million mulattoes in America as a result of miscegenation.

So much then for the aims of the New Negro. A word now about his methods. It is with respect to methods that the essential difference between the New and the Old Negro relates.

First, the methods by which the new Negro expects to realize his political aims are radical. He would repudiate and discard both of the old parties – Republican and Democratic. His knowledge of political science enables him to see that a political organization must have an economic foundation. A party whose money comes from working people, must and will represent working people. Now, everybody conceded that the Negro is essentially a worker. There are no big capitalists among them. There are a few petit bourgeoisie, but the process of money concentrations is destined to weed them out and drop them down into the ranks of the working class. In fact, the interests of all Negroes are tied up with the workers. Therefore, the Negro should support a working class political party. He is a fool or insane, who opposes his best interests by supporting his enemy. As workers, Negroes have nothing in common with their employers. The Negro wants high wages; the employer wants to pay low wages. The Negro wants to work short hours; the employer wants to work him long hours. Since this is true, it follows as a logical corollary that the Negro should not support a party of the employing class. Now, it is a question of fact that the Republican and Democratic Parties are parties of the employing or capitalist class.

On the economic field, the New Negro advocates that the Negro joins the labor unions. Wherever white unions discriminate against the Negro worker, then the only sensible thing to do is to form independent unions to fight both the white capitalists for more wages and shorter hours, on the one hand, and white labor unions for justice on the other. It is folly for the Negro to fight labor organization because some white unions ignorantly ignore or oppose him. It is about as logical and wise as to repudiate and condemn writing on the ground that it is used by some crooks for forgery. As a consumer, he would organize cooperative societies to reduce the high cost of living.

The social methods are: education and physical action in self defense. That education must constitute the basis of all action, is beyond the realm of the question. And to fight back in self defense, should not be accepted as a matter of course. No one who will not fight to protect his life is fit to live. Self defense is recognized as a legitimate weapon in all civilized countries. Yet the Old Crowd Negroes have counselled the doctrine of non-resistance.

As to current movements, the Negro would accept praise and support that which his enemies reject, condemn and oppose. He is tolerant. He would restore free speech, a free press and freedom of assemblage. He would release Debs. He would recognize the right of Russia to self-determination. He is opposed to the Treaty and the League of Nations.

Yet he rejects Lodge's reservations.[6] He knows that neither will help the people. As to Negro leaders, his object is to destroy them all and build up new ones.

Finally, the New Negro arrived upon the scene at the time of all other forward, progressive groups and movements – after the great world war. He is the product of the same world wide forces, that have brought into being the great liberal and radical movements that are now seizing the reins of political, economic and social power in all of the civilized countries of the world.

His presence is inevitable in these times of economic chaos, political upheaval and social distress. Yes there is a New Negro. And it is he who will pilot the Negro through this terrible hour of storm and stress.

The Black Man's Burden (A Reply to Rudyard Kipling) (By Hubert Harrison, *When Africa Awakes*, 1920)

Take up the Black Man's burden—
Send forth the worst ye breed,
And bind our sons in shackles
To serve your selfish greed;
To wait in heavy harness
Be-devilled and beguiled
Until the Fates remove you
From a world you have defiled.

Take up the black Man's burden—
Your lies may still abide
To veil the threat of terror
And check our racial pride;
Your cannon, church and courthouse
May still our sons constrain
To seek the white man's profit
And work the white man's gain.

Take up the Black Man's burden—
Reach out and hog the earth,
And leave your workers hungry
In the country of their birth;
Then, when your goal is nearest,
The end for which you fought

---

[6] Henry Cabot Lodge (1850–1924), US Senator who opposed the Treaty of Versailles on the grounds of US patriotism.

Watch other's trained efficiency
Bring all your hope to naught.

Take up the Black Man's burden—
Reduce their chiefs and kings
To toil of serf and sweeper
The lot of common things:
Sodden their soil with slaughter,
Ravish their lands with lead;
Go, sign them with your living
And seal them with your dead.

Take up the Black Man's burden—
And reap your old reward;
The curse of those ye cozen,
The hate of those ye barred
From your Canadian cities
And your Australian ports;
And when they ask for meat and drink
Go, girdle them with forts.

Take up the Black Man's burden—
Ye cannot stoop to less.
Will not your fraud of "freedom"
Still cloak your greediness?
But, by the gods ye worship,
And by the deeds ye do,
These silent, sullen peoples
Shall weigh your gods and you.

Take up the Black Man's burden—
Until the tail is told,
Until the balances of hate
Bear down the beam of gold.
And while ye wait remember
The justice, though delayed
Will hold you as her debtor
Till the Black Man's debt is paid.

A New Negro for a New Day
(By W. A. Domingo, *The Messenger*, November 1920)

A NEW spirit is abroad in the world. Ancient wrongs and oppressions are melting before the rising wrath of the masses of the entire world. This new spirit is a direct result of the war which destroyed millions of lives and enormous quantities of the products of labor, besides intensifying the sufferings of toilers everywhere. Just as the world war embraced all the races of mankind so have its consequences, typified by the new spirit, permeated all peoples. None is free from its influence; all are making demands for the democracy and justice that were eloquently mouthed by those who had and still have the power to make those words living realities. For the first time in human history have the lowly workers of world asserted themselves and given intelligent expression to their needs. Subject races, small nationalities and oppressed workers are realizing their kinship. The white workers of Russia, the yellow coolies of Korea, the brown ryots of India and the black toilers of Africa, the West Indies and the United States are making similar demands upon their oppressors, although they and their masters in many instances are alike in race, color, language and religion. The former speak the language of the oppressed; the latter the language of the oppressor. Labor is the common denominator of the working class of the world. Exploitation is the common denominator of oppressors everywhere.

Many oppress because they profit from it, or think they do. There is a community of interests between oppressors. The real beneficiaries of exploitation are a small minority. They maintain their position because they control the machinery of government and the vehicles of public information – the school, church, stage, press and platform. These agencies support similar institutions. They defend present economic conditions, defame the working class; white and black, and abase the Negro race as a whole.

As a considerable part of the American working class. Negroes have grievance against those who profit from the present system which operates against the interest of all workers. As Negroes they have specific reasons for desiring the downfall of those who manipulate public opinion for the creation of race prejudice which in turn divides the black and white workers of the country into warring camps. The workers of both races suffer from this vicious propaganda and it is to their interest to change conditions which make it possible. The reason for this propaganda and its resultant division of the working class is to rob them of their labor. And the robbery of the workers of the product of their toil sanctioned by our present system of government. Even if the black and white workers unite industrially, as they are slowly but surely doing, they will still be robbed of some of the product of their toil unless they unite for working-class political action. To stop our present robbery and remove the cause of most of our racial friction it is necessary to change the system which legalizes this robbery.

In our present society most human beings must work to live. They must have access to a job. The private owners of land, factories, railroads, mines and machinery have in their power to deny their fellows work. And without work a man and his family must suffer. Because of the developments brought about by inventions a man can produce more than is necessary for the consumption of himself and his family. But because the things produced do not belong to the producer but to the owner of his job the former finds wages, which represent a small portion of the things he has produced. Insufficient to keep himself and his family in a reasonable degree of comfort. The owners of jobs have common interest and pay only as much wages as they are forced to pay. Their interests are opposed to those of their employees. And color or race makes no difference. Jews underpay Jews, and Negro employers rob their employees regardless of race or color. The interests of all workers are alike. Many workers do not realize this and work against their own interests. They refuse to join labor unions or exclude some workers because of their color. They also vote to strengthen the political chains which enslave them.

This is true of the Negro worker who votes for the Republican party which is frankly the party of Big Business. It is the party of the landlord and banker, black and white, Jew or Gentile. But most Negroes vote for the Republican party because it was the party of Lincoln and because he had freed their fathers. Whatever debt Negroes owed the Republican party has been paid long ago. Besides, it is the Republican party that delivered the Negro into the hands of the South in 1876 when Hayes was seated on condition that he withdraw federal troops from the South. For nearly fifty years the Republican party has been in power controlling the Army, Navy and Supreme Court and during that period the oppression of Negroes has been cumulatively increased.

The only party that can make any appeal to Negroes that is based upon mutual interests is the Socialist Party, it is composed of enlightened workers who repudiate the Du Bois-Gompers tactics of "rewarding friends and punishing enemies." These workers realize that the chain of labor is as strong as its weakest link and from the standpoint of class consciousness Negroes are, through no fault of theirs the weakest link.

If Negroes would be free then they must unite with others who are struggling for freedom. And it is the Socialists who are striving to free America from the throes of wage slavery. The slogan "those who would be free must themselves strike the first blow" gains added importance in the present political struggle. If Negroes think themselves freer than white workingmen then let them vote for Mr. Harding and the Republican party which represent the forces of reaction; if they feel themselves less free than white working class men then let them vote with their fellow workers of all colors who repudiate both the Democratic and Republican tickets and vote for Eugene V. Debs, freedom and progress on November 2.

Wanted – A Colored International (abridged)
(By Hubert Harrison, *Negro World*, 28 May 1921)

All over the world today the subject peoples of all colors are rising to the call of democracy, to formulate their grievances and plan their own enfranchisement from the chains of slavery, social, political and economic. From Ireland and Armenia, from Russia and Finland, from India, Egypt and West Africa, efforts have come looking for their relief from the thralldom of centuries of oppression.

Of all those people the darker races are the ones who have suffered most. In addition to the economic evils under which the others suffer they must endure those which flow from the degrading dogma of the color line; that dogma which has been set up by the Anglo-Saxon peoples and adopted in varying degrees by other white peoples who have followed their footsteps in the path of capitalistic imperialism; that dogma which declares that the lands and labors of colored races everywhere shall be the legitimate prey of white peoples and that the Negro, the Hindu, the Chinese and Japanese must endure insult and contumely in a world that was made for all.

Here in America, we who are of African ancestry and Negro blood have drunk this cup of gall and wormwood to the bitter dregs. Our labor built the greatness of this land in which we are shut out from places of public accommodation: from the church, the ballot and the laws' protection. We are Jim-Crowed, disfranchised and lynched without redress from law or public sentiment, which vigorously exercises its humanity on behalf of the Irish, Armenians and Germans thousands of miles away, but can find no time to concern itself with the barbarism and savagery perpetrated on black fellow citizens in its very midst.

This cynical indifference extends to the leaders of the Christian Church, the high priests of democracy and the conservative exponents of the aims of labor. Thus the Negro is left out of the plans being put forward by these groups for the reorganization and reconstruction of American affairs on the basis of "democracy".

We Negroes have no faith in American democracy, and can have none so long as lynching, economic and social serfdom lie in the dark alleys of its mental reservations. When a president of this country can become famous abroad for his preachments on "The New Freedom" while pregnant Negro women are roasted by white savages in his section of the South with not one word of protest coming from his lips; when a church which calls itself Christian can grow hysterically "alarmed" over the souls of savages in Central Africa, while it sees every day the bodies of its black fellow Christians brutalized and their souls blasted while it smirks in gleeful acquiescence; when the "aims of labor" on its march to justice exclude all reference to the masses of black workers whom conservative labor leaders would condemn in America to the shards and sweepings of economic existence – when such is the great watchword, then we Negroes must be excused for feeling neither love nor respect for the rotten hypocrisy which masquerades as democracy in America.

When we look upon the Negro republics of Haiti and Santo Domingo where American marines murder and rape at their pleasure while the financial vultures of Wall Street scream with joy over the bloody execution which brings the wealth of these countries under their control; when we see the Virgin Islanders in the deadly coils of American capitalism gasping for a breath of liberty, and Mexico menaced by the same monster, we begin to realize that we must organize our forces to save ourselves from further degradation and ultimate extinction.

We have appealed to the common Christian sentiment of the white people for justice, but we have been told that with the white people of this country race is more powerful than religion. We have appealed to the common patriotism which should bind us together in a common loyalty to the practice rather than the preachments of democracy, and in every case we have been rebuffed and spurned. We have depended on protest and publicity, and protest and publicity addressed to the humane sentiments of white America have availed us nothing. We are too weak to wage war against these evil conditions with force, yet we cannot afford to wait for help to come to us from those who are our oppressors. We must, therefore, learn a lesson from those others who suffer elsewhere from evils similar to ours. Whether it be Sinn Fein or Swadesha,[7] their experiences should be serviceable to us.

Our first duty is to come together in mind as well as in mass; to take counsel from each other and to father strength from contact; to organize

---

[7] The Swadeshi Movement was a movement for Indian Independence which orchestrated mass boycotts against British rule in India between 1906–1917.

and plan effective resistance to race prejudice wherever it may raise its head; to attract the attention of all possible friends whose circumstances may have put them in the same plight and whose program may involve the same way of escape. We must organize, plan and act, and the time for the action is now. A call should be issued for a congress of the darker races, which should be frankly anti-imperialistic and should serve as an international center of cooperation from which strength may be drawn for the several sections of the world of color. Such a congress should be worldwide in scope; it should include representatives and spokesmen of the oppressed peoples of India, Egypt, China, West and South Africa and the West Indies, Hawaii, the Philippines, Afghanistan, Algeria and Morocco. It should be made up of those who realize that capitalist imperialism which mercilessly exploits the darker races for its own financial purposes is the enemy which we must combine to fight with arms as varied as those by which it is fighting to destroy our manhood, independence and self-respect. Against the pseudo-internationalism of the short-sighted savants who are posturing on the stage of capitalist culture it should oppose the stark internationalism of clear vision which sees that capitalism means conflict of races and nations, and that war and oppression of the weak spring from the same economic motive – which is at the root of capitalist culture [...]

Enslaved
(By Claude McKay, *The Liberator*, July 1921)

OH when I think of my long-suffering race
For weary centuries despised, oppressed,
Enslaved and lynched, denied a human place
In the great life line of the Christian West;
And in the Black Land disinherited,
Robbed in the ancient country of its birth,–
My heart grows sick with hate, becomes as lead,
For my race, my race, outcast upon the earth.
Then from the dark depths of my soul I cry
To the avenging angel to consume
The white man's world of wonders utterly:
Let it be swallowed up in earth's vast womb,
Or upward roll as sacrificial smoke
To liberate my people from its yoke!

Frightful Friendship vs Self Defense
(By Hubert Harrison, *Negro World*, 18 July 1921)

It was a wise man who said, "God protect me from my friends; I can look after my enemies." We, of the Negro race, are reminded of this old saw whenever a race riot loses its American character of being a one-sided massacre of frightened and defenseless sheep and casualties appear on both sides. The Associated Press and the other news gathering agencies first magnify the Negro's losses and minimize the whites as a fixed policy, whose object is to convince Negroes that fighting back in self-defense is useless and dangerous to them. Then when anyone speaks up in favor of the new policy which American Negroes have been pursuing since 1917, our good white friends insist that that is "bad advice" – for Negroes; although it is the very policy in pursuit of which the United States Government is this year sending ninety-four percent of its revenues on wars past, present and future. The very papers which, like the *Times*, *World* and *Journal*, denounce self-defense for Negroes on the editorial page, carry on the front page, in bold headlines, Secretary Denby's address, in which he upholds and expounds the national policy, "In times of peace prepare for war" "What makes the might differ?"

Every reader of these same newspapers knows that, in the South, the Negro, who is arrested is absolutely at the mercy of any lawless mob. The officers of the law always fail to protect his life. And any colored community in the South may be invaded at any time by armed mobs eager and able to kill, burn and loot, at their own sweet will, unchecked by the legal authorities whose power always breaks down when such colored communities require their protection. Does any white newspaper in America dare to deny this fact? No. Then what can be the objection to Negroes, in such cases, arming in defense of their own lives and the majesty of that law which the mob has outraged? It can not be legality, because every statute book – even in the South – concedes that self-defense is legal and proper. The real reason is, that every one of these fake friends thinks it a lesser evil that law-abiding Negroes should be killed by lawless whites, than that lawless whites should be killed, even in self-defense, by law-abiding Negroes, because this is, after all, "a white man's country." Naturally, we Negroes are, for biologic reasons, unable to concede this point of preference. Therefore, such white newspapers are wasting their time and space advising us to let ourselves be killed. It would be much better if they develop the same amount of time and space to the "cracker" in the South, and the enforcement of law and order among them.

These remarks are called forth as a result of white newspaper comments on the mass meeting held on Sunday, June 5, in New York, under the auspices of the Liberty League of Negro-Americans, and on the speech delivered there by the editor of this section. In that speech, after stating the inside facts of the Tulsa race riots, which the white newspapers had suppressed, I insisted (as I have done since 1916) that since Negroes in America (like Irishmen in Ireland) were the victims of violence because they had been defenceless; that since lynching and pogroms were indulged in because they cost the aggressors nothing; if the prospective victims should put up a stout and costly defense the violence would be indulged in only by those who were willing to pay the price, and would be very much reduced even at that. This seems to rile the *New York World*, the *Times* and the *Journal*. The *Times* lied about our meeting like a Southern Gentleman. The *World* took the *Times*' report as gospel truth, and addressed an allocution to me and to the Liberty League in a rather confused and illogical editorial. The *Journal*, whose owner controls the photoplay "The Birth of a Nation," also rushed into print to protect the dear Negroes from "bad advice." We append the brief editorials of the *World* and the *Journal*, and our answers to the *World* and *Times* that our readers may compare Caucasian and Negro reasoning and decide, for themselves, which is worth their while. We merely observe that the *World* deliberately lies when it says that any of the speakers advocated lawlessness in the East, West, North or South.

Bad Advice to Negroes

World, June 6, 1921

In advising men of his race to arm themselves, Herbert H. Harrison, president of the Liberal League of Negro Americans, gives them the worst possible counsel. In protest against lawlessness in Oklahoma he urges lawlessness by ten times as many in the East. In reprisal for rioting and outrage he outlines a policy that would cause further outrage and inevitably lead to conflict.

Almost as if he welcomed them Mr. Harrison says he would not be astonished "if we saw three splendid race riots by next September." He admits that fifty armed Negroes in Tulsa "went to patrol the jail." This conduct was grossly improper, whether committed by white men or colored. As General Barrett pointed out, the lawless "patrol" should have been at once disarmed and dispersed. Its presence aggravated, if it did not cause, the horrors that followed.

The further troubles to which acceptance of his counsel might lead would undoubtedly swell the membership of Mr. Harrison's organization. But this is bad policy. An American community is either lawless or law-abiding. If it is law-abiding it will not tolerate private armies. If it is lawless there is no safety for civilization except in the return to law.

Bad Advice to Colored Men

To Carry Weapons Provoked Their Use
New York Evening Journal, June 6

H.H. Harrison, president of the Liberty League of Negro Americans, advises his colored friends to arm themselves and get ready for anti-negro riots. Mr Harrison predicted three "splendid race riots by next September."

The advice is quite natural and well meant. But it may prove unwise. Those that have weapons are apt to use them. And for men hopelessly outnumbered, that could by no possibility win in the end, to be armed might be the very worst thing.

Mr. Harrison is quoted as saying that at Tulsa, where serious riots occurred, "a group of fifty colored men merely went to patrol the jail when rumors of intended violence to a colored prisoner reached their ears."

It is possible that a patrol of fifty armed colored men started the riots. It is absolutely certain that the colored men were bound to come out second best when the rioting began.

Livingston, the white explorer, when travelling in Africa, made it a point to carry no weapon. This won the confidence of the natives and in Livingston's opinion contributed to his safety.

The plan that Livingston adopted among the black man in Africa is probably the best plan, and the safest, for a black man among the white men of America.

Negroes and Self–Defense

To the Editor of the *New York Times*:

Dear Sir; – If I submit that the careless reporting of one of your reporters in today's Times has done me and the organization which I represent a grave injury will you be so good as to permit me to offer a few brief corrections? I refer to the report of a meeting held on Sunday in Harlem relative to the Tulsa race riots under the somewhat sensational caption "Urges Negroes Here to Arm Themselves."

In the first place, the meeting was called by the Liberty League of

Negro Americans,[8] an organization with branches extending in flourishing fashion as far west as St. Louis, Mo., and not by the Liberal League. In this next place, it is not true that the speakers were all colored. The white woman who indorsed every step of our program in a brief but able speech is, perhaps, the most famous high school teachers in the state of New York. I withhold her name now only because she might be bothered by the dangerous impression created by the carelessness (or worse) of your reporter.

No funds were solicited, since, as I told the audience, we were not yet sure as to whether funds were needed, or would be welcomed by the Tulsa authorities from outside sources. As soon as we can learn of the need and the desire for such funds we shall raise them. I did prophesy that we would have at least three great race riots in America before September, but I didn't describe them as "splendid." As a man of African extraction I confess myself unable to see anything "splendid" in race riots. And, finally, I did not make any special appeals to Negroes to arm themselves – in New York. A sentence from our telegram to the Governor of Oklahoma will give the basic idea expressed by me and backed by the League.

"If this sort of thing can be done with impunity in a southern state, then it will become necessary for Negroes all over the South to arm for self-defense. Surely no sane man will argue that they must and should die like defenseless sheep. And I certainly believe that, as one of the (white) speakers said, a Negro who shoots down lawless murderers in defense of his home is contributing to the creation of a wholesome respect for law and order and orderly legal processes. Don't you think so too? At any rate, the right of self-defense is conceded by all laws, Southern as well as Northern, and you must have observed yourself that, whether you and I differ or not on this point, my people are defending themselves now, as a last resort. The pity of it is that this should have become necessary in a land where, in theory, all are entitled to the equal protection of the law, but only white men get it – in the South.

Yours respectfully,
HUBERT H. HARRISON.
June 6 1921

---

[8] The Liberty League of Negro Americans was set up by Harrison in 1917.

The Negro and Self Defense

New York City, June 9, 1921
513 Lennox Ave, care of Porro Press,
To the Editor of the *New York World*:

Sir—We, Negroes, thank you very much for the very estimable service which the *World* has been always ready and willing to render us, vis the giving of good advice, which, by the way, costs you absolutely nothing. In regards to your ill-informed editorial of yesterday's date, I was somewhat surprised to see that the writer based himself so solidly upon the news item printed in the *Times* the day before. The *Times'* account was a false and prejudiced one, designed to do as much damage as was possible to the cause of the Liberty League. The *World* has no excuse for writing an editorial based on anything less reliable than its own report. The *Times*, by the way, was one of the papers which had not been invited to send a reporter to the meeting, while the *World* had been invited and sent none.

The people who were present at that meeting will testify that no lawlessness, whether in the East or West, was advocated by any speaker at the meeting of last Sunday, but we do insist all the time on calling the attention of Negroes to the fact that, ultimately, the reason why Negroes or Irishmen are the victims of violence is because they are defenseless. We, therefore, insist Mr. Editor, that one way for Negroes to put down lawless violence is by resisting it to the full with the lawful violence of self-defense. If you and other so-called white friends of the Negro are opposed to this, then you simply stand in the position of one who would look on and see a friend get his throat cut without offering him a gun or a knife to prevent that throat cutting; but as soon as he grabs a gun or takes a knife to save his throat, you will always be found ready and willing to run up and offer against his self-defense the protest which you never offered against the original aggression. And for such frightful friendship the good white people of this country might just as well understand that the Negro of America today does not care two pins.

Yours, very truly,
HUBERT H. HARRISON.
President of the Liberty League.

Liberating Africa
(Editorial, *The Crusader*, August 1921)

All intelligent Negroes are agreed upon the necessity of liberating Africa from the incubus of European capitalist control. Prevailing differences are in regard to the methods by which this liberation can be achieved.

The African Blood Brotherhood and THE CRUSADER believe in utilizing every possible means towards this and, while keeping in mind that in the ultimate final success will depend upon the degree to which the opinion of the Negro masses have been mobilized and their minds prepared for the necessary sacrifice.

We believe that it is essential to the early success of our cause that the Negro seek co-operation with the Indian Nationalists, the Turkish Nationalists, the Persians, the Arabs and all other peoples participating in the common struggle for liberty, and especially with those people whose struggle is against the great enslaver of the darker races – England.

It is our belief that we should make common cause with the Indians and the Irish Republicans, with Soviet Russia and the Turkish Nationalists and with all other forces now, or in the future, menacing the British Empire in particular and the capitalist-imperialist world in general.

Since it is by the British Empire particularly that we are subjugated, we must seek the destruction of the British Empire. And since it is best to fight with allies than without them, we must seek cooperation with all other forces consciously working with the same end in view, and intelligently encourage and stimulate such forces as are working unconsciously to the same purpose.

Since it is under the capitalist-imperialist system that Negroes suffer, we must boldly seek the destruction of that system, and to that end seek co-operation with such other forces – Socialism, Bolshevism, or what not – that are engaged in war to the death with Capitalism.

Since it is the anglo-saxon race that issues the dictum of Negro inferiority and is doing its utmost to bring the French and other Latin peoples around to this anglo-saxon point of view, it is the sensible racial duty of the Negro to work for the isolation and eventual degradation of the anglo-saxon race.

Since the Christian religion, as interpreted in theory and practice by its chief adherents – the white peoples of the world – has time and again given official sanction to the anglo-saxon dictum of Negro inferiority, and support to the idiotic theory that Negroes were specially created by a white-favoring Christian God to be "hewers of wood and drawers of water" for the white race, it is up to intelligent Negroes to seriously study the problem of religion and to weigh the merits of the world's two leading religions – Christianity and Mohammedanism – in their relation to the Negro: one the religion of the white imperial peoples and one the religion of millions upon millions of black, brown and yellow peoples in Africa and Asia; one the religion of Negro inferiority, the other the religion of the equality of all believers.

Since it is to the interest of the white imperial peoples to seek the perpetuation of white world domination and to fight all forces aimed at ending such domination, it is essential that Negroes cautiously examine all those measures which the white press, the white pulpit and white statesmen urge as necessary for "the salvation of (white capitalist) civilization."

It is only by intelligently utilizing all the forces opposed to those who have Africa and the Africans in subjugation that we can hope to achieve the liberation of Africa and the redemption of her races the world over.

Hands Across the Sea
(By Hubert Harrison, *Negro World*, 10 September, 1921)

The most dangerous phase of developed capitalism is that of imperialism – when having subjugated its workers and exploited its natural resources at home, it turns with grim determination towards 'undeveloped' races and areas to renew the same processes there. This is the phase in which militarism and navalism develop with dizzying speed with their accumulating burden of taxation for 'preparedness' against the day when the capitalist class of the nation must use the final argument of forces against its foreign competitors for markets. These markets change their character under the impact of international trade, and are no longer simply markets for the absorption of finished products, but become fields for the investment of accumulated surplus profits, in which process they are transformed into original sources for the production of surplus by the opening up of mines, railroads and other large-scale capitalist enterprises. It becomes necessary to take over the government of the selected area in order that the profits may be effectually guaranteed and 'spheres of influence', 'protectorates', and 'mandates' are set up.

Thus the lands of 'backward' peoples are brought within the central influence of the capitalistic economic system and the subjection of black, brown and other colored workers to the rigors of the 'white man's burden' comes as a consequence of the successful exploitation of white workers at home, and binds them both in an international opposition to the continuance of the capitalist regime. Most Americans who are able to see the process more or less clearly in the case of other nations are unable to see the same process implicit and explicit in the career of their own.

The case of Haiti and the present plight of the Haitian people helps us to see the aims of our own American imperialists in the white light of pitiless publicity. A people of African descent, scarcely seven hundred miles from our own shores, with a government of their own, have had their government suppressed and their liberties destroyed by the Navy Department of the United States without even the slight formality of a declaration of war by the United States Congress as required by the Constitution. In the presidential chair our 'cracker' marines have installed a puppet in the person of Monsieur D'Artiguenave[9] to carry out their will; The legislative bodies of the erstwhile republic have been either suppressed or degraded; unoffending black citizens have been wantonly butchered in cold blood, and thousands have been forced into slavery to labor on the military roads without pay. Here is American imperialism in its stark, repulsive nakedness. And what are we going to do about it?

The fight which will soon be waged in Congress for the restoration of Haitian rights is receiving no help from the millions of Negroes who are presumably interested in the international movement for the practical advancement of people of Negro blood. It is high time that it should. This is an opportunity that lies ready to our hands. And if we would use our votes here in an intelligent, purposeful way we could at least make our voices heard and heeded in Washington on behalf of our brothers in black who are suffering seven hundred miles away. Pending this, we could inaugurate gigantic propaganda meetings in such places as Faneuil Hall, Madison Square Garden, and the Negro Churches; we could in our newspapers and magazines agitate for the withdrawal of the forces of the American Occupation, as the Irish did on behalf of Ireland; we could at least get up a gigantic petition with a million signatures and carry it to Congress. Even a 'silent protest parade' would become us better than this slavish apathy and servile acquiescence in which we are now sunk.

Believe it or not as we will, the Negro American in now on trial before the eyes of the world and if he fails to act he may yet hear the God of opportunity utter those fateful words recorded in the third chapter of

---

[9] Philippe Sudre D'Artiguenave was a president installed by the USA following its occupation of Haiti in 1915.

Revelations concerning the angel of the church of the Laodiceans. For we may be sure that French, British and Belgian imperialism is a limb of the same tree of white domination on which our home-made branch grows.

Negroes have Slumbered for Centuries
(By Marcus Garvey, *Negro World*, 15 April 1922)

Fellow Men of the Negro Race, *Greeting*

It becomes my pleasure to address you once more in the interest of the Universal Negro Improvement Association. We are at this time engaged in an international campaign to mobilize the sentiment of Negroes everywhere in behalf of Africa's freedom.

As we view the great changes that are taking place we conclude that the time has come for the four hundred million members of our race to also change their attitude on world affairs. For centuries we have slumbered in a condition of slavery, paying the extreme price for our lethargy. Today, as mighty changes sweep over the affairs of men, we cannot but arouse ourselves to the consciousness of self determination.

"What Other Men Can Do –"

All peoples are endeavoring to politically free themselves and place themselves so that in the great struggle for the survival of the fittest they may be found among those worthy of holding their own in the affairs of men. Four hundred million Negroes can do nothing more praiseworthy than to seek their own emancipation; to found for themselves a government; to build up a mighty nation that will stand the test of time. All this is the work of the Universal Negro Improvement Association. We are commissioned through this great movement to go throughout the length and breadth of the world, teaching and converting men to this great doctrine. We believe this race of ours should occupy a place of importance in the world second to none. When we think of the glorious achievements of the Anglo-Saxon, the Teutonic race, the Japanese and other races of the world, we cannot but be encouraged in the belief that what other men have done we also can do. We have set ourselves a standard and each and every member of the race must reach up to it. We, as it were, have hitched our wagons to the stars, and we shall continue to climb and climb until we have reached the highest point in the heavenly constellation.

A Practical Dream

An appeal is now made to all the Negro peoples of America, the West Indies, South and Central America, Canada and Africa to line up in every way possible behind this gigantic Negro movement, so as to enable us to put over the program in its entirety. The things we lack now are courage, faith and confidence. If I can get every Negro to feel as George Washington felt when he pictured to himself an independent America; like William Pitt when he pictured a glorious and an extended British Empire; like Napoleon as he pictured the conquest of the air; like Marconi as he pictured the conveyance of transatlantic messages carried on the current of the air, then we can be assured of the immediate conquest of Africa and the emancipation of four hundred million souls. Is there a difference between George Washington and the humblest Negro of today? Between Napoleon and any black man that you see? The answer is NO, but for the fact that Napoleon discovered himself as a man, George Washington discovered himself as a man and declared that what other men have done, they would also do.

The difference between men is that some know themselves, while others do not. The men, the races and nations that know themselves are those that are able to lift themselves from one condition to the other within the scale of human achievement. Those who have never discovered themselves have perished through their indolence, through their neglect, through their lethargy.

The Universal Negro Improvement Association appeals to four hundred million Negroes asking that they get to know themselves, know that God created them men co-equal in rights with the other races of the world, giving to them certain rights that cannot be disputed, and among those rights is the possession of Africa, is the possession of racial freedom. Shall we have Africa? Shall we be free? This must be determined by every black man, woman and child in the world.

The Freeing of Africa

The Universal Negro Improvement Association is making it so that the Negro is fully awake, fully conscious that he has been robbed, exploited and murdered for centuries, and is now preparing himself not to be outdone any longer.

We are living in an age of reorganization, when peoples everywhere are striking out for freedom, for complete independence, as the people of India, of Ireland, of Egypt, and of Palestine. Like the rest who have won their freedom we are agitating for ours, and we feel sure that in a short while we shall become completely free; but the acquisition of our rights, the freeing of ourselves, depends not upon what others will do for us, but what we are willing to do for and by ourselves. We surely shall not expect Great Britain to free Africa, nor America, nor France to Free Africa, nor Italy. It is for four hundred million Negroes to get together the world over; the fifteen millions of America to get together with the twenty-five millions of South and Central America, with the 180 millions of Africa, and then unitedly strike a universal blow for real democracy, for real human freedom.

The Assembling of Legislators

Let every Negro in the world look toward the great International Convention assembled in New York City from the 1st to the 31st of August in the present year. At this convention thousands of delegates who will have come from all parts of the world will raise their voices in solemn protest against the many injustices done to us as a people, and if we must die, then four hundred millions of us shall die so as to insure the freedom of our Motherland Africa and the respect of this race of ours.

I say to Negroes throughout the world, line up behind the Universal Negro Improvement Association with your money, with your education, with your physical strength and let us put this program over. It is not a question as to whether it can be done; it is a declaration that it must be done. The Colonists under the leadership of George Washington did it for America, Tolstoi did it in his preparatory work, Kerensky, Trotsky and Lenin have done it by action for Russia; you and I must do it for Africa.

O Black Men, How Long?

There is work for each and every one of us; no Negro is too old, no Negro is too young not to be able to contribute something in one way or the other toward the work of the Universal Negro Improvement Association, Remember, men, this is not a work for the few, this is not a work for the individual; this is a work for all. In the classification of races we are put down as a part of the great human family, and each and every section in this great family is supposed to lift itself on its own initiative and struggle toward a common standard. The white man has set the standard of the present day the yellow man is climbing up toward the standard – black me, how long can you afford to fall behind? The question of superiority and inferiority of races will linger just so long as the one race remains weak and allow the other races to become strong, but when all races will have on their own initiative gone out and accomplished for themselves, thereby proving the distinctive fitness of each to rise to a common height, then and there will this great difference of races be settled, once and forever. No black man will flatter himself to believe that so long as he lags behind and look to the white man, or any other man, will he get the respect that is due him, but whenever he strikes out on his own account to do for himself, then and there will he be accepted by the rest of his fellow men as an equal, as a companion, as a proper associate.

These are the hopes of the Universal Negro Improvement Association, and I feel that every Negro is going to support that movement to have them all realized. You can help now by giving to us the financial support that is necessary. Send us a contribution to our African Redemption Fund; let it be $5, $10, $20, $30, $50, $70, $100, or send a contribution to the Convention Fund in like amount. This forthcoming convention will be an expensive one; many important propositions will have to be undertaken and properly financed, and the Universal Negro Improvement Association can only carry out the program as far as each and every member of the race will contribute thereto. The time for helping is now. You are asked to do your bit. Write to the Universal Negro Improvement Association, 56 West 135th Street, New York City, N.Y., U.S.A.

With very best wishes for your success, I have the honor to be,
Your obedient servant,
MARCUS GARVEY, President-General, Universal
Negro Improvement Association, Cincinnati, Ohio,
April 4, 1922

Birthright
(By Claude McKay, *The Liberator*, August 1922)

SOME friendly critics think that my attitude towards the social status of the Negro should be more broadly socialistic and less chauvinistically racial as it seems to them. These persons seem to believe that the pretty parlor talk of international brotherhood or the radical shibboleth of "class Struggle" is sufficient to cure the Negro cancer along with all the other social ills of modern civilization. Apparently they are content with an intellectual recognition of the Negro's place in the class struggle, meanwhile ignoring the ugly fact that his disabilities as a worker are relatively heavier than those of the white worker.

Being a Negro, I think it is my proud birthright to put the case of the Negro proletarian, to the best of my ability, before the white members of the movement to which I belong. For the problem of the darker races is a rigid test of Radicalism. To some radicals it might seem more terrible to face than the barricades. But this racial question may be eventually the monkey wrench thrown into the machinery of American revolutionary struggle.

The Negro radical wants more than anything else to find in the working class movement a revolutionary attitude towards Negroes different from the sympathetic interest of bourgeois philanthropists and capitalist politicians. And if this difference is not practically demonstrated, Negro leaders can hardly go to the ignorant black masses and show them why they should organize and work by the standard of the white workers. Karl Marx's economic theories are hard to digest, and Negroes, like many other lazy-minded workers, may find it easier to put their faith in the gospel of that other Jew, Jesus.

The Negroes might remain, in the United States of America, a solid army, twelve million strong, a reactionary mass, men, women and children. They might remain a reactionary fact, distrustful – of the revolutionary activities of the white working class. They might remain the tool of the ruling class, to be used effectively, as in the past, against radical labor. And in that event the black workers will suffer – the white workers will lose – the ruling class will win.

And so it is not only the birthright of the Negro radical to educate the black worker, but it is also his duty to interpret him to the uninformed white radical who is prone to accept the colorful fiction rather than the stark reality of the Negro's struggle for full social and economic freedom. Where the white radical is quite sharp in detecting every bourgeois trap, however carefully hidden, that is set for the white worker, he very often loses his keen perceptions when he approaches the Negro question, and sometimes falls into the trap. And by his blunder he not only aids the bourgeoisie, but also the ultra-nationalist Negro leaders who, in their insistent appeal to the race prejudice of blacks against whites, declare that no class of white people will ever understand the black race.

And such a point of view is quite justifiable if judged by the silly rot about Negroes in general that sometimes gets printed in the radical press. A typical case is an article called "Outcry Against Black Horror" which appeared in the London *Communist*[10] of April 8th under the

---

[10] *The Communist* was the newspaper of the Communist Party of Great Britain from 1920–1923.

endorsement of the editor. With an unconscious sense of the comic the editor of the *Communist* remarks that "it is part of the normal brutality of imperialism to ignore things like those set out herein." But if this communist editor had any real knowledge or judgment or taste or sense of humor he would have recognized the article in question as a patently cheap and vicious sort of bourgeois propaganda document that would disgrace the pages of the most flamboyant Northcliffe or Hearst sheet, and only fit for a publication like *John Bull*.[11] By its ugly phrases and false statements-such as "crime against the white race," "In the Wild West when a colored man outrages a white woman he is lynched without ado," "white people being enslaved by black and colored savages" – and its stirring up of the most primitive racial passions, the article violates every principle of Communism and shows the incompetency of the English editor for his job. It is on a par with the unscrupulous propaganda of Viereck's *American Monthly*.[12]

And another example of this well organized and far flung propaganda is the recent statement in the Japan *Chronicle*, a mouthpiece of·the English bourgeoisie, published in Kobe, blowing hot and cold, liberal where the interests of the British governing class are concerned, but intolerant and hostile towards the interests of the Japanese ruling class, it says that Americans, having been forced to resort to stern measures against Negroes because of the "blacks" abnormal passion for white women, should be foremost in protesting against the presence of colored troops in Germany.

It happens at this moment to be expedient for the Anglo Saxon bourgeoisie (which in its slave-holding and colonial rule has followed a set policy of exploiting and degrading the men and women of the colored masses everywhere) should resent the presence of colored troops in Germany; but the reaction of those Anglo-Saxons who make a profession of communism is not quite so clear.

The truth is, as shown by the statistics of the case, the percentage of crime among the colored troops in Germany is remarkably low in comparison·with that of white occupational troops in India, the West Indies, Africa and other lands over which imperialism holds, sway. And it is very low when set against the natural enemies of any white capitalist army. Lewis Gannett, after an impartial and thorough investigation of the charges against the colored troops in the Rhineland, gave his

---

[11] *John Bull* was a conservative Sunday newspaper in England.
[12] George Sylvester Viereck (1884–1962), later a pro-Nazi propagandist who published 'Would-Be Assassins' in *American Monthly* in 1922.

report in the New York Nation of May 25, 1921, and it discredits all the prejudicial and highly colored accounts that have been written about the crimes of the black troops in Germany. Surely it is the bounden duty of the radicals, having regard to the high purpose of their work, to get the proper information on such important subjects. It is their business to reject the stupid bourgeois custom of general indictment of a nation of people on the basis of the practices of an individual or a minority. From this lowest level of radical absurdity it is pleasing to rise to the higher plane of artistic bourgeois propaganda. "Birthright," a recent novel by T. S. Stribling, is a powerful plea for the preservation of existing Southern standards.[13] The white man, it says in effect, has his own code of morals, a code which makes for a special kind of culture. The black man possesses another, immutably different. They are two streams that will never meet. This is the main theme of the narrative. The hero of the tale, Peter Siner, is quite incidental to the plot. Siner is a mulatto college graduate of weak character. There is nothing very remarkable about him. He might have been white; there are many such people in the world, persons of good intentions who lack the impulse or means to carry them out.

Mr. Stribling believes in the institution of entailment. The white man of the South holds title to his property and culture, which he transmits to his children. The white town also holds Niggertown in fee. Whitetown does not exert itself to work. It lives a leisurely life on the back of Niggertown. Whitetown has a double standard of sex morals by which its best young blood flows regularly into the rising stream of Niggertown and gives America the finest results of mixed mating in the world. Niggertown itself is very dirty, filthy and immoral. It transgresses all the superficial standards of the moral code by which Whitetown lives. Niggertown, according to the standards of Whitetown, is lazy and unthrifty, yet, by its labors, Niggertown keeps Whitetown clean, respectable and comfortable. Niggertown, like most servants' quarters, is ugly because it gives its best time to make Whitetown beautiful.

"Birthright," is a lovely and admirable description of life in the sunny South, where only the white bourgeoisie can afford the luxury of laziness. Mr. Stribling is an ardent advocate of this birthright of the white ruling class. All that is necessary to change the beautiful picture is that the Negroes of the South should realize that they are entitled to an equal share of the white birthright which they have created. The Negroes have

---

[13] T. S. Stribling (1881–1965), writer and lawyer from Tennessee.

the potential power to that share. They need only the knowledge in order to use that power rightly.

And Mr. Stribling gives the key to that power. He says: "No white Southerner knows his own village so minutely as does any member of the colored population. The colored villagers see the whites off their guard and just as they are, and that is an attitude in which no one looks his best. The Negroes might be called the black recording angels of the South. If what they know should be shouted aloud in any Southern town, its social life would disintegrate." Well, for my part, as a lover of humanity and freedom and truth, I say let it disintegrate, and make way for something better and nobler. Let the Black Recording Angel speak out!

The Colonial Congress and the Negro
(By Richard B. Moore,[14] *The Crisis*, July 1927)

The International Congress against Colonial Oppression and Imperialism held in Brussels last February passed a strong set of resolutions on the Negro problem, from which we publish an abstract:

GENERAL RESOLUTION ON THE NEGRO QUESTION

For five hundred years the Negro Peoples of the World have been the victims of a most terrible and ruthless oppression. The institution of the slave trade, as a consequence of the commercial revolution and expansion of Europe was the beginning of a regime of terror and robbery that is one of the most horrible in the history of mankind. As a result of this traffic, Africa lost a hundred million of her people. Four out of every five of these were killed in the bloody business of capture and transport, the survivors being consigned to a most cruel slavery in the New World.

The immense wealth derived from this gruesome trade was the foundation of the wealth and development of European merchants and states. But the development of the African peoples was thereby abruptly arrested and their civilization, which in many areas had reached a high state of advancement, was almost completely destroyed. These peoples henceforward were declared to be heathen and savage, an inferior race,

---

[14] Richard B. Moore (1893–1978) emigrated to the USA in 1909 from Barbados at the age of fifteen. He joined the Socialist Party in 1917 and the African Blood Brotherhood in 1915; like Briggs he went on to join the Communist Party. The 'resolutions' published by *The Crisis* come from Moore's resolution at the International Congress against Colonial Oppression and Imperialism held in Brussels in February 1927 where Moore was a member of the American delegation.

ordained by the Christian God to be slaves of the superior Europeans, without any rights that a white man is bound to respect. And a bitter and hostile prejudice arose against the Negro race which has dominated the feeling of almost all Europeans towards them, causing them to be subjected to numerous unequal, degrading and pernicious prescriptions.

The abolition of chattel slavery freed the Negro peoples only from the thralldom of being legally held as personal property; the enslavement, exploitation and extermination of these peoples continue until the present moment. The process of subjugation was greatly accelerated by the mad scramble of European Powers for African territory between 1880 and 1890. This was due to the desire that financial capital had to put its reserves into the production of raw material, far from those areas of the industries of transformation which had just begun to develop in Europe. Afterwards, for the sake of its own development, industrial capitalism is joined to financial capitalism in the colonial robbery. By force and fraud the independent African states were subjected their lands and possessions almost all forcibly expropriated and distributed among European corporations and persons and their peoples driven by a most brutal and inhuman system to produce immense wealth for their oppressors. Virulent diseases were introduced among the people and devastation can be realized from the fact that despite the great virility and fecundity of the African peoples, Africa is now the least populous of the continents of the world.

Thus were the blessings of Christianity and civilization brought to the Africans. So that today in that vast continent of 11,500,000 square miles only two small states, Abyssinia and Liberia are accounted independent. The former is now menaced by the Anglo-Italian pact and the latter with its customs and constabulary in the hands of American officials and a great concession granted to a Wall Street Corporation can no longer be considered free. The expropriation of the lands and extermination of the people proceeds grimly in Kenya and the Sudan, a suitable reward from the imperialists to the Africans whom they sacrificed in the great World War which was heralded as a war "to make the world safe for democracy and for the rights of weaker peoples".

Similarly the Union of South Africa has recently enacted a Color Bar Bill which prohibits the native from working with machinery and from employment in the civil services, which adds new burdens to these peoples already oppressed by Pass Laws, Hut Taxes and the like and who are herded into miserable reservations and compounds and terribly exploited on the farms and in the mines. Everywhere also in Africa excepting a small area on the West Coast where the lands and customs of the natives have been maintained by them, there exists a rigorous repression of the people under the yoke of foreign imperialists. The productivity of this area which is 8 times greater than that of neighboring areas of European owned plantations, is an irrefutable proof of the utterly wanton and vicious nature of the system of modern slavery.

In the United States, the 12 million "Negroes" though guaranteed equal rights under the Constitution, are denied the full and equal participation in the life of the Nation. This oppression is greatest in the Southern States where the spirit of chattel slavery still predominates. Segregation, disfranchisement, legal injustice, debt and convict slavery and lynching and mob violence degrade and crush these peoples. This vicious system of suppression operates to reduce this race to an inferior servile caste, exploited and abused by all other classes of society. Haiti, established by Toussaint L'Ouverture and his fellow-slaves, the first successful Slave revolution in history, is now crushed and subjugated by the marines of that very power which proclaimed "the war for democracy". More than 3,000 Haitians have been murdered and large numbers are enslaved for the building of military roads under corvée system. They have been despoiled of their lands and liberties and imprisonment and torture is the lot of all who dare to speak for their freedom. In the Caribbean colonies, the Negro peoples are subjected under varying forms of imperialist rule. Limited franchise and oppressive plantation systems reduce these masses to a permanent condition of serfdom and penury. In Latin America, Negroes suffer no special suppression. The cordial relations resulting from the social and political equality in the races in these countries prove that there is on inherent antagonism between them.

For the Republic of Haiti, Cuba, Santo Domingo and for the peoples of Porto Rico and the Virgin Islands, we must demand complete political and economic independence and the immediate withdrawal of all imperialist troops. For the other Caribbean colonies, we must likewise demand and obtain self-government. The Confederation of the British West Indies should be achieved and the Union of all these peoples accomplished.

For the emancipation of the Negro peoples of the World, we must wage a resolute and unyielding struggle to achieve:

1. Complete freedom of the peoples of Africa and of African origin;
2. Complete equality between the Negro race and all other races;
3. Control of the land and governments of Africa by the Africans;
4. Immediate abolition of all compulsory labor and unjust taxation;

5. Immediate abolition of all racial restrictions, social, political and economic;
6. Immediate abolition of military conscription and recruiting;
7. Freedom of movement within Africa and elsewhere;
8. Freedom of speech, press and assembly;
9. The right of education in all branches;
10. The right to organize trade-Unions.

To accomplish these ends ye must prosecute the following measures;

1. The organization of the economic and political power of the people; Unionization of Negro workers. Organization of cooperatives.
2. Organization and coordination of the Negro liberation movements;
3. Prosecution of the fight against imperialist ideology: Chauvinism, fascism, kukluxism and race prejudice;
4. Admission of the workers of all races into all unions on the basis of equality;
5. Unity with all other suppressed peoples and classes for the fight against world imperialism.

Chapter 4

Responses to Garveyism

The responses to Garveyism in the black radical press of the time are a rich source of complex and contradictory assertions of an American politics attuned to anti-colonial struggles abroad. The hostility from the black Left in particular to Garveyism, and Garvey's own distancing of the UNIA from the Left, open up an often unpleasant, but fascinating, space for polemical assertions of the meaning of black freedom both domestically and in the colonies. Claude McKay's characterisation of Garveyism as 'curiously bourgeois-obsolete and fantastically utopian' in his article for *The Liberator* (April 1922) is one which also acknowledges the attraction of Garveyism in the face of US racism. Like many of the texts here, McKay's article demonstrates the significance of Garveyism as an influence on anti-colonial politics and a repudiation of Garveyism as a strategy of resistance to racial oppression at home and abroad. The reaction to Garveyism also opened up a space for prejudice against Caribbean migrants to the USA which is encapsulated in W. A. Domingo's angry letter to *The Messenger* in March 1923 and Chandler Owen's clunky defensive response.

Marcus Garvey
(By W. E. B. Du Bois, The Crisis, December 1920)

MARCUS GARVEY was born at St. Ann's Bay, Jamaica, about 1885. He was educated at the public school and then for a short time attended the Church of England Grammar School, although he was a Roman Catholic by religion. On leaving school he learned the printing trade and followed it for many years. In Costa Rica he was associated with Marclam Taylor in publishing the Blue field's Messenger. Later he was on the staff of La Nation. He then returned to Jamaica and worked as a printer, being foreman of the printing department of P. Benjamin's

Manufacturing Company of Kingston. Later he visited Europe and spent some time in England and France and while abroad conceived his scheme of organizing the Negro Improvement Society. This society was launched August 1, 1914, in Jamaica, with these general objects among others:

"To establish a Universal Confraternity among the race"; "to promote the spirit of race pride and love"; "to administer to and assist the needy"; "to strengthen the imperialism of independent African States"; "to conduct a world-wide commercial and industrial intercourse".

His first practical object was to be the establishment of a farm school. Meetings were held and the Roman Catholic Bishop, the Mayor of Kingston, and many others addressed them. Nevertheless the project did not succeed and Mr. Garvey was soon in financial difficulties. He therefore practically abandoned the Jamaica field and came to the United States. In the United States his movement for many years languished until at last with the increased migration from the West Indies during the war he succeeded in establishing a strong nucleus in the Harlem district of New York City.

His program now enlarged and changed somewhat in emphasis. He began especially to emphasize the commercial development of the Negroes and as an islander familiar with the necessities of ship traffic he planned the "Black Star Line". The public for a long time regarded this as simply a scheme of exploitation, when they were startled by hearing that Garvey had bought a ship. This boat was a former coasting vessel, 32 years old, but it was put into commission with a black crew and a black captain and was announced as the first of a fleet of vessels which would trade between the colored peoples of America, the West Indies and Africa. With this beginning, the popularity and reputation of Mr. Garvey and his association increased quickly.

In addition to the Yarmouth he is said to have purchased two small boats, the Shady-side, a small excursion steamer which made daily excursions up the Hudson, and a yacht which was designed to cruise among the West Indies and collect cargo in some central spot for the Yarmouth. He had first announced the Black Star Line as a Five Million Dollar corporation, but in February, 1920, he announced that it was going to be a Ten Million Dollar corporation with shares selling at Five Dollars. To this he added in a few months the Negro Factories Corporation capitalized at One Million Dollars with two hundred thousand one dollar shares, and finally he announced the subscription of Five Million Dollars to free Liberia and Haiti from debt.

Early in 1920 he called a convention of Negroes to meet in New York City from the 1st to the 31st of August, "to outline a constructive plan and program for the uplifting of the Negroes and the redemption of Africa". He also took title to three apartment houses to be used as offices and purchased the foundation of an unfinished Baptist church which he covered over and used for meetings, calling it "Liberty Hall". In August, 1920, his convention met with representatives from various parts of the United States, several of the West India Islands and the Canal Zone and a few from Africa. The convention carried out its plan of a month's meetings and culminated with a mass meeting which filled Madison Square Garden. Finally the convention adopted a "Declaration of Independence" with 66 articles, a universal anthem and colors, – red, black and green – and elected Mr. Garvey as "His Excellency, the Provisional President of Africa", together with a number of various other leaders from the various parts of the Negro world. This in brief is the history of the Garvey movement.

The question comes (1) Is it an honest, sincere movement? (2) Are its industrialand commercial projects business like and effective? (3) Are its general objects plausible and capable of being carried out?

The central and dynamic force of the movement is Garvey. He has with singular success capitalized and made vocal the great and long suffering grievances and spirit of protest among the West Indian peasantry. Hitherto the black peasantry of the West Indies has been almost leaderless. Its natural leaders, both mulatto and black, have crossed the color line and practically obliterated social distinction, and to some extent economic distinction, between them and the white English world on the Islands. This has left a peasantry with only the rudiments of education and with almost no economic chances, groveling at the bottom. Their distress and needs gave Garvey his vision.

It is a little difficult to characterize the man Garvey. He has been charged with dishonesty and graft, but he seems to me essentially an honest and sincere man with a tremendous vision, great dynamic force, stubborn determination and unselfish desire to serve; but also he has very serious defects of temperament and training: he is dictatorial, domineering, inordinately vain and very suspicious. He cannot get on with his fellow-workers. His entourage has continually changed. He has had endless law suits and some cases of fisticuffs with his subordinates and has even divorced the young wife whom he married with great fanfare of trumpets about a year ago. All these things militate against him and his reputation. Nevertheless I have not found the slightest proof that his objects were not sincere or that he was consciously diverting money to his own uses. The great difficulty with him is that he has absolutely no business sense, no flair for real organization and his general objects are so shot through with bombast and exaggeration that it is difficult to pin them down for careful examination.

On the other hand, Garvey is an extraordinary leader of men. Thousands of people believe in him. He is able to stir them with singular eloquence and the general run of his thought is of a high plane. He has become to thousands of people a sort of religion. He allows and encourages all sorts of personal adulation, even printing in his paper the addresses of some of the delegates who hailed him as "His Majesty". He dons on state occasion, a costume consisting of an academic cap and gown flounced in red and green!

Of Garvey's curious credulity and suspicions one example will suffice: In March,1919, he held a large mass meeting at Palace Casino which was presided over by Chandler Owen and addressed by himself and Phillip Randolph. Here he collected $204 in contributions on the plea that while in France, W. E. B. Du Bois had interfered with the work of his "High Commissioner" by "defeating" his articles in the French press and "repudiating" his statements as to lynching and injustice in America! The truth was that Mr. Du Bois never saw or heard of his "High Commissioner", never denied his nor anyone's statements of the wretched American conditions, did everything possible to arouse rather than quiet the French press and would have been delighted to welcome and co-operate with any colored fellow-worker.

Lessons in Tactics for the Liberation Movement
(By Cyril Briggs, *The Crusader*, November 1921)

WARS are not all won by actual fighting. Propaganda is everywhere recognized as a great weapon. The Negro needs to put our propaganda not only on the inside to wake up the masses and mobilize Negro thought in the Liberation Struggle, but on the outside, among whites, as well.

WE MUST AIM to encourage existent divisions and even to foster new divisions in the ranks of the white race. To this end we must refrain from chauvinistic utterances and threats of 'what we are going to do when we win Africa' etc., that would have the effect of forcing together the much-divided ranks of the white race. We must aim to keep White Labor and Capital apart by showing White Labor that its interests are identical with our own, inasmuch as we are both seeking freedom from Capitalist oppression and exploitation and neither the Negro nor White Labor can achieve that freedom without the aid of the other. So long as Capitalism is allowed to retain its grip on the resources of "the colonies,"

White Labor will find it well-nigh impossible to destroy Capitalism at home. And, in the case of the Negro, co-operation is even more essential since under present conditions of warfare and control of the weapons of destruction we will find it impossible to effect an early liberation of Africa without outside aid in some form or other: the supplying of arms and munitions; the exertion of moral influence by the class-conscious white workers against their imperial governments; or "direct action" against aggressive or subjugating wars, such as forced the governments of France and Great Britain to keep their hands off of Soviet Russia.

NO BUSINESS ENTERPRISE is good enough to base the Liberation Movement and the morale of the Negro Masses upon the success or failure of that enterprise. Of course we must have business enterprises, but let's not link them up directly with the Liberation Movement and thereby stake the entire movement upon their chances of success or failure and at the same time invite white aggression to what may be correctly considered a vulnerable spot in our armor. The sooner the Garvey Section of the Liberation Movement recognizes this the better for that section in particular and the movement in general.

JUST AS THE NEGRO in the United States can never hope to win equal rights with his white neighbors until Africa is liberated and a strong Negro state (or states) erected on that continent, so, too, we can never liberate Africa, unless and until, the American Section of the Negro Race is made strong enough to play the part for a free Africa that the Irish in America now play for a free Ireland. Every Negro in the United States should use his vote – and use it fearlessly and intelligently to strengthen the radical movement and thus create a deeper schism within the white race in America and at the same time make more friendly – by demonstrating his willingness to go half the way – those who are already friendly to his cause.

WE MUST CONSOLIDATE the organized strength of the Negro. And we cannot do this by putting up any one organization as "the organization par excellence" and demanding as a prerequisite to participation in the Liberation Struggle that all other organizations destroy themselves to let their members come into the theoretical "organization par excellence." When it is impossible even to induce all unorganized Negroes to join this organization that sets itself up as "the whole cheese" how can they expect the members of existent organizations to forego their loyalty to their own organizations and destroy all that they have painfully built up to go into another organization whose program – if it has one – may not appeal to them as strongly as does, the program of their own organization? No, the common sense way does not consist in insisting that all other organizations should destroy themselves and ALL Negroes should come into MY organization or YOUR organization – the common sense way is for all Negro organizations to co-operate TO FEDERATE in order to make for effectiveness in the Liberation Struggle. The Federation Plan was outlined in the Bulletins which the A.B.B. issued at the Second Garvey Congress and in the invitation to co-operation sent to Mr. Garvey. It is further explained in this issue.

DESIRABLE AS IT IS that our energies be directed against the enemy and not wasted in fighting among ourselves, it is sometimes necessary to engage in discussion in order that certain vital issues may be clarified and a better understanding gained of the problems with which we are faced. In such discussions the A.B.B. has always, and shall always, confine itself to the issues involved. We have too many arguments in favor of our program to need to descend to mud-slinging, false allegations and abuse. We could call names too, if we wanted to. We could put our false statements, too, and could lie as hard and as fast as the other fellow. But we don't have to. Common sense is overwhelmingly on our side.

APROPOS of making the American Section of the Negro Race strong enough to play its destined important role, all Negroes in America must use their votes. Those who have votes must help the disfranchised ones to get their votes. Those who were not born in the United States and are not naturalized MUST NATURALIZE. Not because it's better to be an American citizen than to be a British subject (or visa versa), but because it's better to be a NEGRO THAN TO BE EITHER OF THE OTHERS, and because the Negro Strength in America MUST BE DEVELOPED before it can exert political, moral or financial influence upon the Liberation Struggle.

THE UNFORTUNATE experience of U.N.I.A divisions in Santo Domingo, where they have been suppressed and their leaders arrested by United States marines, and in Cuba and Costa Rica where they have been persecuted by the United Fruit Company, supply ample proof of the necessity, long ago affirmed by the A.B.B. of underground tactics in certain parts of the world. In those parts it's a choice of one of three things: (1) open organization with fearless operation and resultant persecution by the powers that be; (2) open organization and compromise of principles with the powers that be for the sake of exemption from hampering persecution or (3) underground organization and the ability to "carry on" fearlessly and effectively without compromise and without inviting premature persecution that would hamper and perhaps even cripple the movement in its early stages, before it is strong enough to strike back effectively at its enemies. WHICH IS THE COMMON SENSE WAY?

Will Not Co-operate, Says Garvey
(Editorial, *The Crusader*, November 1921)
Marcus Garvey Evidently Prefers and Enslaved Africa and Race to Liberation through the Only Possible Means: United Effort – Rejects A.B.B. August 1921, Offer of Co-operation.

The following statement appearing in the Negro World of October 22 is evidently Marcus Garvey's final answer to the African Blood Brotherhood's plea for co-operation on the part of all Negro organizations in order to make for effectiveness in the Liberation Struggle.

"The A.B.B. seems to be in desperate straits and to be seeking the co-operation of other racial groups, notably the U.N.I.A., for the 'immediate protection and ultimate liberation of Negroes everywhere.' Large bodies move slowly. The U.N.I.A is one of the very largest bodies among Negroes, and it is making haste slowly. Its work in the direction of racial uplift and advancement is open and above board. It can form no alliance with any organization of Negroes working secretly to attain and enjoy rights and privileges which ought to be won in a manly open fight. It is, therefore, suspicious of any secret organization such as the A.B.B. claims to be, and it is not going to be tainted by personal or official contact with such a body. It does not intend to be trapped by the white man who invented the A.B.B., this year or next year. The A.B.B. ought to be powerful enough to paddle its own canoe without the aid or consent of the U.N.I.A."

At least we are glad that Marcus Garvey himself admits that the A.B.B. has sought "the co-operation of other racial groups, notably the U.N.I.A." for the immediate protection and ultimate liberation of Negroes everywhere. That shows that the A.B.B. is both broad-minded enough to be willing to co-operate with others, and intelligent enough to know that it will take the combined efforts of ALL Negroes to liberate Africa and thus elevate the status of Negroes everywhere. We are glad he admits that we sought co-operation! And we are glad that since he refuses to enter into co-operation with other Negro organizations that he was kind enough to print his refusal in his paper since otherwise the A.B.B. might have found it difficult to convince his followers that Marcus Garvey, with all his blatant talk of "freeing Africa," could really refuse to co-operate with other Negroes working for "immediate protection and ultimate liberation of Negroes everywhere."

For his own selfish advancement, Marcus Garvey has been making the grandstand play of "seeking" the co-operation of all Negroes. But to prove how much he really desires any thing like co-operation at the first offer of co-operation he slams the door and virtually tells the members of the A.B.B. that if Africa can only be freed by the combined power and organized effort of all Negroes, then he would rather not have a free Africa!

But a free Africa and a liberate Negro people there will be – in spite of Marcus Garvey! While Garvey was indulging in loose chatter and mock heroics the A.B.B. was working – working as hard and as fast for the liberation of Africa and the entire Negro people as it worked hard and fast to protect Negroes at Tulsa when first it saw the war-clouds gathering over that Oklahoma city. And the A.B.B. can now announce the successful fruition of its plans for a strong federation of Negro organizations that would bring the majority of organized Negroes into the Liberation Movement without the unpopular expedient of having break up one's own organization to join another organization in order to be permitted to participate in the Liberation struggle. The A.B.B. announces the affiliation of 153 Negro organizations and churches (to date) in the United States, the West Indies, Central America and Africa, with a total membership of FIVE MILLION NEGROES!

If Marcus Garvey prefers to stay outside of such a federation rather than help liberate Africa by the only way it can be liberated – the combined effort of the entire Negro race! – Marcus Garvey is at liberty to stay outside. And if the less than 20,000 paid up members of the U.N.I.A., which their Chancellor's report shows that organization had in August 1921, should prefer to blindly follow Marcus Garvey in his Don Quixotte jaunts of imaginary liberative efforts rather than play a part in the real struggle, why that is their privilege. BUT THE RACE WILL NOT FORGET NOR LIGHTLY HOLD THE FACT THAT THEY WERE TOO PRO-GARVEY TO BE REALLY PRO-NEGRO!

As to Marcus Garvey's reference to the secret phase of the A.B.B., we know by experience that Marcus Garvey is no tactician and will therefore excuse his silly remarks, simply leaving it to our readers to judge between the experience of the U.N.I.A. in the West Indies and Central America where they have been persecuted and many of their divisions repressed as a result of their too open work and "heap too much talk"; and, on the other hand, the experience of the A.B.B. in those same countries where the A.B.B. posts have been able to defy repression because of the secrecy with which they have veiled their activities, seeking to make themselves strong before exposing themselves to the attacks of the new dominant race and thus giving the enemy an opportunity to repress them before they were strongly enough organized to defy repressive efforts.

Just as the workers in the United States are incited to prematurely go out on strike in order that the capitalists can crush them before they are strongly enough organized, so the oppressor has tried to incite the posts of the A.B.B. to premature action in order to crush them in the bud as they have crushed in the bud other organizations doing "heap much too much talk" and no real preparation.

The leaders of the A.B.B. do not lay much store upon the mock heroic phrase of Marcus Garvey about "rights and privileges which ought to be won in a manly open fight." We have no illusions about the Struggle, and we do not care a straw for mock heroics. We seek results, and we use the methods best fitted to attain results! The Sinn Fein (Ireland) had to organize under cover and plan secretly before they became strong enough to match themselves against the tremendous power of the might British Empire. And even at the present day most of their moves are under cover and closely guarded. Marcus Garvey is alone in his beliefs that it is good tactics to blow one's mouth off threatening one's enemy with dire things to come. "To be forewarned is to be forearmed" as Garvey should have learned through the unfortunate experience of his Caribbean divisions and the Black Star Line in Santiago de Cuba.

At any rate our readers now know just where Marcus Garvey stands in the matter of co-operation for more a effective Liberation Struggle. And if they read the editorial, "Is Not This Treason" in the October issue they must know where he stands on a lot of other matters as well. And again we say:

THE RACE WILL NOT FORGET NOR LIGHTLY HOLD THE FACT THAT ANY NEGRO WAS TOO PRO-GARVEY TO BE REALLY PRO-NEGRO.

Garvey Turns Informer
(By C. Valentine (Briggs), *The Crusader*, November 1921)

Marcus Garvey's methods of "liberating" Africa by upholding her oppressors are PECULIAR to say the least. Not satisfied with advising Negroes to be loyal to all flags under which they live, regardless of the fact that it is manifestly impossible for Negroes to be loyal to Great Britain, France, Belgium, etc., and still free Africa from the cruel rule of those nations, Marcus Garvey attempted on October 20 to turn State Witness for the white oppressors of the Negro race, presenting in the 12th District Magistrates Court, New York City, a letter from the Paramount Chief of the African Blood Brotherhood which Garvey claimed was an invitation to him to "join Briggs in the overthrow of white governments," as a means of liberating Africa from those said governments.

This latest Judas-act of Marcus Garvey's is the climax in a long list of traitorous acts enumerated at length in the October *Crusader* and unrefuted by Garvey because irrefutable since based upon Garvey's own statements in his paper, "The Negro World," or over his signature in the white press. Marcus Garvey's attempt to "inform" on one of the boldest leaders in the Liberation Struggle should convince even the most rabid Garveyite of the insincerity of the man. It is high time for every follower of his to take mental stock of himself and try to honestly answer the question *if he is not too pro-Garvey to be really pro-Negro*. Certainly there can be not the slightest doubt of blackest treason on the part of Marcus Garvey to the Negro Race.

Let him that hath eyes read! Let him that has ears heed! Lest it be said of him by embattled Ethiopia in the day of her triumph over her enemies: Eyes hath ye and saw ye not, ears hath ye and heard you not, depart from my sight for ye are not worthy to be my son.

Negro World December 3rd 1921[1]

In three issues this paper published a news release that one "Cyril Briggs, a white man, was passing for a Negro in New York." The Managing Editor Marcus Garvey, was summoned to court for the publication of the said release. Briggs' mother, who attended the hearing, is a colored woman, therefore this paper is now convinced that Mr Briggs is not a white man in race, but a Negro. We gladly make this retraction.

Black Zionism
(By A. Philip Randolph, *The Messenger*, January 1922)

It is barely possible to understand any single problem today without inquiring into the historical background of other contemporary problems that may or may not have certain points of similarity to the problem which you propose studying. An examination of the laws and principles of human association will reveal that the different ethnic, religious and national groups of the world are fundamentally the same. Their aspirations are similar. All mankind consciously or unconsciously

---
[1] In 1921 Briggs sued Garvey for libel after Garvey accused him of being 'a white man passing as a Negro'. Briggs won his case and the *Negro World* was instructed to publish a retraction.

struggle for the attainment of human happiness. By happiness, in the main, we mean: avoiding pain and securing pleasure. The march of the physical and social sciences show that freedom, or the ability of an individual or group to act in accordance with his desires, in religion, industry and politics, is becoming, more and more, the supreme condition and measure of human happiness. Happiness is the end; freedom is the means. Everywhere, among all peoples, in every epoch of human history, this surge against bondage has gone on. The manifestations and expressions of this movement for human freedom, in different lands, among different peoples, have necessarily varied in conformity with the historical, political and economic background of each country and group. For instance, the objective of the Irish, Hindus and Jews is essentially the same, the achievement of independent nationalism: but they differ in methods. The methods of these three world groups were born in the fires of a long, arduous and crucial struggle. Hence, it might not be amiss to survey the strivings of each of these groups against oppression, in order to discover in what essentials, the Negroes struggles for freedom are similar or dissimilar.

The programme of the Zionist movement was laid down at the first Congress, at Basle, in 1807 and is known as the "Basic Programme." The first article states: "The aims of Zionism is to create for the Jewish people a home in Palestine secured by public law." Of means it indicates: (1) The promotion by appropriate means of the settlement in Palestine of Jewish agriculturalists, artisans and manufacturers. (2) The organization and binding together of the whole of Jewry by means of suitable institutions, both local and international, in accordance with the laws of each country. (3) The strengthening of the Jewish national feeling and consciousness. (4) By way of preparation, steps toward obtaining the consent of governments, where necessary, in order to reach the goal of Zionism. Such are the salient aspects of Zionism. In no part of the entire programe, is there suggested a policy of conquest. Palestine is inhabited by more Arabs and Turks than Jews; by peoples speaking a hundred different languages; yet there is no intimation of expulsion. The keen mentality of the Jew recognizes the suicidal folly of such a policy. Neither their economic power nor man-power would justify the adoption of a policy of antagonism against the present Turkish masters of Palestine, although the Turks are among the weakest of the weak World Powers. The Jews take the unassailable position of attacking the problem of re-establishing a home in Palestine from the angle of greatest promise. They are not warlike, hence they do not boast fully about conquest. Nor do the Zionist leaders pretend that a Jewish State will solve all of the economic, political, social, and religious difficulties of the Jews in any of the countries where Jews are oppressed, such as Poland, Romania, or Russia under the Czar.

Zionism does not attempt to absorb all of the energies and funds of the Jews in the achievement of a New Zion to the exclusion and injury of the vital work of combating the evil of pogroms and other anti-Semitic practices in the different countries of the world. To the Jews, Palestine is a living expression of Jewish character and ideas; a sort of measure and spiritual source, if you will, of Judaism. No more than a small minority of Jews are ever expected to migrate back to Palestine. Zionism is chiefly a cultural movement. It cannot solve the problems of the Jewish workers. Under a Jewish State, the same class divisions would reappear that manifest themselves between the Jewish employees and employers in the Western European and American countries. In very truth, wherever the private ownership in the social tools and sources of wealth production and exchange is sanctioned, the irrepressible and irreconcilable conflict appear. From the point of view of Jewish Nationalism, Zionism is severely logical and practical, but from the point of view of the Jewish workers it is no solvent key. Dr Ch. Weizmann, the great Jewish leader, points out that, "the economic problems of the Jews must be solved in the countries where they now live."

Of Sinn Feinism and its methods.

The goal of Sinn Feinism is an independent Ireland. It is radical Irish nationalism. Its birth marked the entrance of the Irish question upon a genuinely uncompromising plane which immediately focused worldwide attention. In the use of methods, the Sinn Feiners were driven to the adoption of tactics similar to those employed by the Ulsterite and Unionist forces – that is, they matched force with force. This, of course, was their only alternative.

It will be interesting, in this connection, to note the attitude of the Irish in America. Their position is, in many respects, similar to that to the Negro. The bulk of them live in the United States, and being of the Catholic faith, they too, in the South, are the victims of a cruel religious prejudice. But I know of no propaganda to ship the Irish in America back to Ireland, either for conquest or to re-settle.

The Irish, while being ardently devoted to the ideal of an Irish State, recognize the utter futility of an Independent Ireland effecting a solution of their economic, political, social and religious problems in the alien lands. De Valera would be repudiated and laughed out of school were he even to suggest such an idea. Thus, in light of their nationalistic struggles there is much to be said in favor of the soundness of Sinn Feinism. But, needless to say, the freedom of the Irish people from British rule, will not ipso facto, emancipate the Irish workers form the tyranny of their industrial masters. Their economic bondage will persist. To illustrate. The American colonies won independence from Great Britain in 1776 and not only did the slavery of Negroes continue, but the white workers too, experienced no signal difference in their exploitation under King George III from their exploitation under their own native masters. Thus we find the American workers, white and black, still struggling for freedom. The march of nationalism has only been of value to the workers throughout the world, to the extent of eliminating the necessity of directing their chief struggle to the overthrow of foreign rule thereby throwing the class struggle in sharp relief, enabling them to focus their attacks upon class despotism, which arises out of the economic system of capitalism, and not out of the fact of alien rule. Irish employers and Irish employees can not escape the inevitable conflict which will flare forth in the form of strikes, lock-outs, boycotts, etc.

Hence Sinn Feinism, like Zionism, as a purifying cultural idealism, have caught the imagination of their respective followers, but hold no promise of economic freedom for the Irish proletariat.

Now as to Gandhism and its non co-operative programme as a basis for the freedom of India. It, too, is a nationalist movement. Gandhi has adopted the non-resistance philosophy to combat the bloody heel of British tyranny in India. I seriously question its effectiveness against British imperialism, and yet one would be rash, indeed, to preach a doctrine of violence to an unorganized, unarmed, unintelligent peasant class against one of the most formidable powers in the world, the British Empire. Gandhism, or the forces it sets in motion, however, may erelong liberate India, after which the problem of the Hindus workers' overthrowing their own Hindus industrial and agricultural masters, will fling itself into the center of the stage. Nationalists, like racial and religious conflicts, cut across class lines and confuse the vision of the workers, making them susceptible to the intrigues and cunning of insincere and un-scrupulous demagogues. Such has been the tragic and hapless fate of all of the world's oppressed and disinherited With the large exception of a few Jewish, Irish, Hindus, and Negro leaders, the tortured masses are bled of their funds; lashed into a frenzy of unreasoning hope of a new day by sensationalist and picturesque demagogues, only to be disillusioned and disenchanted by the costly but effective realism of experience.

Already in one of the biggest movements ever launched among Negroes, the Universal Negro Improvement Association, disintegrating forces are at work, set in motion by the recognition, on the part of an increasingly growing number of its members, that the operation of Black Star Line and the conquering of Africa are not the work of mere phrases. Thus, Garveyism, with its impossible goal of building an African Empire, in a world of ruthless imperialism, is losing its luster and magic appeal to the awakening masses of Negroes.

The project of the Negroes' building an African Empire smacks of the romantic and infantile excursions of Don Quixote. Unlike the Irish, Hindus and Jews whose countries are dominated by only one foreign power, Great Britain, Africa is parceled up by Great Britain, France, Belgium, Portugal, Italy and Spain, who control every inch of land in Africa save 390 thousand square miles of territory which is in the hands of Abyssinia and Liberia. Hence to establish an empire in Africa, is to conquer the armies and natives of the aforementioned countries. For it is to the interest of all to prevent a successful rising of African natives against either of the Powers; as the success of a rising of natives against France would stimulate, hearten and encourage African subjects in the British region to rise against British rule. Hence, it ought to be apparent to even the most ardent and superficial Garveyite that the interest of one Power in preventing the establishment of an African State is the interest of all of the Powers; and if all of the Powers are interested in maintaining the status quo in Africa, that the redemption of Africa by Negroes who are unarmed, unorganized, uneducated, a minority in numbers to their oppressors, divided, both in and out of Africa by languages, custom, history, and habits, is a will o' the wisp, an iridescent dream which could only be born in the head of an irresponsible enthusiast.

Let us take China for example and her struggle for freedom. It is clear to a cursory reader of the news on the Armament Conference that China, though an alleged independent nation, with an army and navy is doomed to be shackled by the chains of financial imperialism through a consortium of British, American, French and Japanese bankers, even more than she was ere she made her advent into the Conference. Now if such is the fate of a country which is recognized, in diplomatic parlance as an independent nation, what hope is there of Africa, which is completely prostrate before world imperialism, building up an African State. It is recognized by all students of world politics that even Liberia and Abyssinia are independent nations in name only. European and American bankers are the real masters in Liberia, Abyssinia, Haiti, Mexico, in most South American countries, also India, China and Germany. No small nation can accept a loan from one of the great powers and remain independent, and when the small countries, rich in raw material, desired by the great Powers, refuse to borrow, then they, like a lamb before a lion, are gobbled up.

Add to the opposition by the great Powers to any plan to oust them from Africa, the problem of conquering the African natives, with their varied tongues and customs, and the stubborn and forbidding aspect of nature in Africa, and you face a obstacle which only a mad man would suggest attacking today, by way of conquest.

But let us grant for the sake of argument that an African Empire can be established, can it, as is contended by Mr Garvey, protect Negroes in foreign lands? We need not go far afield for an explanation. It is at hand in the case of China, Haiti, Germany, Liberia, Abysinnia, and Mexico.

Japan is an empire and a powerful one at that; yet no Japanese will contend that he has not wrongs to redress which are inflicted upon him on American soil. When we examine the record of lynchings in America, Mexican after Mexican is numbered among the victims. It simply proves that mere allegiance to a nation does not automatically insure safety on one in foreign lands. Only power can protect a national in alien lands, and it is certainly not reasonable to believe that an African State would become a full-fledged great world power comparable with Japan or Germany in the course of a generation. Hence it is either sheer ignorance or absolute insincerity to present as reason for Negroes joining a movement to redeem Africa, the hope and assurance of Negroes in America being protected from injustices, insults and lynchings.

Besides the uncertain fortunes of an African State upon a raging sea of imperialism, the class division of Negro worker and Negro employer, will assert itself. A Negro Emperor would be no less ruthless, brutal and despotic to Negro subjects than was Czar Nicholas to the Russian Moujiks, which finally resulted in the Russian Revolution. Just as the Kaiser has been retired to private life and political oblivion by his own white native Germany, so a Negro ruler would also face the hazards of an imperial course.

Thus, it is obvious to the clear thinking than an African Empire is visionary, and that even granting the possibility of its establishment, it would neither be secure from other more powerful States, nor from the revolutionary movements formented and nurtured by Negroes from within.

What then is the hope of the African, the American and the West Indian Negro, you ask? The answer is that the liberation of Africa can only come by allying the Negro liberation movement with the movements for the liberation of all the world's enslaved of all races, creeds and color. Imperialism is at the bottom of African bondage. Only the abolition of imperialism can free Africa. We can not abolish white and yellow imperialism by raising black imperialism any more than you can abolish war by building battleships, or crime by cultivating criminals. First, the black workers in America and the West Indies must change their own social systems. They must raise the workers to power. The workers have no interest in holding colonies in subjection; for they reap no profits. Imperialism is the child of the capitalist system and as long as it continues, imperialism will rob, and exploit Africa, India, China, Mexico and Haiti. Thus, to the end of achieving this goal, Negroes of the world must turn their faces toward the radical international labor and socialist forces of the world. For with the present stages of African economic, political and social development, only a world-wide proletarian revolution can achieve her liberation. An imperialist African state is impossible today. Even Germany began empire building too late, and her ruin was wrought by her rival powers. But Afghanistan, Persia and Russian China were broken away from their Romanoff masters by the revolutionary upsurge of the Russian workers and peasants.

Garveyism will not only not liberate Africa, but it will set back the clock of Negro progress by cutting the Negro workers away from the proletarian liberation movement expressed in the workers efforts, political and economic to effect solidarity, class consciousness, by setting them against instead of joining them with the white workers struggle for freedom. Herein lies the chief menace of Garveyism.

Garvey as a Negro Moses
(By Claude McKay, *The Liberator*, April 1922)

GARVEYISM is a well-worn word in Negro New York. And it is known among all the Negroes of America, and throughout the world, wherever there are race-conscious Negro groups. But while Garvey is a sort of magic name to the ignorant black masses, the Negro intelligentsia thinks that by his spectacular antics – words big with bombast, colorful robes, Anglo-Saxon titles of nobility (Sir William Ferris, K. C. O. N., for instance, his editor and Lady Henrietta Vinton Davis, his international organizer), his steam-roller-like mass meetings and parades and lamentable business ventures – Garvey has muddied the waters of the Negro movement for freedom and put the race back for many years. But the followers of Marcus Garvey, who are legion and noisy as a tambourine yard party, give him the crown of Negro leadership. Garvey, they assert, with his Universal Negro Improvement Association and the Black Star Line, has given the Negro problem a universal advertisement and made it as popular as Negro minstrelsy. Where men like Booker T. Washington, Dr. Du Bois of the National Association for the Advancement of Colored People, and William Monroe Trotter of the Equal Rights League had but little success, Garvey succeeded in bringing the Associated Press to his knees every time he bellowed. And his words were trumpeted round the degenerate pale-face world trembling with fear of the new Negro.

To those who know Jamaica, the homeland of Marcus Garvey, Garveyism inevitably suggests the name of Bedwardism. Bedwardism is the name of a religious sect there, purely native in its emotional and external features and patterned after the Baptists. It is the true religion of thousands of natives, calling themselves Bedwardites. It was founded by an illiterate black giant named Bedward about 25 years ago, who claimed medicinal and healing properties for a sandy little hole beside a quiet river that flowed calmly to the sea through the eastern part of Jamaica. In the beginning prophet Bedward was a stock newspaper joke; but when thousands began flocking to hear the gigantic whiterobed servant of God at his quarterly baptism, and the police were hard put to handle the crowds, the British Government in Jamaica became irritated. Bedward was warned and threatened and even persecuted a little, but his thousands of followers stood more firmly by him and made him rich with great presents of food, clothing, jewellery and money. So Bedward waxed fat in body and spirit. He began a great building of stone to the God of Bedwardism, which he declared could not be finished until the Second Coming of Christ. And in the plenitude of his powers he sat in his large yard under an orange tree, his wife and grown children, all good Bedwardites, around him, and gave out words of wisdom on his religion and upon topical questions to the pilgrims who went daily to worship and to obtain a bottle of water from the holy hole. The most recent news of the prophet was his arrest by the government for causing hundreds of his followers to sell all their possessions and come together at his home in August Town to witness his annunciation; for on a certain day at noon, he had said, he would ascend into heaven upon a crescent moon. The devout sold and gave away all their property and flocked to August Town, and the hour of the certain day came and passed with Bedward waiting in his robes, and days followed and weeks after. Then his flock of sheep, now turned into a hungry, destitute, despairing mob, howled like hyenas and fought each other until the Government interfered.

It may be that the notorious career of Bedward, the prophet, worked unconsciously upon Marcus Garvey's mind and made him work out his plans along similar spectacular lines. But between the mentality of both men there is no comparison. While Bedward was a huge inflated bag of bombast loaded with ignorance and superstition, Garvey's is beyond doubt a very energetic and quick-witted mind, barb-wired by the imperial traditions of nineteenth-century England. His spirit is revolutionary, but his intellect does not understand the significance of modern revolutionary developments. Maybe he chose not to understand, he may have realized that a resolute facing of facts would make puerile his beautiful schemes for the redemption of the continent of Africa.

It is rather strange that Garvey's political ideas should be so curiously bourgeois-obsolete and fantastically utopian. For he is not of the school of Negro leader that has existed solely on the pecuniary crumbs of Republican politics and democratic philanthropy, and who is absolutely incapable of understanding the Negro-proletarian point of view and the philosophy of the working class movement. On the contrary, Garvey's background is very industrial, for in the West Indies the Negro problem is peculiarly economic, and prejudice is, English-wise, more of class than of race. The flame of revolt must have stirred in Garvey in his early youth when he found the doors to higher education barred against him through economic pressure. For when he became a printer by trade in Kingston he was active in organizing the compositors, and he was the leader of the printers' strike there, 10 years ago, during which time he brought out a special propaganda sheet for the strikers. The strike failed and Garvey went to Europe, returning to Jamaica after a few months' stay abroad, to start his Universal Negro Society. He failed at this in Jamaica – where a tropical laziness settles like a warm fog over the island. Coming to New York in 1917, he struck the black belt like a cyclone, and there lay the foundation of the Universal Negro Improvement Association and the Black Star Line.

At that time the World War had opened up a new field for colored workers. There was less race discrimination in the ranks of labor and the factory gates swung open to the Negro worker. There was plenty of money to spare. Garvey began his "Back to Africa" propaganda in the streets of Harlem, and in a few months he had made his organ "The Negro World," the best edited colored weekly in New York. The launching of the Black Star Line project was the grand event of the movement among all Garveyites, and it had an electrifying effect upon all the Negro peoples of the world – even the black intelligentsia. It landed on the front page of the white press and made good copy for the liberal weeklies and the incorruptible monthlies. The "Negro World" circulated 60,000 copies, and a perusal of its correspondence page showed letters breathing an intense love for Africa from the farthest ends of the world. The movement for African redemption had taken definite form in the minds of Western Negroes, and the respectable Negro uplift organizations were shaken up to realize the significance of "Back to Africa." The money for shares of the Black Star Line poured in in hundreds and thousands of dollars, some brilliant Negro leaders were drawn to the organization, and the little Negro press barked at Garvey from every part of the country, questioning his integrity and impugning his motives. And Garvey, Hearst-like, thundered back his threats at the critics through the "Negro World" and was soon involved in a net of law suits.

The most puzzling thing about the "Back to Africa" propaganda is the leader's repudiation of all the fundamentals of the black worker's economic struggle. No intelligent Negro dare deny the almost miraculous effect and the world-wide breadth and sweep of Garvey's propaganda methods. But all those who think broadly on social conditions are amazed at Garvey's ignorance and his intolerance of modern social ideas. To him Queen Victoria and Lincoln are the greatest figures in history because they both freed the slaves, and the Negro race will never reach the heights of greatness until it has produced such types. He talks of Africa as if it were a little island in the Caribbean Sea. Ignoring all geographical and political divisions, he gives his followers the idea that that vast continent of diverse tribes consists of a large homogenous nation of natives struggling for freedom and waiting for the Western Negroes to come and help them drive out the European exploiters. He has never urged Negroes to organize in industrial unions.

He only exhorted them to get money, buy shares in his African steamship line, and join his Universal Association. And thousands of American and West Indian Negroes responded with eagerness.

He denounced the Socialists and Bolshevists for plotting to demoralize the Negro workers and bring them under the control of white labor. And in the same breath he attacked the National Association for the Advancement of Colored People, and its founder, Dr. Du Bois, for including white leaders and members. In the face of his very capable mulatto and octoroon colleagues, he advocated an all-sable nation of Negroes to be governed strictly after the English plan with Marcus Garvey as supreme head. He organized a Negro Legion and a Negro Red Cross in the heart of Harlem. The Black Star line consisted of two unseaworthy boats and the Negro Factories Corporation was mainly existent on paper. But it seems that Garvey's sole satisfaction in his business venture was the presenting of grandiose visions to his crowd.

Garvey's arrest by the Federal authorities after five years of stupendous vaudeville is a fitting climax. He should feel now an ultimate satisfaction in the fact that he was a universal advertising manager. He was the biggest popularizer of the Negro problem, especially among Negroes, since "Uncle Tom's Cabin." He attained the sublime. During the last days he waxed more falsely eloquent in his tall talks on the Negro Conquest of Africa, and when the clansmen yelled their approval and clamored for more, in his gorgeous robes, he lifted his hands to the low ceiling in a weird pose, his huge ugly bulk cowing the crowd, and told how the mysteries of African magic had been revealed to him, and how he would use them to put the white man to confusion and drive him out of Africa.

Garvey Unfairly Attacked
(Editorial, The Messenger, April 1922)

We hold no brief for Marcus Garvey or the United Negro Improvement Association. No publication in America has given such painstaking analysis of the good points and the bad points of Garvey and his movement as the MESSENGER. The article in the September, 1921, MESSENGER, by A. Philip Randolph, is easily the masterpiece of the Garvey movement.

Nevertheless we oppose unfair tactics, such as the recent attacks upon Garvey's nativity by Roscoe Conkling Simmons in the *Chicago Defender*. The merits and demerits of Garveyism are not lessened or increased because he is a West Indian. Nor is it any sensible argument to say: "If Garvey doesn't like this country, let him go back to Jamaica, where he came from." It would be just as logical to say, If Randolph doesn't like segregation in New York, let him go back to Florida where he came from. If Du Bois doesn't like the Ku Klux Klan in New York, let him go back to Atlanta University.

If Kelly Miller[2] doesn't like the Jim Crow Car of Maryland, let him go back to South Carolina where he came from. If Robert Bagnall[3] doesn't like the Jim Crowing in Loew's Alhambra Theatre in New York, let him go back to Virginia. If Owen doesn't like the reluctant service in Child's Restaurant, let him go back to North Carolina. If Pickens[4] doesn't like

---

[2] Kelly Miller (1863–1939), African American intellectual.
[3] Robert Bagnall (1883–1943), Director of Branches of the NAACP.
[4] William Pickens (1881–1954), Field Secretary of the NAACP.

segregated schools in Kansas or St Louis, let him go back to Alabama. If James Weldon Johnson[5] is not satisfied with everything in the North and West, let him go back to Florida.

All such argument (if it can be dignified by that name) is petty, cheap, vapid, effete. A man has a right and a duty to fight to improve his conditions wherever he is. He has a right to fight to improve not only his home but any other home he may be able to help. If a Negro is in Georgia and the hill billies, instigated by silk-gloved "respectable citizens," decide to lynch him, he is simply a "nigger" whether he comes from Georgia or Georgetown, British Guiana. They care nothing whether he is from Jamaica or Florida, Trinidad or Tennessee, St Kitts or Mississippi, Barbados or Alabama. All Negroes, wherever they are, are born, suffer from common proscriptions, wanton narrowing of opportunities, segregation, discrimination, Jim Crow cars, laws against inter-marriage. Race and color determine the classification – not the place of birth.

It needs to be said that at times Mr. Garvey unfortunately resorts to similar tactics. Witness his calling Cyril Briggs a white man, and his charging the National Advancement Association with his hiring persons to dismantle the machinery on his ships – both of which statements Mr. Garvey knew to be absolutely false.

Our position is that Mr. Garvey has done much good, but also much harm. His opposition to social equality is abominable. His African Empire dream is obsolete and undesirable. His "Negro first" policy is not defensible, is unsound in theory and in practice. His steamship line is not only impracticable, but would have no effect on the Negro problem if successfully established because the Negro problem is not one of transportation.

In spite of all this, Garvey has done much good work in putting into many Negroes a backbone where for years they had only a wishbone. He has stimulated race pride. He has instilled a feeling into Negroes that they are as good as anybody else. He has criticized the hat-in-hand Negro leadership. He has inspired an interest in Negro traditions, Negro literature, Negro art and culture. He has stressed the international aspect of the Negro problem.

If we American Negroes are to attack Garveyism, do it like the MESSENGER editors. Be fair. Don't appeal to nationality – that patriotism which Dr Johnson called "the last refuge of a scoundrel." The

---

[5] James Weldon Johnson (1871–1938), leading member of the NAACP and author of *The Autobiography of an Ex-Colored Man* (1912).

West Indians are among the foremost fighters in all cities for racial rights. They are assiduous workers, vigorous fighters, diligent and able students.

Let Roscoe Conkling Simmons meet Garvey on a fair field. It was Robert G. Ingersoll who once said: "I like black friends better than I do white enemies." So we like West Indian friends better than we do Native Negro enemies. We have heard too much talk of anti-West Indian intolerance. We take no stock in this argument. Rather do we regard it as "a little barrack behind which mental impotency hides when it cannot answer logic."

Hon. Marcus Garvey Tells of Interview with Ku Klux Klan (abridged)[6]
(*Negro World*, 18 July 1922)

LIBERTY HALL, Sunday Night, July 9, 1922 – Unusual interest was centered in tonight's meeting. It having been previously announced that the President General. Hon. Marcus Garvey, would speak about his interview with the Imperial Wizard of the Ku Klux Klan in the city of Atlanta, Ga. A record-breaking crowd was therefore in attendance, and the white press, which has displayed much concern about the affair, sent its representatives to get first hand news of the much discussed interview between these two national figures in American life.

Mr. Garvey, without any preliminaries, plunged directly into his subject and for three-quarters of an hour told of the interview – the motives that inspired it, his impressions of the interview, the attitude of the Ku Klux Klan towards the Negro, what the Klan stand for, and the influence it wields on the country at large. He spoke with a clarity of expression which could leave no doubt that his genius had enabled him to get at the bottom of the whole matter and discover the real truth of this secret organization which has puzzled the country. In this Mr. Garvey has displayed an undaunted courage which is characteristic of a real leader and done what the self-appointed, weak-kneed, spineless leaders of the race have never had the pluck to attempt, namely, to get at the root of an organization which is outwardly hostile to the Negro, and understand it so that proper measures may be made to combat it.

---

[6] Garvey's meeting with the KKK in July 1922 horrified his opponents.

Mr. Garvey made some startling disclosures which sent shock after shock through the audience. Consternation was stamped upon the face of everyone when he declared most emphatically that "the Ku Klux Klan is really the invisible government of the United States of America." "There are more people," he said, "identified with the Ku Klux Klan than you think, and there is more sympathy in this country for the Ku Klux Klan than the ordinary illiterate Negro newspaperman thinks and sees on the surface." This was substantiated by the fact that since the recent exposures made by white newspapers in different parts of the country the Klan, according to figures given him by the acting Imperial Wizard (Edward Young Clarke) had increased by a large percentage and had taken a firm grip in the North and West, where hitherto its activities were unknown.

He, however, made the bland statement that the Klan is not organized for the absolute purpose or for the purpose of interfering with Negroes or for the purpose of suppressing Negroes; but is organized for the purpose of protecting the interests of the white race in America.

Mr. Garvey gave as his impression of the Ku Klux Klan that it is a mighty white organization in America, organized for the purpose of upholding white supremacy in this country – organized for the purpose of making America a white man's country, and that the Klan represents the spirit, the feeling, the attitude of every white man in the United States of America. That being so, the Negro's attitude toward such an organization should not be to stand off, not knowing its program and saying and writing all kinds of things against it, with the intention of aggravating its attitude toward the race, but the duty of the leadership of the Negro race finding itself in such an unenviable position, is to study the thing and get as much information as possible about the thing in their own interest.

After making a logical and searching analysis of the underlying causes of the Ku Klux Klan, which hinged entirely upon white supremacy Mr. Garvey said the best thing that could be done is to get down to a sober understanding of the Klan and try to the best of our ability to solve the question that concerns us; and the Universal Negro Improvement Association says the only way the problem can be solved is for the Negro to create government of his own strong enough on the continent of Africa that can compel the respect of any people in any part of the world. While the Ku Klux Klan, Mr. Garvey declares, desires to make America absolutely a white man's country, the Universal Negro Improvement Association wants to make Africa absolutely a black man's – country.

The speech throughout was a masterpiece of eloquence, and was delivered with all the fervor of a leader whose entire life is wrapped up in the cause which he is espousing.

[...]

HON. MARCUS GARVEY'S SPEECH

Hon. Marcus Garvey spoke as follows: In keeping with my duties as leader of a large movement, as one of the advocates of Negro rights and Negro liberty, as an officer of the largest Negro organization in the world, I became interested in the activities of an organization known as the Ku Klux Klan, not because I wanted to be a member of the Klan, but because I wanted to know the truth about the Klan's attitude toward the race I represent.

Conference with Head of Ku Klux Klan

For that reason a conference was arranged between the Acting Imperial Wizard of the Ku Klux Klan and myself, which took place in Atlanta, Ga., on the 28th of June. The interview or the report of the conference is to be published in The Negro World, the official organ of the Universal Negro Improvement Association, and I believe it will also be published in the searchlight, the official organ of the Ku Klux Klan. Unfortunately, because of the pressure of business, I have been unable to read the interview as held to send a copy back to the Imperial Wizard for his correction as well as for my own, in that it was arranged that the interview would be handed to each party concerned for his approval or correction before it was made public. Up to now the corrections have not been made, and I am to speak tonight not so much from the reported matter of the interview as from my impression of the Ku Klux Klan as gained through contact with the leaders of the Klan.

You will understand what it means when two parties enter into an agreement that no public announcements should be made of certain things until the two parties had the opportunity of looking over the copies concerned referring to the matter or the thing; and that has not been done yet; but since my return to New York I discovered that a large number of the colored people here are very curious as to the nature or visit and what happened, and since I returned to New York I have received copies of Negro newspapers that have published me as joining hands with the Ku Klux Klan. I know and you know the attitude of the Negro press in America – a senseless, ignorant attitude – an attitude that does not tend to help educationally in the development of this race of ours in America, especially to a young, growing race as ours.

His Impressions of the Ku Klux Klan

From my impressions, from my observations, from my understanding the Ku Klux Klan is a mighty white organization in the United States of America, organized for the purpose of making America a white man's country pure and simple. The organization has absolutely no apology to make as far as its program is concerned – a program of making America a white man's country. In America we have twelve or fifteen million in a population of 105,000,000 people. The Ku Klux Klan represents the spirit, the feeling, the attitude of every white man in the United States of America, Now what should be the Negro's attitude toward such an organization?

Negro's Attitude Toward the K.K.K.

The Negro's attitude toward such an organization should not be to stand off, not knowing its program, not understanding it and saying and writing all kinds of things against it with the intention of aggravating its program and its attitude toward the race, but the duty of the leadership of the Negro race, finding itself in such an unenviable position, is to study the thing, to understand the thing and to get as much information as possible about the thing in your own interests. Aggravating the Ku Klux Klan or aggravating any organization in the world organized for the specific purpose of white supremacy is not going to help the race in America, placed at a disadvantage as it is. There is much more beneath the surface of the Ku Klux Klan than you can see on the surface. Some of us Negro leaders and some of us Negro newspaperman get crazy because the New York World and New York America about two months ago tried to expose the activities of the Ku Klux Klan. Now let me tell you that the World nor the American has absolutely no intention to put down the Ku Klux Klan to please Negroes. The World and the American exposed the activities of the Ku Klux Klan for their own set reason, for their own set purpose, without having in mind the good that would accrue to Negroes by the putting down of the Ku Klux Klan; and let me tell you this; that it was not so much the real intention of their expose to put down the Ku Klux Klan. Negro editors and Negro leaders got wild and started to lambaste the Ku Klux Klan, and write all kinds of things against them. Let me tell you this; that the Ku Klux Klan is really the invisible government of the United States of America, and that there are more people identified with the Klan than you think; that there are more people in sympathy with the activities of the Ku Klux Klan than you think, and that there is more sympathy in this country for the Ku Klux Klan than the ordinary illiterate Negro newspaperman thinks and sees on the surface.

As proof that the Ku Klux Klan is a worthy organization in the opinion of the white leaders of this country, the expose of the New York World led to what? Led to an investigation of the activities of the Klan by the Congress of the United States; and what has happened up to now? The Ku Klux Klan has grown twice as strong since the expose as before. The expose of the Ku Klux Klan was solely a skillful method of advertising the activities of the Klan at very little cost to the Klan.

After the activities of the Ku Klux Klan were exposed, California was besieged with the Ku Klux Klan and New York itself became a stronghold of the Klan, and if I am to take the words of the acting Imperial Wizard, the Ku Klux Klan is stronger in the Northern States than it is in the Southern States of the United States of America.

The Correct Attitude of the Negro

Now what are you going to do about it? Stand off and refuse to investigate and refuse to understand the attitude of the Klan toward you and in that way expect to solve the problem? Our belief is that the leadership of a large group of people must be intelligent enough to be on guard in protecting the interests or the rights of the people. Because of that intention, because of that feeling, because of that attitude, I interviewed the Imperial Wizard of the Ku Klux Klan to find out the Klan's attitude toward the race. You may believe it or not – I made several statements to him, in which he said this: That the Klan is not organized for the absolute purpose of interfering with Negroes – for the purpose of suppressing Negroes, but the Klan is organized for the purpose of protection the interests of the white race in America. Now anything that does not spell the interests of the white race in America does not come within the scope of the Ku Klux Klan.

Purely a Racial Organization

I found out, therefore, that the Ku Klux Klan was purely a racial organization standing up in the interests of others. You cannot blame any group of men, whether they are Chinese, Japanese, Anglo-Saxons or Frenchmen, for standing up for their interests or for organizing in their interest. I am not apologizing for the Klan or endeavoring to excuse the existence of the Klan, but I want a proper understanding about the

Ku Klux Klan so that there can be no friction between the Negroes in America and the Ku Klux Klan, because it is not going to help.

The Invisible Government of America

The Ku Klux Klan is not an ordinary social club organized around the corner. The Ku Klux Klan is the invisible government of the United States of America. The Ku Klux Klan expresses to a great extent the feeling of every real white American. The attitude of the Ku Klux Klan is that America shall be a white man's country at all hazards, at all costs. The attitude of the Universal Negro Improvement Association is in a way similar to the Ku Klux Klan. Whilst the Ku Klux Klan desires to make America absolutely a white man's country, the Universal Negro Improvement Association wants to make Africa absolutely a black man's country. (Great applause) Whether you wish it or not, that is not the point, because your wish does not amount to anything. The wish of fifteen million Negroes in America does not amount to anything when 95,000,000 other folds wish the thing that you want. That is the disadvantage. We wish liberty; we wish to be good American citizens; we want to be President of the United States; we wish to be Congressmen; we wish to be Senators; we wish to be governors of States; we wish to be mayors of cities; we wish to be police commissioners. It is a wish, all right, but the other fellow wishes the same thing. Now, is he going to allow you to have your wish? That is the attitude. The white people of this country are not going to allow Negroes ambitious and educated Negroes – to have their wish, and the wish of the educated, ambitious Negro of America is that the Negro has as much right to be President of the United States as President Harding has. The ambition and wish of the Negro in America today is that the Negro has as much right to be a member of the Cabinet as any white man. Now that is your wish. Will the other fellow accede to your wish?

K.K.K. Interprets Spirit of White Man

The Ku Klux Klan interprets the spirit of every white man in this country and says "you shall not pass." What are you going to do? You have the wish, but the odds are against you.

Negro Press and Leaders Working on Surface

Some of us Negro leaders, some of us newspapermen before we get down to a serious study of the question and adopt the best possible means of solving the problem we are working on the surface. My suit is mine, but if a bully comes along and tears it off me it is mine but it is his now. All of us know that America is as much the Negro's as the white man's, but the white man says, "I am going to make this a white man's country." The only thing for you to do is to get hold of him, beat him and take it away. But can you do that? You cannot do that. Therefore the best thing you can do is to get down to a sober understanding of the Klan and try to the best of your ability to solve the question that concerns you. And the Universal Negro Improvement Association says the only way the problem can be solved is for the Negro to create a government of his own strong enough on the continent of Africa that can compel the respect of all men in all parts of the world.

We are not going to have any fight as an organization with the Ku Klux Klan because it is not going to help. The Ku Klux Klan, as I said a while ago, is the invisible government of the United States of America. What do I mean by that? The Klan represents the spiritual feeling and even the physical attitude of every white man in this country. There are hundreds of other organizations that feel as the Ku Klux Klan feels. There are millions of individuals in America who feel as the Ku Klux Klan feels, but those individuals, those organizations are not honest enough to make the confession that the Ku Klux Klan makes. I prefer and I have a higher regard for the man who intends to take my life who will warn me and say, "Garvey, I am going to take your life," so as to give me time to prepare my soul for my God rather than the man who will pretend to be my friend, and as I turn my back he ushers me into eternity without even giving me a chance to say my Lord's Prayer.

The Ku Klux Klan comes out openly and says this: Negroes, we are going to make this country a white man's country; so long as there is a white man in America a Negro shall not be President of the United States; so long as there is a white man in America a Negro shall never be a member of the cabinet; so long as there is a white man in America a Negro shall never again be a Congressman or Senator; so long as there is a white man in America a Negro shall never again be a Governor or a Lieutenant-Governor of a State. Now the man that says that gives you enough information about yourself and about him as to enable you to make some plans to help yourself one way or the other; but the other fellow who comes and says nothing to you, but, on the other hand, flatters you and says, "I am your friend and have the same feeling or attitude toward you as the other fellow who told you" – which is the better friend, the one who tells you or the one who keeps the information from you but means the same thing?

I asked the Acting Imperial Wizard of the Ku Klux Klan, whether he was interpreting the spirit of just a few people who make up his organization or not, and he said "no; we are interpreting the spirit of every true white American; but we are honest enough to say certain things that others do not care to say." Now in a nutshell you have the situation. What is the use of staying outside not understanding the attitude and lambasting those people who are in power. Sentiment cannot put down the Ku Klux Klan; newspaper writings cannot put down the Ku Klux Klan. The Ku Klux Klan is expressing the feeling of over 95,000,000 people. No law can put down the prejudice of a race. You may legislate between now and eternity. If I hate you, no law in the world can make me love you. If I am prejudiced against you for reasons, no law, no constitution in the world can make me change my attitude toward you

K.K.K. Represents Sentiment of White People

The Ku Klux Klan is therefore expressing the feeling and the sentiment of a large number of people in this country towards us as a race – the attitude of refusing to allow the Negro to enjoy political, economic and social equality. The Ku Klux Klan made me to understand that their attitude is based on the assumption that this country was discovered by white men; this country was first peopled and colonised by white men; that this country's existence was brought about by white men fighting, suffering and dying to create a government of their own and because of the suffering of white men in the past to bequeath to their children of today a country of their own, the children of today are not disposed to give up their rights racially to any other race whether it be Negro Japanese or any other race on the face of the globe [...]

A Symposium on Garvey by Negro Leaders
(The Messenger, December 1922)

In late September Chandler Owen, Executive Secretary of The Friends of Negro Freedom, sent a questionnaire to twenty-live prominent Negroes of America to see what they thought of Marcus Garvey.

Accompanying the questionnaire was a personal letter and a set of facts, which, it was hoped, would assist those who were not so well posted on Garvey's antics, in framing their reply.

The letter sent was as follows:
Dear Sir
No doubt the sending of the human hand by the Ku Klux Klan A. Philip Randolph, leader in the fight against Marcus Garvey directing him to cease his attacks in his MESSENGER Magazine and immediately become a paid-up member of the Garvey machine, – has brought forcibly to your attention the fight of the Friends of Negro Freedom has been waging against the Garvey menace since last July. Associated in this campaign are Chandler Owen, co-editor of the MESSENGER, Robert Bagnall, director of branches of the National Association for the Advancement of Colored People, and Prof. William Pickens, field secretary of the N. A. A. C. P.

The Friends are fighting Garvey because of his nonresistant policy toward the Ku Klux Klan, and because of his flagrant squandering of funds in his Black Star Line and other fantastic schemes.

Garvey denies that he is allied with the Klan, but does not condemn it. He says let it alone. He says do not blame white people for mistreating us. He says this is "a white man's country" and the Negro has nothing and should get out and – "go back to Africa."

We believe the future of the American Negro is here in America, We believe it only takes time to work out this future. We want to know what YOU think. Kindly use the enclosed blank for that purpose.

    Very truly yours,
    (signed) CHANDLER OWEN. Ex. Sec. *The Friends of Negro Freedom.*

P.S. – This letter is being sent to other prominent Negroes for the purpose of a symposium to be published in the MESSENGER Magazine.

The accompanying set of facts was as follows:

1. Last June Marcus Garvey held a secret conference with the Acting Imperial Wizard Edward Young Clarke of the Ku Klux Klan at Atlanta, Ga. He has never made public that interview although he promised to do so.

2. Shortly after the interview Garvey made a speech at New Orleans in which was this statement :

"This is a white man's country. He found it. He conquered it, and we can't blame him if he wants to keep it. I am not not vexed with the white man of the South for Jim-Crowing me, because I am black.

"I never built any street cars or railroads. The white man built them for his own convenience. And if I don't want to ride where he's willing to let me ride, then I'd better walk."

3. On September 5 A. Philip Randolph received through the mails a

human hand, accompanied by a letter signed by the Klan saying he had better be a paid up member in the Garvey organization ("your nigger improvement association") "within a week." A second letter came on September 12 postmarked New Orleans, from which the first was postmarked.

* * *

The questionnaire was as follows.
1. Do you think Garvey's policy correct for the American Negro?
2. Do you think Garvey should be deported as an alien creating unnecessary mischief?
3. Remarks:

* * *

Of the twenty-five persons to whom the letter was sent fourteen replied. The replies are as follows:

HARRY H. PACE
President, the Pace Phonograph Corporation
New York City

Replying to your inquiry concerning Marcus Garvey I beg to advise that I do not think the Garvey policy is the correct one for either the American Negro or any other kind of Negro. Mr. Garvey took advantage of the unrest among Negroes immediately following the world war when they like every other people were clamoring for new ideas and new things. He had enough semblance of substance in his doctrine to make them appeal to the unthinking, but everybody knows how foolish it is to think of any back to Africa movement. The whole scheme of an African Empire is absurd and is merely a romantic ideal with which to separate fools from their money. Garvey has linked idealism with commercialism and has failed in both things. He had a fine chance to be a huge commercial success had he continued his business as a business proposition instead of as a financial scheme. With the organization and with the start that he had he ought to have been a tremendous factor for good in the race.

It seems to me that it ought to be suggested very forcibly to him that he adjourn to Africa, himself, taking with him the faithful who want to go and it would be much better for both him and those of us who desire to remain behind. He has already done untold damages to the race and has destroyed friends for us whom we never thought could be reached.

* * *

CARTER G. WOODSON
Editor, *The Journal of Negro History*
Washington, D. C.

Replying to your communication of September 21. I beg leave to say that I have given such little attention to the work of Marcus Garvey that I am not in a position to make an estimate of his career.

* * *

CARL MURPHY
Editor, *The Afro-American*
Baltimore, Md,

To question No. 1: "No"
To question No. 2: "No"
To Remarks: "I think the authorities of New York should see to it that Mr. Garvey's stock schemes are kept within the bounds of the law."

* * *

O. A. FULLER
Dean, Bishop College,
Marshall, Texas.

To question No. 1:

It is absolutely incorrect, and too wide of the mark to be called really a policy, if what I have seen in print is the thing he is advocating

To question No. 2:

I really do think that he is an undesirable citizen, if he can be called a citizen, and if not a citizen he should be handled for disturbing what may be termed peaceful relations that we are striving to establish between the races.

To remarks:

I have answered the above questions in the light of the information brought me through your recent letter. I have been too busy during the summer months to read anything about Mr. Garvey. I have read a few unfavorable comments in *The Richmond Planet*. I have not the information at hand that I desire. But taking facts as I have been able to see and get hold of them I am of the opinion that Marcus Garvey is a dangerous character. I think the American people can and will be able to settle all of their differences without any interference from abroad, such as Marcus Garvey is advocating.

* * *

W. E. B DU BOIS
Editor, *The Crisis*
New York City

I have published from time to time my opinion of Mr. Garvey in *The Crisis* and shall add to that in the future.

* * *

R. R. CHURCH
Politician. Real Estate
Memphis, Tenn.

In reply to your questions of September 27 I beg to advise that my answer is "no" to both of them.

* * *

ARCHIBALD H. GRIMKE
President, District of Columbia Branch, NAACP
Washington D. C.

To question No. 1:
I do not. It is a collosal folly.
To question No. 2:
I think not. The State and Federal laws ought to be sufficient to take care of him without resort to deportation

* * *

ROBERT S. ABBOTT
Editor, *The Chicago Defender*
Chicago, Ill.

Mr. Abbott desires to acknowledge receipt of your favor from September 20th.

You will note from new, articles carried the columns of *The Defender*, that we have kept pace with most of the information contained in your letter.

I think Mr. Abbott believes that Mr. Garvey's policy is not correct for the American Negro, and I am sure that he feels that any individual who desires to assume a position of leadership for American Negroes, ought to show his sincerity by becoming a citizen of the United States. The question of deportation, is one which I do believe he cares to give an expression on.

THE ROBERT S. ABBOTT PUB. CO.
(Signed) A. L. Jackson, Asst. to Pres.

* * *

J. B. BASS
Editor, *The Californian Eagle*
Los Angeles, Cal.

To question No. 1 : I should say not.
To question No. 2 : Yes!
To Remarks :
I must heartily approve of the gallant fight which you are making against the pernicious propaganda of Garvey. The straw that broke the camel's back was his assimilation of the Ku Klux Klan. He has become a menace to the future progress of the Negro race.

* * *

EMMETT J. SCOTT
Secretary-Treasurer, Howard University
Washington, D. C.

I hold the definite and positive opinion that a too intensive *intra-racial* struggle is most destructive. It opens wider the opportunity for that *inter-racial* struggle which we all agree is the greatest menace from which we colored Americans suffer. Naturally our race must be and is divided into several schools, or groups of thought, each urging a policy which it believes strikes at a common wrong. What we need therefore is a more charitable understanding within and among our race groups. It is just possible and highly probable that there is much right and much wrong in all of us, which is treated with the alchemy of *intra-racial* tolerance and mutual respect will yield a product most serviceable to the race as a whole.

The following are my thoughts with reference to the questions submitted by you:

1: In re Marcus Garvey's policy for the American Negro:

I do not for one moment believe that any benefit is to come to Colored Americans in the matter of undertaking to set up a government on African soil. The international questions involved are too great and require no statement from me. There is not a foot on African soil not already claimed by European or other governments. I regard even the suggestion as a fantastic dream.

2. In re Marcus Garvey's deportation:

Our government was founded upon the principle of free speech and tolerance of individual opinion. However much as I may discredit Marcus Garvey's preachings, I am disposed to be tolerant, feeling that the acid test of truth and time will prove what is right and what is wrong therein. We cannot wander far from the teachings of Gamaliel in such matters. Garvey has set men thinking, and nothing helps a race and nation so much as serious thought.

* * *

THOMAS W. TALLEY
Professor of Chemistry and Biology,
Fisk University Nashville, Tenn.

I am in receipt of your communication of September 21. I am enclosing the data-sheet sent me. On its face will be found my estimate of all men of the Garvey type.

To question no. 1: "No"

To question no. 2: "Yes"

To Remarks: Thomas Jefferson, in penning the Declaration of Independence, wrote: "We hold these truths to be self evident: That all men are created equal; that they are endowed by their Creator with certain unalienable rights; that among these are life, liberty and the pursuit of happiness."

This is pure unadulterated Americanism. It is the standard set up for and by our government at its very beginning. The loyal American white man and the loyal American Negro have joined hands in an earnest endeavor to bring the masses into harmony with this their rich heritage. There is therefore no place in the American thought and plan for men of the Garvey type who freely pour their oil of vitriol on men of one color while they pat the men of another color on the back until they can empty their pockets; and then, when they have emptied the pockets of these, wantonly appeal to the worst in those whom they have once abused with the hope of somehow reaping a new rich harvest through their chicanery.

* * *

JOHN E. NAIL
Nail & Parker. Real Estate
New York City

To question no. 1: "No"

To question no. 2: "No"

To remarks : I believe Mr. Garvey's first program for economic organization of colored peoples in America was sound, but he has deviated considerably from that program and developed a visionary one without substance.

* * *

KELLY MILLER
Dean, Junior College, Howard University
Washington, D. C.

To question No. 1:

The redemption of Africa through Negro initiative and genius is worth the strivings of the race for the next half thousand years. While Garvey did not originate this idea, he has given it expression and emphasis beyond all others. It is difficult to disentangle the good from the evil of the Garvey propaganda. In so far as it stimulates Negro initiative and self-realization, good; in so far as impossible hopes may mislead the simple, bad. The movement lacks the practicality and freedom from the taint of suspicion to warrant adoption in its present form as a race policy.

To question No. 2:

I do not think that Garvey should be deported and am surprised that the suggestion should come from any Negro. I do not believe that any individual should he banished from America or put in the penitentiary because of his belief or the expression of it. I do not believe in the imprisonment, expulsion or suppression of ideas. Freedom of speech is the bulwark of the weak; suppression is the weapon of the strong. If Garvey's doctrine's are false, combat them with the truth; if his dealings are devious, correct them with the law; if he mislead the simple, show them the more excellent way. But by no means should the oppressed become oppressor, nor the persecuted turn persecutor.

* * *

ROBERT W. BAGNALL
Director of Branches N.A.A.C.P
New York City

To question No.1:

Garvey's policy is, in my opinion, a great menace to the progress of the Negro here and elsewhere.

To question No. 2:

Most definitely he should be deported. He has already increased the friction between the races and race antipathy. He has also essayed to introduce the West Indian problem of color within the race. He has robbed many Negroes of patriotism by developing a cult which believes Africa their country, and America "the white man's country." He has, beyond doubt, made an alliance with the Ku Klux Klan, an organization hostile to all Negro advancement here.

To Remarks:
Not only is Garvey a menace, but so is Garveyism. It fundamentally stands for segregation, the root of all our evils. It is undermining a quality which must be preserved in the American Negro.

THE ANSWER
(The Importance of Being White)

"A white worm and a black worm lived in a clod:
The white worm to the black worm wouldn't even nod,
For the white worm, you know, was the Chosen One of God:
But along came a man with feet stoutly shod,
And both the little worms without preference trod,
Now squashed together they fertilize the sod;
O dear! What a fate for the Chosen One of God."
                    JOSEPHINE COLDWELL
San Francisco, Cal.

The Only Way to Redeem Africa (abridged)
(By A. Philip Randolph, *The Messenger*, December 1922)
[*Mr. Randolph this month disturbs Brother Marcus's sleep by rubbing the paint off his beautiful "400,000,000 Negro" doll, cutting his rotten "anti-white man" apple, and becoming a nightmare in general to the Imperial Black Kluxer*]

All Africans Not Negroes

All anthropologists know that all Africans are not Negroes, any more than all Europeans are Nordics or all Asiatic are Mongols. Arabs are not Negroes, Egyptians are not Negroes. Yet these groups possess more power than the Negroid groups in Africa. Nor are Berbers classified ethnologically and anthropologically as Negroes. Thus the absurdity of Mr. Garvey's claim when he speaks of 400,000,000 Negroes, assuming as he does that all Africans are Negroes, and that by adding the population of Africa to the Negro population in the United States, South and Central Americas and the West Indies, it will give that sum.

Besides, these different racial and national groups in Africa are as hostile as are the racial and national groups in Europe, the scene of the recent great World War. African history is replete with the inter-tribal wars between Zulus, Kaffirs, Bantus, Bastutos, Herreros, Hottentots, Berbers, Matebeles, clinging steadfastly, as it were, to their respective tribal customs, languages, "will" and land. It is also a matter of common historical knowledge that the Africans have fought heroically against white domination. The military Bantus especially are known to have fought the Boers for four long years to preserve their sovereignty. Now if the Africans will fight among themselves to maintain their respective tribal authority; if they will battle against British and Dutch control for decades, what evidence, may I inquire, is there that they will supinely submit to the blatant "138th Street Wind-jammer"? But, of course, these facts carry no force to this Harlem-African Black Ku Klux Emperor who can certainly boast of having no inconsiderable amount of African "ivory" doing duty for brains.

At this point, then, I will go specifically into an examination of the Garvey program.

First, a word about what brought it forth. It grew up during the turbulent days of the war – a period of political, economic and social unsettlement. Then the wide masses were fed up on flowing, rainbow promises of happy days, days of liberty, justice and democracy after the war. This was a war to end war, to usher in a "new day." Needless to say that the unsophisticated peoples believed all this. But, as time has shown, they were mere promises such as are made by the paytrioteers in all wars. Still these promises served the purpose of stirring the oppressed in all lands of all races and religions. Out of this titanic upheaval sprang the Russian Revolution with its ringing, militant slogan: "No annexations, not punitive indemnities, self-determination for smaller nationalities." This became the fountain-head of a world wide move of revolt. The Irish Easter Rebellion had also proclaimed to the world that a wild-eyed spirit of discontent was abroad in the land. Add to this the collapse of the ancient, historic house of the Hapsburgs of Austria-Hungary: the exile of the German Kaiser which followed hard upon the heels of the passing of the wicked and corrupt regime of Czar Nicholas of Russia, and one can visualize to some extent the forces of unrest that had been unleashed.

Besides, there were ample facts of injustice and wrong perpetrated upon the weak and ignorant in the name of humanity that needed only to be presented to stir the fires of revolt. Witness the march of nationalism in Egypt under the leadership of Zaglul; the non-cooperation movement whose prophet is Mahatma Gandhi in India; the rising tide of Islamism in the East; the protests of Korea and China against Japanese dominion' and, the outcry of the workers in the respective capitalist countries against the industrial despotism; all indicating the prurient readiness and eagerness on the part of the disinherited for a program to satisfy their high hopes; to salvage the wreckage of the world wrought by the mad "dogs of war." Even the romantic vagaries of D'Annunzio,[7] as well as the hateful, criminal policies and practices of the Ku Klux Klan in America and the notorious bands of murderous Fascisti in Italy, may be ascribed to the upturned state of affairs precipitated by the war and its aftermath. Thus it is not strange that a monstrosity as the Garvey movement should have been born among the Negroes during this world debacle.

The Negroes, then, like other peoples, were not critical. Like the exploited and outraged everywhere they were weary, distraught and impatient. They were looking for a program, a leader. They were willing to heed any voice which rang out above the din and clangor of confusion and conflict.

Rise of a Demagogue

Hence it was no difficult task for anyone, sufficiently unscrupulous, reckless of fact and truth, deft in the misrepresentation of sound measures and honest, intelligent leaders; possessed with upon the instinct of race loyalty, to capture the ignorant and uninitiated among the Negroes everywhere. Such is the reason for the rise of Garveyism.

Any thoughtful person who reads the Garvey utterances will instantly realize that the man is a typical demagogue. Ready and willing to say well nigh anything, at any time, in order to achieve a moiety of advantage. Sensational statements, and posing as a martyr are his stock and trade. All demagogues dig up some illusory, impossible, visionary, unattainable goal to be purveyed up to the lambs upon the plate of a 100 percent fetishism, whether national, racial or religious, such as "Negro First," "Back to Africa," "the purity of Nordicism," and "100 percent Americanism." And it will be seen that every aspect of the movement partakes of the demagogic character of the self-elected savior of the so-called 400,000,000 Negroes in the world.

Nature of Program – Foreign and Domestic

Every plan and measure are formulated and adjusted to satisfy the ends of the main doctrine or supreme crux: "Back to Africa." Africa is sufficiently far distant and invested with the halo of mysticism as to ensnare

---

[7] Gabriele D'Annunzio (1863–1938), Italian nationalist.

the unsuspecting. The foreign, too, has a touch of novelty among Negroes. It has, not as yet, become worn and hackneyed. Besides, Africa is not accessible to the ignorant masses of Negroes so that they could themselves see the utter folly and absurdity of the project. They can only be disillusioned by the slow process of education, which is invariably a costly one.

But I need make no labored argument to establish that no movement whose program is essentially foreign will ever command the interest and support of the American Negro. While I recognize the international character of the Negro problem that does not imply that the national, or more immediate and concrete aspect is to be ignored. Frenchmen are interested in foreign questions, but that does not make them sacrifice their vital, domestic problems. What is true of the French is also true of the British, Russian and American. A consideration of both aspects, domestic and foreign, must go hand in hand.

But it takes no strained interpretation to see that Garvey has no domestic program; that he is not concerned, here or there, with the fate of American Negroes. Nor is he bothered about the problems of the West Indian Negroes. All of the money, which the U.N.I.A. secures from the credulous Negroes, is used to pay fat salaries, to take pleasure jaunts throughout the country, the West Indies and South and Central Americas in the interest of collecting more money to enable Brother Marcus to yell more lustily about going "back to Africa." In short, everything that is done in America is done with a view to hastening the exit of the Negro from America. This explains the non-citizenship character of the U.N.I.A. This is why Mr. Garvey does not advise his followers to become citizens of the United States.

Out of the slogan "Back to Africa," all his senseless doctrines have grown. First and foremost of which is the "anti-white man's" doctrine. This is based upon the assumption that all white men are the enemies of all Negroes, (except, of course, the Ku Klux Klan which was discovered by the imperial Black Blizzard Garvey in secret conference with the imperial white Wizard Kleagle Clarke.) *This pro Ku Klux Klan attitude of Mr. Garvey's is either the result of ignorance or dishonesty, either of which is detrimental to the Negro. If it is the result of ignorance, it is proof that he does not know how to lead the Negro; and if, on the other hand, it is the result of dishonesty, it is evidence that he cannot be trusted to lead the Negro. Thus, his unfitness for leadership is established upon the establishment of either assumption, one of which is unquestionably true, and both of which are probably true.*

As to the "anti-white man's" doctrine, no intelligent Negro needs to be told that this is both dangerous and false. It is dangerous because it pits whites against blacks; it engenders and fosters a virulent race prejudice, the very menace which we are trying to eradicate, and gives birth to such destructive and violent race riots as East St. Louis, which was a conflict between black and white workers.

It is false because there is ample history to prove the contrary. One has but to mention the names of John Brown who sacrificed his life to emancipate Negro slaves, William Lloyd Garrison, Wendell Phillips, and Lovejoy[8] who suffered but fought unselfishly for the cause of Negro liberty. Then there is Eugene V. Debs and a host of American and European Liberals and radicals who have nothing to gain by taking an attitude of justice the Negro. Only a knave or a hypocrite would argue the contrariwise. To be sure it is good propaganda for one who wants to exploit racial chauvinism for profit; but it is dynamite, which, when once exploded will work havoc in the land, spreading death and destruction everywhere. He who would sacrifice the Negroes' welfare by building up a tinder box of race hatred is not his friend, but his foe. Garvey selected this slogan of "whites against blacks" because he knew that the history and conditions of the Negro would give it some color of truth, and that he could collect more money from Negroes by pandering to their feeling of race hatred than by seeking to abolish it, the only rational program.

Now, out of this "anti-white man's" doctrine grows the subsidiary or corollary doctrine of "Negro First." Let us see how sound this is. Obviously for anyone to assume that he is "first" provokes a similar attitude on the part of everybody else.

[. . .]

And for the chief Mogul, Potentate and Supreme Psha! What shall we call him? I am amazed that he didn't have the gizzard to request the Imperial White Wizard Clarke to knight him as the Infernal Blizzard of Black Ku Kluxism and also to take his title of the Exalted Ruler of the Most Dishonorable Order of Skinners, Fakirs, Hot-Air and Buncombe Dispensers.

---

[8] Prominent white abolitionists.

W. A. Domingo and Chandler Owen's Debate
(*The Messenger*, March 1923)

Mr. Domingo's letter
Editorial, *The Messenger:*
It is upon the principle that "a man's best friend is one who tells him his faults" that I am moved to write you this open letter. I have debated with myself the expediency of so doing since last October, and hesitated upon the supposition that reason would conquer pique and sound public policy outweigh personal prejudices. But as there might be misunderstandings as to my attitude towards some of the newer policies of the magazine on which I am listed as a contributing editor, I am compelled to state my position as clearly and uncompromisingly as possible. I refer to the fight that The Messenger is waging against Garvey and the doctrines that have flowed from his oblique intellect. No one who knows me privately or publicly can accuse me of being in the remotest sense a subscriber to the illogical, race-injuring and dangerous ideas of Mr. Garvey. It is public knowledge and a matter of record that in New York City, as early as the Fall of 1919, I raised my voice in protest against the execrable exaggerations, staggering stupidities, blundering bombast and abominable asininities of our black Barnum, culminating in Thomas Potter and myself being assaulted, kicked, and placed under arrest by Garveyites in the Spring of 1920. Not a bit daunted by my experiences which brought me no fame as a leader, scholar, martyr or orator, I persisted, published and edited The Emancipator (for which you both write), and have not let up a single instant in my unequivocal opposition.

My position is, I think, clear, Garvey's doctrines are dangerous to Negroes everywhere, but more so to those in the United States and Africa; his doctrines and many disgraceful failures have resulted in giving partial confirmation to the Negrophoists' claims as to our essential inferiority and have been the means of weakening us politically, financially and racially by driving away white friends and importing schisms into our ranks.

But I am not discussing Garvey's doctrines, for we are agreed as to their intrinsic worthlessness. I am concerned about the doctrines of *The Messenger.*

I am a West Indian. I am so through no act of mine, and am neither proud nor ashamed of what is purely an accident. It is not the fault of Mr. Randolph that he was born in Jacksonville and nor Rosewood, Florida. Mr. Garvey was born in Jamaica, but according to him, he had rather been born in Africa. Despite his Jamaican birth, I, a Jamaican, find myself differing from him even as most native Negroes no doubt differ from Perry Howard, whom you have bracketed with Garvey as being of the same sinister sort. Difference of opinion is purely a mental quality, and may exist between twin brothers and the closest relatives. Opinions are personal, not national.

Since *The Messenger* began its belated fight to rid the race of the disgrace of Garveyism, I have noticed that many of the articles dealing with that subject have stressed Mr. Garvey's nationality. I have ascribed this to the early reactions of human beings who are engaged in a controversy with an unscrupulous antagonist, but the persistent and regular recurrence of this particular emphasis forces me to ignore past relationships and register my emphatic protest. Behind the unnecessary emphasis, the Cato-like repetition, there seems to lurk a national animus that finds a convenient vent in this particular subject. Believing that the Editors of THE MESSENGER who wrote an editorial as recently as last summer protesting against the *Chicago Defender's* irrational assaults upon Garvey's nationality, are amenable to unemotional, dispassionate argumentation, I desire to draw their attention to phases of the question that they may have overlooked.

In your righteous denunciation of Garvey you excoriate his demagogy, but with a strange inconsistency resort to the very methods you condemn. If Garvey is guilty of imitating white people with his black this and black that, aren't you emulating him when you adopt his own reprehensible methods of popular appeal without regard to principle? Isn't this a case of the oppressed becoming oppressors and the lynched becoming lynchers.

In the January MESSENGER there is an editorial entitled "A Supreme Negro Jamaican Jackass," which reads in part: "Of course, no American Negro would have stooped to such depths . . . It was left for Marcus Garvey from Jamaica, etc." Yet in another editorial, "The Gyer-Johnson-Howard Triangle," speaking of Perry Howard,[9] of Mississippi, U.S.A, you say, "Negroes of this country . . . should hereafter class him along with Marcus Garvey." Elementary logic records an inconsistency here. If Howard is equal to Garvey in infamy, then Jamaica is not the only place to produce Jackasses of Garvey's type! And to give Jamaica a monopoly in the production of Jackasses after placing Perry Howard in

---

[9] Perry Howard (1877–1961), prominent African American member of the Republican Party.

parity with Garvey is to involve yourselves in a contradiction! No; traitors and fools may be found anywhere and everywhere.

Youth can ever learn from age, and I refer you to your last issue and advise you to ponder over the reply of Kelly Miller to your own questionnaire, which, by the way, elicited a majority of answers that were a complete repudiation of your own policy on the question of deportation of Garvey.

You argue for equality with white people, yet by giving their nationality unfavorable emphasis you deny equality to West Indians, and insinuate that only a West Indian would be guilty of the things you charge against Garvey! Consistency thou art indeed a jewel!

In the past you have called the 90 percent white people of this country cowards for their oppression of the 10 percent Negroes, and yet you advocate a policy, and practice a method, that carried out logically, will mean the oppression of 90,000 foreign-born Negroes (many of them citizens and fighters for your rights) by their 12,000,000 native-born brothers! Which is the greater oppression, nine oppressing one, or four hundred oppressing three?) Suppose Garvey were an American, would you emphasize that fact? If not (and you could not), why emphasize his foreign birth?

I will not point out that it is incompatible with your professed Socialist faith for you to initiate an agitation for deportation or to emphasize the nationality of anyone as a subtle means of generating opposition against him, but I certainly maintain that to oppose Garvey on the score of his birthplace is to confess inability to oppose him formidably upon any other ground. By the penalties you advocate and the arguments you stress against Garvey one can determine what you regard as his greatest offense, namely, his nationality. Certainly there is enough error and weakness in Garveyism for you to find a more intellectually dignified method of assault; and certainly the people you hope to rouse against this monstrous thing are sufficiently intelligent as to be entitled to a higher form of propaganda!

What is the object of emphasizing the nationality of an offender; to build up a feeling against the offender or against his nationality? The National Association for the Advancement of Colored People is interested in creating an unfavorable public opinion against Perry Howard, but do the leaders Johnson, Du Bois and Pickens, always refer to their quarry as Mississippian? Emphasizing nationality unfavorably can have only one result, whether it is desired or not, namely, extend public hostility from an individual to his group. Need I amplify this further when it is remembered that one of the greatest grievances of American

Negroes is against white newspapers forever stressing the race of colored criminal? Need I point out that the policy you are now pursuing will logically culminate in dissension within the race, and if sufficiently disseminated, make the life of West Indians among American Negroes as unsafe or unpleasant as is the life of American Negroes among their white countrymen?

THE MESSENGER for which I wrote and which I loved, prided itself upon its internationalism, and valued this quality as its hall-mark of superiority: but today it seems to have fallen from its former high estate. So international was it that it formulated plans for the guidance of Negroes everywhere and catered foreign subscribers; today its policy is one that is more intolerant and aggressively anti West Indian than even those papers that it formerly condemned. Comparisons are odious but they can serve to drive home a point. *The Crisis* is no less opposed to Garvey, but neither Mr. Johnson, Mr. White, nor Mr. Du Bois has forgotten the instincts of fair play, chivalry and *noblesse oblige*, and appealed to popular protest against wholesale denunciation of West Indians for the sins (!) of one of their group.

How can THE MESSENGER reconcile its demand for the deportation of West Indians then un-convicted of crime, made in the November and December issues, with its fight against the deportation of Alexander Berkman, the Russian anarchist, in 1919, a man who had served nearly twenty years in prison for attempting to murder Henry C. Frick, the Pennsylvania steel magnate? How can it reconcile its opposition to a group of Negro aliens while soliciting and accepting financial support from white aliens? And what of the financial, moral and intellectual support these black aliens gave the MESSENGER and it editors from 1916 to the present time?

And aren't these the same West Indians whom you praised during that period for their independence, radical tendencies and lack of enervating traditions? Must I conclude that you only admire these traits when they coincide with your interests or promote any cause you espouse? Suppose those who now support the Universal Negro Improvement Association joined the Friends of Negro Freedom would you sanctify them and render them acceptable to your new-born chauvinism? E tu Brute?

It is surprising to learn at the Friends of Negro Freedom that the West Indians are a menace to the progress of American Negroes. Perhaps such careful, modest and reliable scholars as W.E.B Du Bois and Carter Woodson, PHD, are in error when they stress the part "played by West Indians" in the up-building of the race in this country. Have you ever read the famous passage in "the Souls of Black Folk" in which the author refers to the contributions by West Indians in the early portion of the last century in formulating the manhood policies of native Negroes? Would the progress of American Negroes be greater without the achievements of foreign-born Negroes like Nathaniel Dett, Bert Williams, Prince Hall, Peter Ogden, Claude McKay, Straker, Crogman, Matzeliger, Russwurm, Marcus Wheatland, M.D., Bishop Derrick, Denmark Vesey, Dr. M.A.K. Shaw, Margetson, F. Burton Ceruti, Giles of Ocala, Fla., and hundreds of teachers, doctors, minister, lawyers, dentists, business men and progressive folk in other walks of life? Since when has meritorious achievement become a detriment to progress? And what of those like James Weldon and Rosamond Johnson, William Stanley Braitwaite and Robert Brown Elliot with foreign-born parents? And Du Bois with his Haitian-Bahaman ancestors? If The Messenger is ignorant of these elementary facts, its knowledge of the race it affects to speak for is comparable only with the more complete unacquaintance with facts revealed by its *bête noir*, Marcus Garvey. The sober sense of The Messenger must deprecate anything that tends to destroy racial unity upon essential questions like lynching; and viewed by their consequences, would anyone seriously argue that Garvey's ravings are as dangerous to American Negroes and the unspeakable and despicable treachery of Perry Howard? Are his words more truckling than Moton's "Be modest and unassuming"? If not, why emphasize the former's birthplace and ignore that of the latter? Or is discrimination inside the race another newly acquired policy of The MESSENGER.

Let us face certain fundamental facts regarding Garvey. Only so can we arrive at the truth and thus evolve a sound policy. Who are the bitterest and most persistent opponents of Garvey? Aren't they West Indians like Cyril V. Briggs, R.B. Moore, Frank R. Crosswaith, Thomas Potter and myself? Who caused his arrests and his indictments? West Indians: Grey, Warner, Briggs and Orr! Who conducts the *Crusader Service*, Garvey's veritable Nemesis? Briggs, assisted by the writer. The January *Crisis*, in justice to truth and elevated journalistic principles, concedes part of the work I did in unmasking Garvey.

Let us view the question from another angle: Who are the journalistic janissaries of Garvey, his intellectual bodyguard who play the role of his *diablous advocates?* "Sir" John F. Bruce (Grit), "Sir" R.L. Poston and "Sir" W.H. Ferris! Of what nationality are a majority of those be(k)nighted by Garvey? His Dukes, Ladies and Clowns? Who subscribed the larger portions of his many funds? (Read the lists in the *Negro World*.) Are West Indians numerous in strongholds like Pittsburgh, Cincinnati and Cleveland? But these facts do not constitute an indictment of American Negroes. Not a bit. One can understand how a people burdened with the naked and bitter realities of race prejudices and with traditions of despair and suffering will embrace something as chimerical and unsubstantial as the Black Star Line and an empire in Africa. It explains why they respond to Garvey's appeals even as they responded to those of Chief Sam, Bishop Holly, Bishop Turner, and the others related by Woodson in his book on Negro migration. It explains, too, to a degree, the gullibility revealed by William Pickens in his article in the *Nation* a year ago. Mr. Pickens, migrating from South Carolina to Arkansas, where he had to be acclimatized, had, buried somewhere in his subconscious self, some of the pioneer's optimism and became so enthusiastic over Garvey as to describe him as being "as brave as a Numidian lion." Mr. Pickens has seen the light since.

In the light of the foregone facts, historical and otherwise, is it hoping too much for me to expect that The Messenger will change its new policy of shifting personal responsibility to a group and penalizing a people who, despite their many faults and their misfortune in not choosing to be born in Mississsippi or Alabama, so well described by Mrs. Ratliff and Clement Wood in the *Nation*, or Arkansas, whose eloquent description by Pickens in the January Messenger I richly enjoyed, are, when all is said and done, just as human as their brothers in the United States?

New York City   W.A. Domingo

Mr. Owen's Reply (abridged)
In the first place, Mr. W.A. Domingo gives as the reason for his writing the preceding letter his apprehension lest "there might be misunderstandings as to my [Domingo's] attitude towards some of the newer policies of the magazine [The Messenger] on which I am listed as a contributing editor." This is a novel reason to say the least. We have never heard that contributing editors were responsible for all the policies of a publication. Even the editors, as a role, do not stand as sponsors for the articles of the contributing editors. The Messenger editors require the following conditions only from their contributing editors: They must steer clear of libel, keep within the bounds of civil decency, maintain a reasonable dignity, know *all* they write, but not write all they *know* (otherwise we would lack the space, and people would not have time to read it), write well, using the King's or the Queen's English, and make their presentation with cogent logic and comprehensive information.

"I am a West Indian"

Mr. Domingo continues: "I am a West Indian . . . *Difference of opinion is purely a mental quality and may exist between twin brothers and closest relatives. Opinions are personal, not national.*" Apparently, however, Mr. Domingo places some emphasis upon nationality, as shown in his utterance: "I am a West Indian." Probably one of the real reasons for his letter. Again, while difference of opinion may be purely a mental quality from the point of view of *effect*, national influences are frequently the causes of those differences. And Garvey's case is just about as good a citation as could be summoned. For instance, Garvey is from Jamaica, British West Indies. The British are the leading shipping and maritime nation; hence the natural suggestion of some form of shipping by a British subject, namely, the Black Star Line. The British Empire has a royal court, so Garvey imitates with his royal black court. The British Potentate, as it were, creates Knights, Dukes, Peers, Counts and Ladies, so Garvey makes black k(nights), dukes, peers, counts and ladies. In his cabinet Garvey again mimics the British. To illustrate, America has a Secretary of the Treasury, but Great Britain has a Chancellor of the Exchequer; so Garvey creates a chancellor of the U.N.I.A. exchequer. Even the so-called "Provisional President of Africa" is a British counterfeit. It grew out of the existence of De Valera, then provisional president of Ireland. De Valera represented the president of a British possession who was not in the country over which he was supposed to preside. Hence Garvey decided that he, also a British subject, and desirous of claiming control over territory held largely by Great Britain, would copy the title of De Valera. Sir Feris, Sir Bruce and Sir Poston are British "Sirs," and there is no other way by which to explain the Garvey schemes without a resort to nationality. His opinions may be personal, but they are produced by national influences.

Next Mr. Domingo remarks: "Since The Messenger began its *belated* fight to rid the race of the disgrace of Garveyism." . . . Let us stop right here. The Editor of The Messenger was the first person to suggest and inaugurate the fight upon Garvey's nebulous schemes and dreams. Too often we have heard Domingo stress this. In fact, our systematic, unremitting opposition to Garvey is a matter of record which may be easily verified by referring to The Messenger files.

"A Supreme Negro Jamaican Jackass"

Mr. Domingo's national bias is evident in his objection to an editorial in the January Messenger entitled: "A Supreme Negro Jamaican Jackass." There is no objection to our referring to Garvey as a jackass; none to his racial identity as a Negro; but mention of his nationality is taboo. Here our contributing editor is more concerned about nationality – the great island of Jamaica – than the entire Negro race. Is Jamaica a more sensitive and tender darling than the Negro?

Mr. Domingo has set himself up as the high priest of logic and is sure he finds an inconsistency in our editorial on Perry Howard (from Mississippi, U.S.A.,– don't forget the state or the nation!) where we say: "*Negroes of this country . . . should hereafter class him (Perry Howard) along with Marcus Garvey.*" Commenting upon this sentence Mr. Domingo proceeds as follows: "*Elementary logic records an inconsistency here. If Howard is equal to Garvey in infamy, then Jamaica is not the only place to produce Jackasses of Garvey's type!*" The fault here is with Mr. Domingo's logic. There are degrees even among classes. There are jackasses and jackasses! To illustrate: Students in Columbia University who make from 90 to 100 are put in Class A; those who make from 80 to 90 in Class B; those from 70 to 80 in Class C, while all below that are dropped. It is obvious that one student may make 90 and another 99 but both would be in class A, even though the student making 99 would have made the higher average. Likewise one student may make 68 and another 34, to use an extreme case. The student making 68 will have an average twice as high as the one who makes 34, yet both will fall under the "dropped" class. So with Garvey and Perry Howard. *Both are racial outlaws*, but then again there are outlaws and outlaws! This, of course, is no argument against Jamaicans; it is simply a puncturing of Dominigo's "*elementary logic.*" America is certainly capable of producing Negro and white jackasses. She has provided enough for centuries to come
[. . .]

"Should Marcus Garvey Be Deported"

It is not incompatible with Socialist faith to advocate deportation any more than it is to urge imprisonment. That there was no evidence to that effect which Mr. Domingo could find is evidenced by his not referring to it, despite his having searched for some since August 27th, when we first presented our reasons on that question. It might be well here and now too, to make our position crystally clear: *Even if it were against alleged Socialist principles to advocate what we regard just and right, we would still advocate it, because we accept no Bibles or creeds even in Socialism.* We support Socialism because of our faith in its general principles, but do not accept it with every dot of the "i" and crossing of the "t" as our objector does the tenets in Moscow.

Socialism recognizes that a tool is good or bad according to the use to which it is put. It opposes the imprisonment of men for expressing political and class war views, but urges the Democratic district attorney of New York City to arrest and imprison the ballot thieves who robbed their candidates of election. Socialists oppose injunctions against peaceful picketing of labor unionists, but not the injunction secure by Morris Hillquit (prominent Socialist attorney) for the International Ladies' Garment Workers' Union (largely a Socialist Union) against the Clothing Manufacturers of New York. Socialism opposes the deportation of I.W.W., Communists, Socialists and others, for the expression of political and war-time opinions, but *not* the deportation of Charles Morse (banker and shipping magnate) from France, to be tried in the United States for defrauding the government and using the mails to defraud. Our answer, therefore, is that Mr. Domingo is in error in believing that Socialism favors deporting a white man who is indicted for using the mails to defraud, but against meting out similar punishment to our "black Barnum" Marcus Garvey, also indicted for using the mails to defraud. *Moreover, if we regard our position correct, no fealty to creedish faiths of any kind would permit us to falter and swerve in the performance of our recognized duty.*
[...]

To All Oppressed Peoples and Classes
(*The Crisis*, October 1927[10])

THE MORE one reads the literature as sent out by the Brussels Congress against Colonial Oppression, the more one is impressed by its

---

[10] This manifesto came out of the World Congress Against Colonial Oppression and Imperialism in Brussels in February 1927, where the American delegation included Richard B. Moore (see footnote 14 on p. XXX). It is included here as the conference is an important link between the politics of the early 1920s and the alliances and groupings formed in the 1930s.

earnestness and ability. A "Manifesto to All Oppressed Peoples" is the latest offering from which we quote:

The proud edifice of European and later of American capitalism has been erected on the sweat and blood of the colonial peoples. Horrible slavery, inhuman maltreatment, forced labor and in some cases the complete extermination of whole races and cultures so that scarcely the name remains, have been the means to this end.

The end of the 19th and the beginning of the 20th century saw the final division of the world between a group of imperialist powers. A few great powers at the bidding of a small group of individuals controlling immense stores of accumulated capital, brought the whole worlds under their control with the assistance of rifles and bayonets and the most modern murder technique. The struggle of these imperialist powers amongst themselves for the last stretches of undivided land. And the demand of countries more recently imperialist for the redivision of the world led finally to the greatest catastrophe and greatest crime in the history of the world – the great World War.

But this fearful cataclysm which drenched the land of the two Continents with blood did not abolish the awful system of which it was itself the fruit. The imperialist powers are grimly hanging on to the booty which threatened to slip from their hands and which they paid so much to retain. The murder of millions of men, including hundreds of thousands of colonial slaves from India and the African possessions of France, did not end the mad scramble for possession. Fascist Italy has taken the place of imperialist Germany in the struggle for colonial possessions. Even in Germany itself, the privileged classes who have restored their economic and political power and forgotten the bitter taste of foreign rule are again striving to win for themselves the right to oppress other peoples.

That is the inexcusable logic of the system under which mankind is groaning. The present economic system which exhausted the European masses during the war is today less than ever able to exist without the subjection of whole nationalities and the resulting excess profits. The less capitalism is in a position to ensure the well-being of the European masses and above all of the proletarian masses the more it is compelled to seek markets for its goods on foreign continents which can be controlled by force. The development of monopolist capital transformed a small clique in the imperialist countries, above all in the Anglo-Saxon countries, into the masters of the world.

The World War shoed the deep divisions of world capitalism, but not only that, the imperialists were compelled to set up the slogan of self-determination as a way out of their difficulties. After the war, the oppressed and enslaved peoples took the imperialists at their word. A might movement for national emancipation passed over immense territories in Asia, Africa and America. The banner of revolt was raised in China, India, Egypt, North-West Africa, Indonesia and the Philippines. This great movement received a mighty impetus from the Russian revolution which smashed the power of Russian imperialism, freed hundreds of races and Nationalities exploited by the Tsarist Empire and established the rule of the proletariat upon the basis of a free federation of free peoples. The Workers State is the flaming torch lighting the oppressed peoples of the world along the path to freedom and independence.

This might will to freedom and independence will never again be broken. Only fools can believe that the civilization of today and of the future will be confined to Europe and the United States of America. The struggle of the Asiatic, American and African peoples for national emancipation in alliance with the proletariat of the imperialist countries, is the force which will abolish international capitalism and civilize the whole world.

Part II
Anti-Colonialism and Anti-Racism 1929–1937

Chapter 5
Transnational Anti-Racism

At the Sixth Congress of the Third International in 1928 the CPUSA adopted the self-determination of the Black Belt thesis. This argued that African Americans in the southern states constituted an oppressed nation possessed of the right to self-determination, and that those in the north constituted a national minority who were denied social, political and economic equality. This policy of self-determination, for all its complications, was an important recognition of African Americans as a particular oppressed group in the USA and positively impacted on the credibility of the CPUSA as an organisation which placed race politics at the centre of their praxis. The articles below focus on those articulations of interconnected histories which inflect international struggles to speak to the condition of African Americans. More detailed reports of the political situations in both the Caribbean and Africa are presented in both *The Communist* and *Negro Worker*. The fluctuating policies of the Stalinised Comintern impact sharply on the politics of this period and the articulations of black radicalism are more directly associated with fortunes of the Soviet Union (as opposed to the example of the Bolshevik revolution) than in the earlier period.

ANLC Organizes Labor Unions in West Indies
(By O. E. Huiswoud,[1] *The [Harlem/Negro] Liberator*, 7 December 1929)

In the West Indies the workers and farmers are awakening to the realization that only through effective organization can they wage a real fight against their oppression and exploitation.

---

[1] Otto Huiswoud (1893–1961), born in Surinam Huiswoud emigrated to the USA in 1910, and was a member of the ABB and a founding member of the Communist Party in 1919. Along with Claude McKay, Huiswoud was a delegate at the 4th Comintern Congress in Moscow in 1922. He was a leading member of the ITUCNW in the 1930s.

Victims of a vicious colonial policy which keeps them as an army of slaves producing huge profits for the absentee landlords and big foreign corporations working under a broiling sun for the most miserable wages, denied political control of their own country, these oppressed workers are becoming conscious of the fact that only thru their organized power can they hope to gain any betterment of their conditions.

On the plantations these farm laborers are working under semi-slave conditions. Paid a mere pittance for their toil, they are at the complete mercy of the land owners and their agents. The city workers fare little better. They are paid a very low wage (one to two dollars per day) and forced to toil under the most oppressive conditions. They are compelled because of the low wages to live in crowded, unsanitary and disease breeding hovels. Practically unorganized, they are unable to resist the encroachment of the employers who take every advantage of this situation to keep them at a starvation level.

Despite this, many spontaneous strikes occur, which are often brutally suppressed by the government. This situation makes it imperative that the workers in the West Indies organize themselves into powerful unions in order to combat the exploitation of the employers and to better their living conditions.

Recently the American Negro Labor Congress, through its Field Organizer, aided the workers in Jamaica to organize a union. Workers from all trades and occupations responded splendidly to the call for organization. The need for a real strong union, fighting in their behalf, was long felt by the masses. A number of mass meetings were held and the workers demonstrated their interest and appreciation in attending in hundreds. Committees comprising thirteen trades and occupations, such as carpenters, longshoremen, bakers, dressmakers, trainmen, etc., were formed charged with the task of organizing local unions in their respective occupations. An enlarged committee with the purpose of supervising, coordinating and federating these local bodies was organized. The work of these committees has made rapid progress. The workers have shown their enthusiasm by forging ahead in order to build a real trade union movement in Jamaica. Out of these committees has developed a permanent organization, "The Jamaica Trades and Labor Union."

The workers in Jamaica are showing real spirit and are determined to build a movement that will lift them out of the mire of poverty and degradation and be a powerful instrument in destroying the shackles of wage slavery.

Lenin
(Editorial, *The [Harlem/Negro] Liberator*, 18 January 1930)

Millions of workers throughout Africa, Asia, Europe and America will take part during the present month in the Lenin Memorial meetings being held all over the world under the auspices of the Communist Parties, the vanguard in each country of the exploited working class.

Vladimir Ilyich Lenin was without doubt the greatest fighter for the emancipation of the world's oppressed that imperialism has even had to contend with. Lenin was a most relentless enemy of world imperialism and its exploitation and oppression of the workers of the "home" countries and the peoples of the colonies and semi-colonies. A thorough Marxist he was absolutely clear in his attitude towards imperialism and grimly uncompromising in the struggle for its overthrow.

It was Lenin who laid the basis for that whole-hearted support which Communist parties throughout the world have given to the nationalist movements in Turkey, China, Haiti, Morocco, India, Egypt, Korea and other oppressed countries, as well as for a free black republic of South Africa, self-determination for the Negro people of the Southern United States and complete racial, social and political equality for the Negro, north and south. This support it was which made possible the successful struggles of China and Turkey against the imperialists of Great Britain, France, Japan, the United States, etc. Lenin clearly laid down the principle of cooperation with and full support for these struggles. In his book "Socialism and War," soon to be published in English, Lenin laid it down that:

"The Socialists cannot reach their great aim without fighting against every form of national oppression. They must therefore unequivocally demand that the Social-Democrats of the oppressing countries (of the so-called 'great' nations, in particular) should recognize and defend the right of the oppressed nations to self determination in the political sense of word, i.e. the right to political separation. A Socialist or a great nation or a nation possessing colonies who does not defend this right is a chauvinist."

That he intended recognition of the right of oppressed peoples to revolt to go further than mere words, Lenin makes clear in speaking of the imperialist slaughter of 1914:

"Whoever justifies participation in this war, perpetuates imperialist oppression of nations. Whoever seeks to use the present difficulties of the governments in order to fight for a social revolution, is fighting for the real freedom of really all nations, a freedom that can be realized only under Socialism."

Lenin was the leader not only of the heroic Russian workers and peasants who have attained their freedom by the overthrow of Russian imperialism, but he was pre-eminently the leader of the world's toilers of all races and countries in the world-wide struggle against imperialist oppression and exploitation. Lenin is dead. But his example and his teachings have inspired countless millions of the oppressed to militant struggle for the final overthrow of the system under which they are oppressed.

The Negro and the Struggle Against Imperialism (abridged) (By James W. Ford,[2] *The Communist*, January 1930)

THE so-called Negro "problem" has been consistently misstated for so long that a survey of it is needed, especially with regards to the Negro under imperialism. We are in the period of the general decay of capitalism; sharpening of antagonisms are producing a real serious crisis in capitalism and imperialism which really characterizes capitalism at the present time. This period is of tremendous significance to the international working class and oppressed peoples and is of very great importance to the Negro people themselves. The future history of the Negro in the struggles for liberation, for political, social and economic advancement depends immeasurably upon how they estimate the present period of imperialism, the concrete organization tasks they put before themselves in order to achieve these things and the unity they establish with the international struggle against imperialism. Indeed, the Negro people are passing through one of the most important periods of struggle for liberation. We have already seen the great struggles of the Chinese workers and peasants; we see rising waves of revolt and struggle in India; we are witnessing great waves of revolt in the working class and proletariat in the home lands of imperialism.

---

[2] James W. Ford (1893–1957) prominent African American Communist, who stood as the Party's vice presidential candidate in 1932, 1936 and 1940. He edited the early editions of *Negro Worker* before being replaced by George Padmore. In 1937 Ford went to Spain to support the Republican forces in the Civil War.

Imperialism and the Negroes

For our purpose in dealing with the special question of the Negro, imperialism is that stage of capitalism when the whole globe has been divided and distributed amongst a few of the greatest capitalists powers, and especially the territory of Africa; and when there is going on amongst the Negroes of America class changes, the development of a Negro bourgeoisie which, subordinating itself to the big white bourgeoisie, causes a more intense exploitation of the Negro toiling masses of America. Imperialism nurses and stimulates racial hatreds by means of racial oppression
[...]

Policy of Imperialism

What is the present policy of imperialism with regards to the Negro peoples? Whereas in early history of India, England followed a policy which uprooted and tore down old customs and institutions and feudal systems which amounted to a social revolution, in Africa, excepting possibly South Africa, British imperialism is following a policy of maintaining the old customs and hindering the industrial development of the country as was done previously in India, and is ruling the country through native chiefs while she sucks profits from the territories, thus degrading and perpetually carrying on a policy which hinders the advancement of the toiling masses of Africa. French imperialism, while tearing down old customs, is at the same time in actuality exterminating whole territories of the population.

The policy of imperialism is, in actuality, a policy of retarding the industrial development of the country, a policy which results in retarding and hindering the advancement of the African people, and standing in contrast to it is the agrarian policy–the policy of maintaining Africa as the "countryside" for the European imperialists, as the leading source of raw materials, as market centers, as centers for surplus investments of capital accumulations gained through the exploitations of the workers in the home countries. The latter of these conditions, i.e., as sources of raw materials, as market centers and as centers for surplus capital accumulation, is leading to intense rivalries and contradictions amongst the imperialists themselves, and is the determining factor leading to another war
[...]

The liberation movements of the Negro masses take different form in different sections. The essential characteristic of Negro Liberation movements must be that the central question is the question of relationship to the Negro masses, and must be based upon the great bulk of the Negro population, their demands, their specific and special demands. Liberation movements cannot hope to be successful unless they have this characteristic. Liberation movements cannot go far, cannot play a final role in the liberation of the Negroes representing partial, middle class demands. If the middle class and intellectuals wish to serve in the liberation of the masses they must be organizers and servants of the masses. The liberation movements also demand programs that offer the masses real assistance in their desperate needs and conditions.

The liberation movement must be a struggle towards social liberation. Social liberation like economic liberation must lead towards self-determination, towards the elimination of all of those social fetters that are confining the Negro masses to narrow and limited paths, into "ghetto" life, into isolation whereby they can be more easily exploited, into places of oppression, into narrow political surroundings. All of these demands means, in actuality, a struggle for separation from imperialist domination; for imperialists foster these conditions for the specific reasons of oppression and exploitation. [...]

The Revolutionary Movement in Africa
(By George Padmore,[3] *Negro Worker*, June 1931)

The revolutionary movement in Africa is rapidly assuming new forms of a higher political character. The anti-imperialist struggle is passing over from the agitational stage to open mass demonstrations of the workers and peasants, as well as armed clashes with the military forces of imperialism.

South Africa

The revolts which have broken out in various sections of Africa, during the past year show the wide extent to which the militancy and radicali-

---

[3] George Padmore (1903–1959) was an enormously influential pan-Africanist who was born in Trinidad and went to the USA in 1924. He joined the CPUSA in 1927 and broke with the Communist movement in 1934 over what he perceived as the abandonment of the colonial question in the era of Popular Front imperatives of the USSR in its relationship to Britain and France. This led him to be cast by the *Negro/Harlem Liberator* in July 1934 as 'petty bourgeois with connections with agent provocateurs and enemies of the Negro liberation struggle'.

sation of the Black toiling masses is taking place. For example, in the Union of South Africa, the struggles between the native population and the British and Boer imperialists are more acute today than ever before. Several armed clashes have occurred in the most important industrial centers of the country between the black workers and the armed forces of South African fascist dictatorship.

These struggles culminated in one of the most militant demonstrations in Durban on Dingaan's Day (December the 16th, 1930). Despite the attempt of the police to prohibit the workers from demonstrating, thousands of natives headed by the Communist vanguard bearing a red banner defied the police and took possession of the streets. Hundreds of police re-enforced by armed bands of fascist-hooligans made a vicious assault upon the demonstrators who stood their grounds and retaliated, blow for blow.

East Africa

Revolutionary ferment is also assuming wider and wider proportions in East Africa. The British so-called Labour Government tries to conceal its repressive colonial policy with "left" phrases about "paramountcy of native interests", but the conditions of the toiling masses in Kenya and the other colonies is hardly any better than slavery. The Kenya Government tries to crush all manifestations of political awakening among the natives by suppressing their organizations of struggle, but the revolutionary movement continues to bring in increasing masses of toilers. Because of this general unrest, the British "Labour" Government through its colonial minister, Lord Passfield,[4] has recently enacted a law which makes it a criminal offense for natives to collect funds for any purpose except religious. The object of this law is to prevent the workers, especially the agricultural labourers, who are semi-serfs on the plantations of the white landlords from developing any effective organized methods of struggle. For instance, the Kikuyu Central Association, the only revolutionary political organization among the natives of Kenya has been declared illegal. Yet in the face of this open imperialist terror and oppression, MacDonald has the nerve to talk about "trusteeship of native interests", in the recently published White Papers. The Africans, however, can no longer be fooled by such hypocritical gestures

---

[4] Sidney James Webb, 1st Baron Passfield (1859–1947) was Secretary of State for the Colonies in the second Labour government of Ramsay MacDonald (1866–1937) between 1929–1931.

of the social-fascist, the open defenders of British imperialism. The East African toilers are still carrying on agitation on the plantations and on the reserves, and will find new forms and methods of organizing their forces in order to drive the landlords and the official representatives and agents of British imperialism out of their country.

British West Africa

In order to find a solution of the present financial situation the British colonial governments, as well as the various commercial interests who dominate the economic life of West Africa are cutting their African staffs, while at the same time the governments are increasing taxation on the toiling population. This led to a revolt in the South Eastern province of Nigeria, in December 1929. The peasant women refused to pay the special tax which the government attempted to impose upon them. Over 30,000 women demonstrated and drove the tax collectors away from their villages. Native soldiers commanded by European officers were used against the demonstrators. About 83 women were shot and 87 others wounded before the uprising was suppressed.

The most recent peasant outbreak occurred in Sierra Leone during the middle of February 1931. This was one of the most serious outbreaks which has broken out in the West Coast since the crisis. Despite the attempts of the British Government to suppress all information about the uprising, the native petty-bourgeois press of Sierra Leone openly writes that the principal causes for the revolt were economic. Hundreds of natives led by a battalion of 50 men armed with guns invaded the Kambia District in Sierra Leone which lies next to the neighbouring French colony of Guinea. In February the peasants under a man called Hydare, a Negro moslem leader who is reported to have had tremendous influence over the natives of Kambia, thousands of whom he converted to Mohamedanism, organized an anti-imperialist movement against the British government. After arming his followers Hydare raised the standard of revolt by calling upon the peasants to refuse to pay their hut taxes and to drive the British officials away from the province. Hydare also demanded that all crown land in the protectorate of Sierra Leone be confiscated and divided up among the landless peasants in order that they might be able to grow food to feed themselves in view of the fact that the palm kernels industry which is their chief source of income, has completely collapsed due to overproduction. In order to avoid starvation the peasants are turning their attention to the cultivation of food crops, such as rice, but the government officials, are opposed to this and are demanding the immediate payment of taxes. Hydare's agitation had tremendous influence throughout the Kambia province. The British Government attempted to arrest him, but the natives threatened death to all Europeans who entered their territory. The situation became so alarming that the Central Government in Free-Town ordered a detachment of the Royal West African Frontier Force to the scene of the rebellion. The soldiers, mostly natives drawn from the other sections of Sierra Leone, commanded by British officers, while attempting to embark in Kambia were fired upon by the insurgents. Skirmishes followed during the course of which several natives and soldiers were killed including Hydare and Captain H. J. Holmes, the English officer in command of the troops. After several days of fighting the soldiers thanks to their overwhelming numbers and superior arms were able to put down the revolt. After this the most repressive campaign was launched. Hundreds of huts of natives who took parts in the uprising were burnt to the ground, and men and women arrested and thrown into jail or deported from the territory.

Task of International Revolutionary Labour Movement

The international revolutionary movement, especially the Communist Party of Great Britain and the Britain Section of the League Against Imperialism must render every possible assistance to this growing revolutionary movement in Africa.

Increase and Spread the Scottsboro Defense[5]
(Editorial, Negro Worker, July 1931)

The storm of international protest against the planned execution of 8 young Negro workers on a frame-up charge, at Scottsboro, Alabama, that has arisen throughout the world and grows in volume, has shocked the bourgeoisie ONLY MIGHTY MASS PROTEST OF THE INTERNATIONAL PROLETARIAT CAN STOP THE EXECUTION OF THE 8 BLACK PROLETARIANS! Mass demonstrations and meetings of workers of all races as well as stormy scenes before American consulates have been held throughout Europe and America, and in South

---

[5] The Scottsboro trials dominated CPUSA activities in the early 1930s. The Communist International Labor Defense, a radical legal-action organisation both represented many of the defendants and organised mass rallies and campaigns.

Africa and Latin America, protesting indignantly against the frame-up of their class brothers and demanding their release. NOTHING LIKE THIS HAS EVER HAPPENED BEFORE! The bourgeoisie has been astounded at this wonderful demonstration of international solidarity – AT THE SPECTACLE OF WORKERS OF ALL RACES RAISING THEIR FISTS IN DEFENSE OF 8 NEGRO PROLETARIANS.

At Berlin workers, under the leadership of the Communist Party and the International Labour Defence, made mighty demonstrations before the American consulate.

At Paris a demonstration before the American consulate was broken up by the police.

In South Africa native and poor white workers themselves ground down under the heel of Boer and British imperialism raised their protest.

At Hamburg and extending into the country districts over 5 huge mass meetings and demonstrations have been held; comrade Andre, the well known leader of the Red Front Fighters, and others have spoken; Altogether over 20,000 workers have taken part, and the wave of protest has been great.

On July 9th a great mass meeting was held at the International Seamen's Club at Hamburg in which African seamen took part. Representatives of the International Labour Defence and the International Trade Union Committee of Negro Workers spoke on the history of the case and its class significance. The mass of workers expressed their indignation by protest resolutions denouncing the frame-up of these boys by the American capitalists and demanding their immediate release. On the same day a demonstration was held at the American consulate.

At Dresden and Cologne, Germany, windows of the American consulates were broken in and the workers hurled bottles into the windows containing messages **Stop the Lynching! Hands Off the 8 Negro Workers!** In these and many other towns of Germany the workers have demonstrated under the leadership of the Communist Party and the International Labour Defence.

At Geneva, Switzerland, on the occasion of the holding of the International Conference on African Children, the frame-up was denounced before this body by the representative of the League Against Imperialism. On the following day a protest meeting was held in Geneva at which a representative of the International Trade Union Committee of Negro workers spoke. Under the Leadership of the Swiss Section of the International Labour Defence, workers demonstrated before the American consulate. They paraded through the streets despite the police order against it and then held their meeting before the Consulate. The police tried to break up the meeting but the workers fought back, several were arrested. The walls of the American consulate building were painted with Big Red letters: **Down with Lynch Rule in the U. S. A! Stop the Murder of the 8 Negro Boys!**

Workers in many other countries in England, Cuba etc., have joined in the International protest. In Moscow and Leningrad and many other cities and factories throughout Russia mighty mass demonstrations arose in indignant protestation against this most brutal frame-up of 8 children by American capitalism.

Comrades, this international spirit of solidarity is the only kind of language that the bourgeoisie will heed. This mass movement bringing about the solidarity of workers throughout the world, will bring so much pressure upon the blood thirsty capitalist bosses of the U.S.A. that they will be forced to release our class brothers.

Telegrams and cables have poured in upon the Governor of Alabama from over the world. A cable of protest was received from a group of scientists with the name of Albert Einstein, the famous German scientist at the top. At Leningrad there was a great protest of the toiling cultural and scientific workers engineers, technicians, educational and art workers.

This has been a mighty demonstration of world sympathy and international solidarity.

But comrades and fellow workers, the boys are still in the clutches of the fiendish boss class. Only an appeal to a higher court has delayed the case so far. There is nothing but capitalist "justice" in these courts. This means that the boys will be executed unless we raise a mightier international protest for their actual release.

The International Trade Union Committee of Negro Workers calls upon the international proletariat to increase its vigilance, to increase its protests. Demonstrate before American consulates! Let the bosses feel the mighty fist of the international proletariat!

To the workers of Alabama both white and black, organize Self-Defence Corps composed of both white and black workers. Defend your right to assembly! Defend your meetings! Demonstrate for the release of the boys! You are fighting for bread and life. The bosses are trying to hide from you unemployment and starvation. They are trying to divide you and thereby destroy your movement.

Down with white terror and lynching, Death to Lynchers!

Long live International solidarity!

What is the International Trade Union Committee of Negro Workers?
(*Negro Worker*, December 1931)

The Negro Workers Committee was formed in July 1930 at an international conference of Negro toilers held in Hamburg, Germany. The Committee is not a race, but a class organization, organizing and leading the fight in the interests of Negro workers in Africa, the West Indies and other colonies. The aims of the Committee are as follows:

1. Abolition of Forced Labour, Peonage and Slavery.
2. Equal Pay for Equal Work – Irrespective of Race, Colour or Sex.
3. Eight Hour Day.
4. Government Relief for Unemployed, – free rent, no taxes.
5. Freedom to organize trade unions, unemployed councils and peasant committees, – right to strike.
6. Against racial barriers in trade unions and colour bar in industry.
7. Against capitalist terror – lynching, police and soldier terrorism, arrest and deportation of foreign workers.
8. Against confiscation of peasant and communal lands, against taxation of the Negro workers and peasants.
9. To promote and develop the spirit of international solidarity between the workers of all colours and nationalities.
10. To agitate and organize the Negro workers against the imperialist war in China and the intervention in Soviet Russia, in which the white capitalist exploiters intend to use black workers as cannon-fodder as they did in the last war.
11. To defend the independence of Liberia, Haiti and other Negro States and to fight for the full independence of the Negro toilers in Africa and the West Indies, and their right of self-determination in the Black Belt of U. S. A.
12. The Committee also fights against white chauvinism, (race prejudice) social-reformism and the reformist programmes of the Negro capitalist misleaders, and the missionaries, preachers and other agents of imperialism.

These misleaders, instead of organizing the Negro masses to fight for their freedom are the very ones who help the capitalists by preaching obedience, and loyalty to imperialist rule:

Negro Workers, organize the fight against imperialism!
Support the Revolutionary Trade Union Movement!
Fight for the Freedom of the Working Class

Trouble in the West Indies
(By George Padmore, *Negro Worker*, May 1932)

We have repeatedly pointed out in the columns of this journal, the terrible economic exploitation and imperialist policy of oppressive taxation imposed upon the workers and peasant masses in the Caribbean, and the burning necessity for the West Indian workers at home and abroad to wake up and take a more active part in the building up of an anti-imperialist movement which will alone enable them to meet the tyrants on an equal footing.

Elsewhere in this issue appears an appeal by the Editor of the "Grenada West Indian" which confirms the warning which we have always given to the West Indian workers. The "Negro Worker" is in profound sympathy with the toiling masses of Grenada, but we do not agree with the methods of meeting this imperialist offensive, as indicated by Mr. Marryshow.[6]

We have absolutely no illusions about sending a delegation to the Colonial Office. We have seen too many of these useless excursions coming to London, not only from the West Indies, but from the African colonies. Not many weeks ago we happened to run across a group of these "loyal subjects of the King" from Trinidad. From all indication it appears that all that came out of this mission was, that two lawyers and a labour fakir – who for years played the role of lackey to such notorious Labour imperialists as MacDonald and Passfield – got a free trip across the Atlantic out of funds subscribed by a starving population.

It is high time that West Indians who pose as leaders stop this kowtowing business of sending memoranda, petitions, and deputations to England. It is no use kidding ourselves that we can at the same time fight our oppressors and beg them for favours. We must stop this monkey business of appealing from Cesar to Cesar. Furthermore, this kind of humbug merely creates much harm, for it helps to support the illusion which missionaries and other so-called friends of the colonial peoples try to foster among the masses that the Secretary of State is different to the bureaucrats on the spot. The truth is that such people as Vans Best[7] and Blood,[8] the appointees of Downing Street, are only able to run amuck in

---

[6] T. A. Marryshow (1887–1958), key anti-colonial activist and journalist and President of the Grenada Workers Association.
[7] T. A. Vans Best, Colonial Secretary in Trinidad.
[8] Sir Hilary Blood (1893–1967), Colonial Secretary in Grenada.

Grenada, because they know damn well that they have the support, not only of that die-hard-red-neck Tory slave driver, Cunliffe Lister,[9] but also such imperialist parasites, as Sir Samuel Wilson, the notorious ex-governor of Trinidad who is the real czar of the West Indies Department of the Colonial Office, and the very man under whom Vans Best served as Colonial Secretary in Trinidad. They are all birds of the same feathers.

West Indian workers, whether at home, in America or England, must learn from the experiences of India and Ireland. They must not put their faith in the lying promises of the British imperialists and their touts, whether white or black. They must depend upon their own organized might, which alone will enable them to rid their island homes of such bloodsuckers as Vans Best and Blood.

Workers, peasants and militant intellectuals of Grenada, organize your ranks into an anti-imperialist movement. Demonstrate on the streets, as you have recently done, in order to dramatize before the whole world the sufferings of a starving, bankrupt, ruthlessly crushed down and exploited people. If need be you must prepare to call a general strike. Grenada will have the sympathy and the support of the working class throughout the world, especially the British workers, who, after their bitter betrayal of the Labour Party, and their ever increasing misery are learning to realize that they will never be able to emancipate themselves unless they support the struggles of the colonial peoples for freedom and self-determination.

For Self-Determination in the Black Belt
(Editorial, *The [Harlem/Negro] Liberator*, 1 August 1932)

In an immense territory of the South, a territory commonly known as the Black Belt, live millions of Negro workers and farmers. These Negroes build and man the factories of this territory. The Negro farmers and tenants till the land of this territory. They produce the wealth of this territory.

But the rulers of this territory are not Negroes. The factories that the Negroes man, belong to white owners. The land that the Negroes till, and water with their sweat, belongs to white landlords. The officials of the territory, from the governors of states down to the holders of the lowest local offices, are white men. The courts of this territory are

---

[9] Philip Cunliffe-Lister (1884–1972), Secretary of State for the Colonies between 1931 and 1935.

presided over by white judges. The police and the sheriffs of this territory are white.

A handful of white bankers and landlords have imposed upon the millions of Negroes a foreign bondage. And in order to maintain this bondage, Negroes are held in slavery on the land, starved on the farms, whipped on the chain-gangs, hanged from trees or legally lynched in the courts.

The land of the Black Belt rightfully belongs to the millions of Negroes who till it. These Negroes should own the land in this territory; they should rule its territory and make its laws and sit in judgment in its courts. They should have the right to determine what form of government they desire: and should they decide upon a government separate from the United States, they must be free to act upon their decision.

This is, briefly, what is meant by the demand raised by the Communist Party: the right of self-determination in the Black Belt. This demand is part and parcel of the demand of the working class Party for equal rights. Without the right of self-determination in the Black Belt, all talk of equal rights is empty and futile.

But this slogan horrifies, not only the white bosses and landlords who grow fat by keeping the Negroes in subjection, but likewise the supporters, open and concealed of these bosses and landlords. And one of those who cry out against the right of self-determination is Haywood Broun, mouthpiece of the Socialist Party.

To Broun, the idea of a handful of white bosses ruling millions of Negroes, is entirely acceptable. But when the proposition is made that the Negroes of this territory shall govern this territory in which they are a majority and govern the handful of white men who live there – then Broun, and all his fellow-faker, are alarmed.

"It means a new form of Jim-Crowism," says Broun. Broun does not cry out against Norman Thomas, Socialist candidate for President who regularly segregates Negroes in his meetings in the South. And although he has frankly stated that he is opposed to enforcement of the fourteenth and fifteenth amendments, Broun is much "concerned" over "Jim-Crowism" in the Black Belt.

Does the right of self-determination mean Jim-Crowism? It means the opposite – freedom from bondage and inequality. The rule of Negroes in the Black Belt does not mean the setting aside of this territory for the Negroes alone, and forcing Negroes to live there. Equal rights for the Negroes in every part of the United States, with freedom to come and go as they wish – this is one of the main aims of the Communists. But the demand for equal rights is a hollow mockery unless the Negroes can throw off their backs this handful of white rulers who keep them in bondage. That is the meaning of the demand of the Communists: Equal for Negroes, self-determination for the Black Belt.

How the Empire is Governed
(By George Padmore, *Negro Worker*, July 1932)

British Imperialism is no infant. It is full grown. So full grown that it is becoming senile and thanks to the blows which it is receiving from its more verile rivals, especially the U. S. on the one hand, and the revolts of the toiling masses under its yoke on the other, is beginning to totter. Even the blind can see that its fall is inevitable. However, while it lasts, let us briefly review how it is governed.

* * *

For centuries the ruling class of Britain through wars with rival imperialist powers, military expeditions, frauds, corruption and trickery, especially of British merchant-capitalists and missionaries in Africa and India, has been planting the Union Jack in other peoples' territories. It is in this way the so-called mighty British Empire has been carved out.

During these centuries of colonial domination and exploitation, the imperialists of Britain can truly be said to have learnt the art of "governing". Their policy in a dual one. On the one hand, they maintain their domination over the colonial masses through deceit, hypocrisy and corruption. And when these methods fail, brute force, and terrorism, backed up by machine guns and bombing planes are brought into action in order to maintain the authority of these white overlords.

* * *

Now let us see how the first method of British domination is being concretely applied in various parts of the Empire.

In **India**, the imperialists have been able to maintain a stranglehold over three hundred millions people by exploiting religious differences among the toiling masses, through organized pogroms. When the true history of India comes to be written, the facts will reveal that the agents of the British Rajah have been as skilful provocateurs as those of Nicolas II. Let no one be so naive as to think that the British are in India for India's good. That is what the missionaries and other middle-class people who masquerade as "friends of India" would have the world believe. And it is just because of this kind of humbug that these people must be branded as some of the greatest enemies of the Indian masses. In this respect the diehard Tory imperialists are by far more honest than these ecclesiastical and petty-bourgeois charlatans. Some years ago, the late Sir Joynson-Hicks, Secretary of State for Home Affairs publicly declared:

"We did not conquer India for the benefit of the Indians. I know in missionary meetings it is said that we conquered India to raise the level of the Indians. That is cant!

"We conquered India as an outlet for the goods of Great Britain. We conquered India by the sword, and by the sword we shall hold it," (Shame.)

"Call it shame if you like, I am stating facts, I am interested in missionary work of that kind, but I am not such a hypocrite as to say that we hold India for the benefit of the Indians. We hold it as the finest outlet for British goods in general, and for Lancashire cotton goods in particular."

And just because of this, as long as India remains under British domination, so long will we witness Hindus flying at Mohammedans threats, and vice versa. For back of every communal riot in this land of misery, and hunger, stands the agents-provocateur of British Imperialism. Believe it or not!

A Tass message from Rome published in the "**Pravda**" of June 26, states: –

"Italian divers who are employed in the Bay of Biscay on the salvage of cargo from the Egypt, which was sunk some years ago on a voyage from England to India, state that the steamer was loaded with arms and munitions, although the official bills of lading and customs documents show a different cargo.

The Italian Press calls attention to the fact that the English customs issued false documents, and points out that, with the sanction of the English authorities, the steamer was carrying arms for the Indian Moslems for the purpose of provoking religious conflicts.

Referring to the recent bloody events – in Bombay, "**Stampa**" writes: – "This episode throws some light on the eastern policy of England, which sends millions of bullets and arms to the Indian Moslems, although no trace of such a transaction is to be found in the ship's documents. It is possible that some individuals who thought that their secret was buried at the bottom of the sea will be very much disconcerted by this compromising discovery."

* * *

What applies to India also occurs in **Ireland**. Wherever the British imperialists have conquered a people of homogenous racial stock, they have utilized religion as the wedge to carry through their policy of "divide and rule". In India it is Hinduism against Mohammedanism. In Ireland it is Protestantism against Catholicism. For nobody realizes more so than the hypocritical puritanic British capitalists the truism, that "religion is the opium of the people". And they are out to exploit it to the fullest.

Ireland, one of the oldest nations in the world has not only been robbed and plundered for centuries; its peasantry starved and driven off the land; millions forced to migrate to America; – but the British bond holders and absentee landlords have torn the country in two. "Protestant" Ulster versus the "catholic" South! Just recently, during a religious congress in Dublin, we witnesses the extent to which religious fanaticism has driven bleeding Ireland. Irish protestant workers and peasants, misled by British imperialist agents attacked groups of Irish catholic workers and peasants, simply because religion has been used to poison them against their fellow-exploited countrymen. Thanks to these artificial barriers fostered and maintained by an alien conqueror, these arrogant British slave holders, through their agent, J. H. Thomas, have the impudence to threaten the toiling masses of the Irish Free State to pay them 3 million Pounds annual tribute, under the farcical display of indignation that the Irish people are violating their "sacred" obligations. Such hypocritical phrase mongering by this ex-socialist and traitor of the British workers is enough to turn the stomachs of all decent minded and freedom loving peoples.

* * *

What applies to India – and Ireland, equally applies to **Africa**. It is quite true that the methods used by the British exploiters and oppressors in Africa are not so much based upon religion, but the policy of "divide and rule" is the same.

Let us see: In those parts of Africa where the British invaders found economic and social system with a sufficiently, developed political organization, through which they could operate, – as in Northern Nigeria, they introduced the "unique" system of "Indirect Rule", Lord Lugard was the father of this ingenious form of colonial plunder. The lands were confiscated from the natives and the chiefs were stripped of all of their traditional authority, and turned into tax-collectors and forced labour agents, behind whom, the European officials have been able, not only to extort tribute from the workers and the peasants, but to make slaves out of them.

In other colonies, especially in East Africa (Kenya) the same policy has been applied. The natives have been driven away from their best lands, which have been turned over to white landlords, for the development of plantations with forced labour.

At the present moment, the British imperialists are attempting to introduce the same methods into the Gold Coast, Here we witness some of the most brazen methods utilized by the imperialists to carry out their aims.

Thanks to the world economic crisis, the Gold Coast, like other African colonies, is faced with a tremendous financial deficit. So in order to find the money to maintain the state apparatus with its fabulous salaries for the European officialdom, the late Governor, Sir Ransford Slater attempted to introduce direct taxation in the form of **Income Tax**. This however, met with spontaneous mass opposition. The workers and peasants in Cape Coast staged monster demonstrations and protested against the enactments of the Bill.

Faced with a threatened revolt of the great mass of the population, the government made a temporary retreat. Governor Slater paid a hasty visit to Nigeria and after a conference with Sir Donald Cameron, the governor of that colony, returned to the Gold Coast well armed with the weapon of indirect policy which Lugard has saddled upon Nigeria.

Slater held a conference with the native chiefs, and by promising them certain privileges succeeded in driving a wedge among the Gold Coast people. The new scheme is to enact the original **Income Tax Bill** under the title **of Native Revenue Bill**. Through this vicious piece of legislation, the British imperialists tell the chiefs that they would be given the right to impose taxation upon the people and as reward for this, they would get a certain percentage for their local administration.

Although there is still much opposition against this new manoeuvre, the government has succeeded to some extent in splitting up the united front which formerly existed amount the chiefs. Those of the Eastern provinces, enamoured by the opportunity of becoming His Majesty's tax collectors are in favour of enforcing the new Bill when it becomes law with the aid of armed police and the West African Frontier Force.

The danger of increased taxation still menaces the Gold Coast people. The toiling masses must realize that the imperialists do not give a tinker's damn about individual African "leaders", no matter how big or powerful they may consider themselves. What they are afraid of, however, is the organized mass action of the workers and peasants. For at heart, every tyrant is a coward.

Furthermore, the British rulers in Africa also try to maintain their domination over the masses through other forms of corruption. For example: Where the prestige of the chiefs can no longer be utilized to rob the toiling population, the governments try to alienate certain sections of the intellectuals from the broad masses and thereby undermine the nationalist movement and put a brake upon the ever increasing anti-imperialist struggle for freedom and self-determination.

This is done in the following way: The government buy over these intellectuals by promising them jobs or a career in the colonial service. Already a number of them, who were at one time considered opponents of British imperialism, and champions of the people, have been won over by the skilful manoeuvring of the white officials and missionaries, – agents of the imperialists.

These native traitors have either been given decorative seats on Legislative Councils, petty positions, such as police magistrates, and other minor state offices, or otherwise decorated with some medal or title O. B. E., a Knighthood, etc., which George Vth is so fond of dishing out on his birthday. These British imperialists certainly know the art of effectively applying in their colonial policy semi-feudal titles and decorations in corrupting the upper-class Negroes.

* * *

In the West Indies this method of corruption is even more wide spread than in Africa. The Negro bourgeoisie and upper middle class is the most bribable strata of the population. The former without any substantial independent economic base and the latter saturated with all the ideology of exploiters themselves, from their very birth aspire to serve His Majesty in some form or the other. Throughout the West Indies and British Guiana the greatest ambition of the average middle-class Negro is to play the role of the King's monkeys by dressing up in ancient frock coats, silk hats and gold brade a la Marcus Garvey and strutting about as "honourable" members of Legislative or municipal Councils. When they fall short of this, they make a compromise with some provincial position in the state apparatus. But here again, the British overlords have been able to resort to an artificial method of splitting up the population and thereby prevent the crystallization of any dangerous anti-imperialist united front. This is done through the **Colour Caste System.** This is wide spread in the West Indies, especially in Jamaica, Barbados and the Windward Islands. Since the majority of the population of these islands are Negroes, the imperialists see to it that the mulattoes are put against the blacks, and vice versa. This is skilfully carried out in the following way. The dominant economic and political power is vested in the hands of Europeans, who in turn appoint the mulattoes to positions immediately be low them; and in this way, use the mulattoes as overseers to keep the black masses in subjection. So whenever the black workers and peasants revolt against oppressive taxation or other forms of imperialist robbery, they invariably find that the ones who are directly applying the policy which they are in rebellion against, are native mulattoes who shelter the real bloodsuckers, the white imperialists. What applies to the State policy, is even more openly manifested in the commercial life of the islands. It is a well known fact that the majority of banks, shipping companies, stores, and commercial houses of the British capitalists make it a policy only to employ mulatto men and women. Who, because of their more privileged economic position, in turn despise the darker skinned Negroes and help their masters to ruthlessly exploit them.

* * *

Hand in hand with their policy of "divide and rule", the British imperialists foster many illusions among the Negro colonial masses, which serves as a tremendous bulwark behind which millions and millions are deceived as to the true mission of these whites in the colonies. In order to put these humbugs over, the churches, the missionary schools the boy scouts and girl guides-movements, flag waving ceremonies, especially Empire Day, are all brought into full play in the service of British imperialism. For example, one of the most widespread illusions to be met with in Africa and the West Indies (and we presume the same thing applies to India) is, that there is no colour prejudice in England. That the Union Jack is the symbol of "justice'" and "fair play" for all, whether white or black, rich or poor, high or low. This kind of bunk is repeated so often, that although the Negroes are treated hardly any better than chattel slaves, or a pariah race, the vast majority of so-called educated Negroes still believe in this nonsense.

As we have already stated, the British bourgeoisie is shrewd and cunning. They are not of yesterday! They are one of the oldest ruling classes in the world, with centuries of colonial experience. Furthermore, they are past masters in the art of hypocrisy, and when compared with their American rivals, they can truly be said to be in a class by themselves. For example: A yankee imperialist will openly treat coloured people in America, as well as the colonies (Haiti, Hawaiian islands, Philippines) as an "inferior" race to be exploited. The typical American colonial official does not disdain to wound the sensibilities of the Negroes people under the "Stars and Stripes" by referring to them as "niggers". The British imperialists and their colonial lackeys do not differ with the Yankees in their mental attitude toward the darker colonial peoples, but being more cunning and hypocritical, they try to create the impression that Negroes and Indians are the equals of the other peoples of the Empire. While an American imperialist will openly refuse to associate with the Negroes of Haiti, or elsewhere, the English exploiter would shake hands and even dine with some bourgeois Negro in Jamaica, or one of the other colonies who could be used as a tool to further the interest of British imperialism. But you may rest assured that as soon as the Negro's back is turned, the European "gentleman" runs to the first wash basin to clean his hands from the contamination of a "nigger". This, in brief, characterizes the difference in outward attitude between these two types of imperialists – British and American. But because the Negro bourgeoisie and middle class, belly-crawling, kow-towing Negroes in Africa and the West Indies have been so saturated with British imperialist propaganda that they are not able to see through the fraud and deceit of these colonial robbers. And it is just because of this, such types of Negroes can never carry on a real militant struggle for our freedom.

These are only some of the many ways through which the rulers of this "mighty" British Empire are able to maintain their yoke over hundreds of millions of human beings in the colonies.

* * *

It is hardly necessary for us to record the other method which British imperialism utilizes when the so-called peaceful methods fail to achieve the required results. This is too well known. To record the occasions on which the strong armed policy of British imperialism have been applied would fill volumes. It is sufficient to recall the "Black and Tan" regime in Ireland; Amritsar and the present reign of terror in India; the incarceration of 33 labour leaders in Meerut prison; the 40,000 Indians in His Majesty's prisons for the "crime" of expressing their right to live as a free and independent people; the thousands of peasants bombed on the North-West frontier and other parts India; the recent massacre of unarmed Negro women in Nigeria; the mass terrorism in South Africa; the forceful confiscation of lands of thousands of East African toilers, and their enslavement on European plantations and mining companies; the denial of every elementary right of freedom of speech, public assembly, organization and press; the administration of "justice" through Ordinances that can only be equalled during the vilest regime of reaction under Tsarism – this is only a mild picture of the British Empire over which its defenders and upholders boast that the sun never sets.

* * *

It is from this yoke of slavery that hundreds of millions of black, white, yellow, brown, toiling humanity are struggling for national freedom and social emancipation. This struggle can only be successfully carried through by cementing the closest bonds of international solidarity between the toiling masses, whether Indians, Negroes or Whites in the colonies and the metropolis against the common enemy – **British Imperialism.** For us, the issue is clear. The Negro masses in Africa and the West Indies can never free themselves from their tyrants single handed. Victory can only be achieved when the workers of India, the workers of Ireland, of Britain and other parts of the Empire realize that theirs is a common struggle with ours. That the same rulers who oppress them, also oppress us. And that as long as the British imperialists are able to keep our struggles divided from each other, so long will they be able to maintain their domination over all of us. Therefore, let us join hands in **the** common struggle against **The Common Enemy**.

A New Song
(By Langston Hughes, *The [Harlem/Negro] Liberator*,
15 October 1932)

I speak in the name of the black millions
Awakening to action.
Let all others keep silent a moment
I have this word to bring,
This thing to say,
This song to sing:
Bitter was the day
When I bowed my back
Beneath the slaver's whip.

That day is past.

Bitter was the day
When I saw my children unschooled,
My young men without a voice in the world,
My women taken as the body-toys
Of a thieving people.

That day is past.

Bitter was the day, I say,
When the lyncher's rope
Hung about my neck,
And the fire scorched my feet,
And the oppressors had no pity,
And only in the sorrow songs
Relief was found.

That day is past.

I know full well now
Only my own hands,

Dark as the earth,
Can make my earth-dark body free.
O thieves, exploiters, killers,
No longer shall you say
With arrogant eyes and scornful lips:
'You are my servant,
Black man—
I, the free!'

That day is past—

For now,
In many mouths—
Dark mouths where red tongues burn
And white teeth gleam—
New words are formed,
Bitter
With the past
But sweet
With the dream.
Tense, silent,
Without a sound.
They fall unuttered—
Yet heard everywhere:

Take care!

Black world
Against the wall,
Open your eyes—

The long white snake of greed has struck to kill!

Be wary and
Be wise!
Before
The darker world
The future lies.

Equality Land and Freedom: A Program for Negro Liberation
(extracts from a pamphlet)
(League of Struggle for Negro Rights,[10] 1933)

For three hundred years the American Negroes have been enslaved – The same blow which struck the shackles of chattel slavery from them hammered on the chains of a new slavery. After three-quarters of a century of supposed freedom the Negro people must still fight for that liberty which should rightly have been theirs after the Civil War.

Today they again stand on the field of battle. They face the alternative: either a determined fight for freedom, or submission to further enslavement, degradation and poverty.

Squarely facing this issue, the League of Struggle for Negro Rights comes forward with a program for the liberation of the Negro people based upon the experiences and traditions of three centuries of struggle against slavery and oppression.

We proclaim before the whole world that the American Negroes are a nation – a nation striving to manhood but whose growth is violently retarded and which is viciously oppressed by American imperialism. The program here presented outlines the only course of action which guarantees the development of the American Negroes to full nationhood, which will elevate them to that rightful place of equality before all and subservience before none.

Land, freedom and equality – the watchword of the ex-slave during the period of Civil War and Reconstruction – still remains the watchword of the embattled Negroes today. The so-called emancipation of the slaves did not bring freedom, because without the means of livelihood, without land, there could be no freedom.

The ex-slaves fought heroically during the Civil War and the Reconstruction period for the land, for citizenship, for equal rights. The Northern Republicans took the Negroes as allies against the slave-owners, and supported their demands only because they needed the help of the Negro people in order to defeat the slavocracy decisively. When the domination of the South had been assured to the Northern capitalists, they cast their Negro ally aside and deserted him to the tender mercies of the K.K.K. and his former masters. The Proclamation of Emancipation and the 13th, 14th and 15th Amendments to the Constitution of the

---

[10] The LSNR was a Communist Party black civil rights organisation of which *The [Negro/Harlem] Liberator* was the official newspaper.

United States were but pieces of paper. The plantation system with all its horrors – share-cropping, peonage, chain gangs, convict labor – was the new freedom of the Negro after the Civil War.

That glorious Civil War decade when the embattled Negro fought with gun in hand against the bloodhounds of reaction for the rights of citizenship and for land, and enjoyed these rights for a time, shall always remain an heroic, revolutionary and living example firing the aspirations of the Negro people for freedom.

Today nine and a half million Negroes still live in the prison of the South, stifled by oppression, cut off from even a breath of freedom. The chains which bind the Negroes as serfs upon the plantations of the Southern Black Belt stretch out like arms of an octopus to enslave the Negro no matter in what part of the country he has sought refuge.

When the Negroes entered upon their mass exodus from the South, they hoped to find that liberty so long denied them. Northern capitalists, however, sought out for them the meanest and lowest place in industry. The Negro worker found that the exploiters of labor did not intend to permit him to rise to a plane of equality with his white fellow-worker. Instead, all the tricks at the disposal of the white ruling class were used to force the Negro into a lower position, to create antagonism and hatred between him and his fellow white workers.

The stifling lynch atmosphere of the South hangs like a cloud over the whole country. Crowded into segregated residential districts, restricted in their social, political and economic activities, insulted at every turn, burdened with a double weight of exploitation and oppression, the Negro masses in the North find that the liberty they have sought remains an illusion – The half-slave conditions in the Southern Black Belt continue to set the pattern for the economic and social oppression of the Negroes in the North as well.

The destruction of the plantation system in the South, the division of the land among the Negro farmers, among the croppers and tenants, would destroy the most important material basis, the basis for the oppression of the Negro people in the United States. It would, at the same time, spring the whole system which dictates inequality for the Negro in all walks of life, which condemns him to live a segregated, jim-crowed existence.

The League of Struggle for Negro Rights therefore demands the confiscation without compensation of the land of the big landlords and capitalists in the South and its distribution among the Negroes and white small farmers and share-croppers.

These plantations are concentrated in what is known as the Black Belt

– that continuous territory stretching from the eastern shore of Maryland through the southeastern corner of Virginia, cutting a strip through North Carolina and comprising practically the whole state of South Carolina, passing through central Georgia and southern Alabama, engulfing Mississippi and the delta regions of Louisiana and Arkansas, including the southwestern tip of Tennessee, and driving a wedge into Texas.

On this continuous strip of land the Negro people form the majority of the population. In fact, from the time of the earliest settlement of this land the Negroes were in the majority. They tilled its soil, created the first large cotton plantations. They till its soil today. This is the homeland of the American Negro people, comprising some 350 counties, cutting across existing state borders. This is the soil upon which the historic battles for freedom took place seventy years ago, where these battles have been re-joined by the heroic Negro share-croppers of Elaine, Arkansas, in 1919, and of Tallapoosa County, Alabama, in 1931 and 1933. This is the breeding ground of lynching and of the vilest degradation of the Negro people. It is from this soil that there arose the giant structure of the Scottsboro Case, broadcasting to the whole world the stirring cry for freedom.

The League of Struggle for Negro Rights declares that the territorial unity of this continuous stretch of land must be proclaimed and established. It declares that upon this territory must arise that political state over which the Negro majority will have governmental authority.

The Negro nation cannot be free as a people until they have complete right to set up their own government [. . .]

A Century of Emancipation
(Editorial, *Negro Worker*, August 1934)

August 1st 1934 marks the 100th anniversary of the emancipation of the chattel slaves of the British Empire. One hundred years ago, the British slave owners were paid the handsome sum of 20 million pounds for the loss of their property – 700,000 black slaves who were manumitted. The barbarous system of slavery, in which not only the landowners and merchants but also the clergy and missionaries had heavy investments had served the depopulation of the African Coast by at least 60 million people, most of whom perished in the raids and on the high seas because of the extremely cruel and unsanitary conditions to which they were subjected.

The tremendous profits derived from the enslavement of Negroes can be gleaned from a statement which appeared in *The Spectator* of May 12, 1933. "The total shipments from Africa alone must have exceeded 9,000,000 slaves, and their value at, say 40 pounds a head would amount to over 350,000,000 pounds (at present day values something like 1,500 million pounds)."

Today, after 100 years of "freedom" the native masses in the colonies are groaning under a system of semi-feudal exploitation and oppression which is very little different from the days of chattel slavery. They are no longer chattel slaves. They are poverty-stricken, wage slaves, forced to toil for a mere pittance for the capitalist, imperialist rulers who coin super profits out of their labour.

Under the semi-slave system which they live, they are denied the most elementary human rights. Poverty, hunger, disease, illiteracy are the heritage of the 'free' Negro under the rule and domination of British imperialism.

Only when the colonial toilers organize and unite their forces, will they be able to deal a death blow to the system of capitalist slavery and usher in the day of real emancipation.

TOILERS OF AFRICA AND THE WEST INDIES

The slave rebels in West Africa, in Barbados, Dominica, Jamaica etc, who fought so heroically against the plantation owners have left you a glorious tradition. You must follow in their footsteps and through your organized power strike a blow for freedom and complete independence.

Negroes Speak of War
(By Langston Hughes, *The [Harlem/Negro] Liberator*,
24 February 1934)

When the time comes for the next war, I'm asking you, remember the last war. I'm asking you, what you fought for, and what you would be fighting for again? I'm asking you how many of the lies were told, do you still believe? Does any Negro believe, for instance, that the world was actually saved for Democracy? Does any Negro believe any more, in closing ranks with the war makers? Maybe a few soldiers believed Dr. Moton when he came over to France talking about "Be nice and fight for the nice white folks. Be meek and shoot some Germans." But do any Negroes believe him now, with lynched black workers hanging on trees all around Tuskegee? I'm asking you?

And after the Chicago riots and Washington riots and the East St.

Louis riots, and more recently the Bonus March, is it some foreign army needs to be fought?

And listen, I'm asking you, with all the war ships and marines and officers and Secretary of the Navy going to Cuba, can't they send even one sergeant after sheriff Shamblin[11] in Alabama?

And with all the money they got to buy bombing planes, why in the hell can't they pay the teachers for my kids to go to school?

And even if I was studying fighting (which I ain't) why couldn't I do a little killing in the navy without wrassling with pots and pans, or join the marines (the lily white marines) and see the world or go in the air force where you never admitted Negroes yet? I'd like to be above the battle toe. Or do you think you gonna use me for stevedoring again?

And speaking of France our once beloved ally where Negroes can still eat in the restaurants in spite of Woodrow Wilson – don't let that fool you. Somebody ought to put the French black Africans wise to the fact that they OUGHT to treat them well in Paris when they are drilling them by the hundreds of thousands to stop bullets with their breasts and bombs with their heads and fill the frontline trenches for dear old France (that only a handful of them have ever seen) in the next war. Or have they got a French Dr. Moton to lie to black Africans too. I'm asking you?

And when the next war comes, I want to know whose war and why. For instance if it's the Japanese, you're speaking of – there's plenty of perils for me right here at home that needs attending to what about them labor unions that won't admit Negroes? And what about all of them factories where I can't work, if even there was work? And what about the schools I can't go to, and the states I can't vote in, and the juries I can't sit on? And what about all them sheriffs that can never find out who did the lynching? And what about something to eat without putting on a uniform and going out to killing folks I never saw to get it? And what about them "separate colored" codes in the NRA? And what about the voice in whose running this country and why – before I even think about crossing the water and fighting again?

Who said I want to go to war? If I do, it ain't the same war that the president wants to go to. No sir, I been hanging on a rope in Alabama too long.

---

[11] Sheriff Shamblin was widely seen as conspiring in the lynching of three African American men, Dan Pippen, A. T. Harden and Elmore Clark in Alabama in August 1933.

Going South in Russia
(By Langston Hughes, *The Crisis*, June 1934)

To an American Negro living in the northern part of the United States the word *South* has an unpleasant sound, an overtone of horror and of fear. For it is in the South, that our ancestors were slaves for three hundred years, bought and sold like cattle. It is in the South today that we suffer the worst forms of racial persecution and economic exploitation – segregation, peonage, and lynching. It is in the Southern states that the color line is hard and fast, Jim Crow rules and I am treated like a dog. Yet it is in the South that two-thirds of my people live: a great Black Belt stretching from Virginia to Texas, across the cotton plantations of Georgia and Alabama and Mississippi down into the orange groves of Florida and the sugar cane lands of Louisiana. It is in the South that black hands create the wealth that supports the great cities – Atlanta, Memphis, New Orleans, where the rich whites live in fine houses on magnolia shaded streets and the Negroes live in slums restricted by law. It is in the South that what the Americans call the "race problem" rears its ugly head the highest and, like a snake with its eyes on a bird, holds the whole land in its power. It is in the South that hate and terror walk the streets and roads by day, sometimes quiet, sometimes violent, and sleep in the beds with the citizens at night.

Two springs ago I came almost directly out of this American South to the Soviet Union. You can imagine the contrast. No need for me to write about it. And after a summer in Moscow, I found myself packing up to go South again – but this time, South under the red flag. I was starting out from Moscow, capital of the new world, bound for Central Asia to discover how the yellow and brown peoples live and work there. I wanted to compare their existence with that of the colored and oppressed peoples I had known under capitalism in Cuba, Haiti, Mexico, and my own United States. I wanted to study the life of these dark people in the Soviet Union and write a book about them for the dark races of the capitalist world.

On the train I had a lot of time to think. I thought how in the thirty years of my life I had seldom gotten on a train in America without being conscious of my color. In the South, there are Jim Crow cars and Negroes must ride separate from the whites, usually in a filthy antiquated coach next to the engine, getting all the smoke and bumps and dirt. In the South, we cannot buy sleeping car tickets. Such comforts are only for white folks. And in the North where segregated travel is not the law, colored people have, nevertheless, many difficulties. In auto buses they must take the seats in the rear, over the wheels. On boats they must occupy the worst cabins. The ticket agents always say that all other accommodations are sold. On trains, if one sits down by a white person, the white person will sometimes get up, flinging back a insult at the Negro who has dared to take a seat beside him. Thus it is that in America, if you are yellow, brown or black, you can never travel anywhere without being reminded of your color, and oft-times suffering great inconveniences.

I sat in the comfortable sleeping car on my first day out of Moscow and remembered many things about trips I had taken in America. I remembered how, once as a youngster going alone to see my father who was working in Mexico, I went into the dining car of the train to eat. I sat down at a table with a white man. The man looked at me and said, "You're a nigger, ain't you?" and left the table. It was beneath his dignity to eat with a Negro child. At St. Louis I went onto the station platform to buy a glass of milk. The clerk behind the counter said, "We don't serve niggers" and refused to sell me anything. As I grew older I learned to expect this often when travelling. So when I went South to lecture on my poetry at Negro universities, I carried my own food because I knew I could not go into the dining cars. Once from Washington to New Orleans, I lived all the way in the train on cold food. I remembered this miserable trip as I sat eating a hot dinner at the diner on the Moscow-Tashkent express.

Travelling South from New York, at Washington, the capital of our country, the official Jim Crow begins. There the conductor comes through the train and if you are a Negro, touches you on the shoulder and says, "The last coach forward is the car for colored people." Then you must move your baggage and yourself up near the engine because when the train crosses the Potomac River into Virginia, and the dome of the Capitol disappears, it is illegal any longer for white people and colored people to ride together. (Or to eat together, or to sleep together, or in some places even to work together.) Now I am riding South from Moscow and I am not Jim-Crowed, and none of the darker people on the train with me are Jim-Crowed, so I make a happy mental note in the back of my mind to write home to the Negro papers: "There is no Jim Crow on the trains of the Soviet Union."

In the car ahead of mine there is a man almost as brown as I am. A young man dressed quite ordinarily in a pair of tan trousers and a nondescript grey coat. Some Asiatic factory worker who has been to Moscow on a vacation, I think. We talk a little. He asks me what I do for a living, and I ask him what he does. I am a writer. He is the mayor of

Bokhara, the Chairman of the City Soviet! I make a note in the back of my mind: "In the Soviet Union dark men are also the mayors of cities," for here is a man who is head of a very famous city, old Bokhara, romantic Bokhara known in stories and legends the world over.

In the course of our conversation, I learned that there were many cities in Central Asia where dark men and women are in control of the government. And I thought about Mississippi where more than half of the population is Negro, but one never hears of a colored person in the government. In fact, in that state Negroes cannot even vote. And you will never meet them riding in the sleeping car.

Here, there were twelve of us going South from Moscow, for I was travelling with a Negro group from Mezhrabpom Film[12] on a tour of the United States.

Kurbanov, for that was the name of the young Uzbek from the Bokhara Soviet, came often to talk to us. He was a mine of information about the liberation of Central Asia and the vast changes that have come about there after the Revolution. Truly a land of Before and After. Before the Revolution, emirs and khans, mullahs and boys. After the Revolution, the workers in power. Before, one-half of one per cent of the people literate. Now fifty per cent read and write. Before, education solely for the rich, mostly in religious schools; and no schools in the villages. Now, free schools everywhere. Before, the land was robbed of its raw materials for the factories of the Russian capitalists. Now, there are big plants, electric stations, and textile mills in Asia. Before, Kurbanov said, the natives were treated like dogs. Now, that is finished, and Russian and native, Jew and gentile, white and brown, live and work together. Before, no intermarriages of white and brown, now there are many. Before Kurbanov himself was a herd-boy in the mountains. Now, he is the Chairman of a city soviet, the mayor of a large and ancient city. Truly, Soviet Asia is a land of Before and After, and the Revolution is creating a new life that is changing the history of the East.

We gathered these things not only from our Uzbek comrade, but from many other passengers we met on the long train during the five days and nights southeast to Central Asia. There was a woman librarian from Leningrad, who had been home on a vacation going back to the work of which she spoke with pride – the growth of the library at Tashkent, the large number of books in the native languages with the new Latin alphabet that were now being published, and the corresponding growth of native readers. There was a young Red Army man who

---

[12] Revolutionary German-Russian film studio.

told us of the camaraderie and understanding of growing up between lads of widely different environmental backgrounds in the Red Army school at Tashkent. There was a Russian merchant privileged to help in the building of new industries in an ancient and once backward, but now awakening Asia. And there were two young Komsomol poets going from Moscow to work on publications for the encouragement of national literature in the young writers of Soviet Asia.

One night, we held a meeting with the members of the train crew not then on duty. Our Negro group and the workers of the express exchanged information and ideas. They told us about their work and their part in the building of socialism. We told them about the conditions of Negro labor in America, about the crisis abroad, about Al Capone and the Chicago bandits and the bootleggers and bankers of Broadway. We found that they knew, as their comments and questions indicated, a great deal more about America than the average American knows about the Soviet Union. And we learnt that their working conditions are superior to those of American railway workers – particularly in regard to the train porters. Here, in each coach, there is a compartment with berths where the night crew might rest. The Negro porters on American trains have no such convenience. Here, on the sleeping cars, there are two attendants. In the U.S.A. a single man takes care of a car, working throughout a long trip, and perhaps managing to catch a little sleep on the bench in the men's toilet. Our porters depend on tips for a living, their wages being extremely low. These things we told the crew of the Moscow-Tashkent express and they, in turn, sent back through us their greetings to the Negro railway workers of America.

So, with our many new and interesting comrades of the train, the days on the road passed quickly. Fist, the rich farm lands slid by outside our windows; stations where peasant women form the kolkhozes sold chickens and cheese and eggs; then the Volga at sunset, famous old river of song and story; a day or so later, Orenburg where Asia begins and camels are in the streets; then the vast reaches of the Kirghiz steppes and the bright tip of the Aral Sea like silver in the sun.

On the day when we passed through the Kazakstan desert, the Fortieth Anniversary of Gorky's literary life was being celebrated throughout the Union. The Komsomol poets and the crew of our train organized a meeting, too. At a little station where the train stopped in the late afternoon, we all went on to the platform and short speeches were made in honor of Gorky and his tremendous work. (Even in the heart of the desert, this writer whose words throb with the lives of the common people, was not forgotten.) Nomad Kazaks, the men in great coats of skins, the women in white headdresses, gathered around, mingling with the passengers. One of the young poets spoke; then a representative of the train crew; and someone from the station. My speech in English was translated into Russian, and again into Kazak tongue. Then the meeting closed. We sent a telegram to Comrade Gorky from the passengers of the train, and another from our Negro group. And as the whistle blew, we climbed back into our coaches, and the engine steamed on through the desert pulling the long train deeper into Asia. It was sunset, and there was a great vastness of sky over sand before the first stars came.

Late the following afternoon, we saw a fertile oasis of water and greenery, cotton growing and trees in fruit, then crowds of yellow faces and bright robes at the now frequent stations. At evening we came to the big city of Tashkent, the great center of the Soviet East. There we were met by a workers' delegation including brown Asiatics, fair-skinned Russians, and an American Negro engineer, Bernard Powers, from Howard University, now helping to build roads across Asia.

The Role of Proletarian Fraternalism in the Liberation Struggle of the Negro People (abridged)
(By Louise Thompson,[13] *The [Harlem/Negro] Liberator*, 28 July 1934)

To win the Negro masses for a genuinely proletarian fraternal practice is the important task facing the International Workers Order.[14] Bourgeois fraternalism which has a strong hold on the Negro people, jim-crows them and wins them for petty bourgeois Negro nationalism, the while it further inoculates white workers with the virus of "white supremacy". The International Workers Order is the only fraternal order which sweeps aside all racial, political and religious barriers erected by the white master class to divide the working class and unites Negro and white, native and foreign born workers on the basis of their proletarian fraternal interests. The International Workers Order recognizes that as a working class conscious fraternal order it must destroy racial antagonism

---

[13] Louise Thompson (1901–1999), African American Communist and activist who was a central figure in the Harlem Renaissance and the radical campaigns of the Depression. In addition to travelling to the Soviet Union (with Langston Hughes), she also visited Spain during the Civil War. She wrote for a variety of publications including *The Crisis*.

[14] International Workers Order (IWO) (1930–1954) was a Communist Party-affiliated insurance, mutual benefit and fraternal organisation. In addition to low-cost life and health assurance the IWO also sponsored educational and cultural activities.

with the white members of our Order taking the lead in fighting racial discrimination and in demanding equal rights for the Negro people. Bourgeois fraternalism, both among white and Negro workers is against the liberation movement of the Negro people. Ready proof of this is found in the Scottsboro case. The International Workers Order placed its entire membership solidly behind the International Labor Defense in the fight to free the Scottsboro Boys; not one fraternal order under white bourgeois leadership has contributed to the defense. The leadership of Negro fraternal orders has resorted to every kind of maneuver to hold their membership from any participation in the defense and to keep those loyal to the National Association for the Advancement of Colored People, the organization leading the attack upon the militant program of the International Labor Defense. Thus we can say that bourgeois fraternalism is an excellent weapon in the hands of the white master class with which to combat the liberation struggle of the Negro people, an obstacle which must be swept aside by winning both the Negro and white workers for working class conscious fraternalism

The International Workers Order can be of real service in meeting the pressing need of the Negro masses for low cost insurance protection. Hand in hand with this economic exploitation has gone the most crass exploitation of the Negro by the big insurance companies. Because of this great economic security, the Negro worker has been ready prey to any and all Insurance schemes and buys proportionately more insurance than other workers. Any Negro worker's family could paper a room with insurance policies bought at some time of momentary prosperity, later allowed to lapse or kept up through the most stringent sacrifices. For all workers insurance costs are higher than for the rich or middle class and it is upon the industrial insurance sold to workers on the weekly payment plan that insurance companies have made fat profits. But the Negro worker pays even higher rates, because say the insurance companies, his sick and death rates are greater, implying physical inferiority of the Negro people rather than exposing the actual environmental conditions which make for any difference. Thus the Negro worker is forced to bear the whole burden of his economic super exploitation, congested and unsanitary jim crow housing, lack of adequate hospitals and medical care, malnutrition. Where he looks to Negro fraternal orders for protection the Negro worker will find many of these orders in bankruptcy because of unsound insurance practices and speculation and graft with benefit funds. The International Workers Order has stripped insurance costs of all the lavish overhead expenses of the commercial insurance companies and bourgeois fraternal orders for salaries, dividends etc – Negro and white, native and foreign born.

The International Workers Order also has the task of winning the millions of Negro and white workers in bourgeois fraternal orders for the fight for social insurance, showing them that without social insurance there is no real protection for workers in capitalist society, and that the only way for workers under capitalism to get social insurance is by their own mass pressure. Unemployment and old age create the greatest economic insecurity of the working class and a social problem that can be handled only by society and its agency, the Negro worker who as the "first to be fired", the first to be cast in the dump heap needs social insurance most. The International Workers Order is the only fraternal order which can lead the workers in the bourgeois fraternal order into united action for social insurance. In this way will the Negro and white workers come to recognize the International Workers Order as their order because it fights for their interests as workers. In this way will the International Workers Order break through the barriers separating these workers and unite them in the struggle for these common interests. [...]

From the Colonies
(The [Harlem/Negro] Liberator, 20 September 1934)

This column opens a regular weekly feature of the *Negro Liberator*. It will contain news and comments on the conditions of Negro workers throughout the world and especially in the colonial countries of Africa, the West Indies and South America. It will review the struggles of the Negro people and other colonial workers throughout the world to throw off the enslaving chains of American, British, French, Italian and Japanese imperialism.

We urge those foreign publications which are not yet on our exchange list to communicate with us immediately and regularly hereafter.

* * *

It took Sir P. Cunliffe-Lister, colonial secretary of British imperialism to pay *The Negro Worker* a very complimentary tribute. Answering an African Coast delegation which came to England to protest against the Sedition Bill adopted in that colony to muzzle the growing struggles of the natives against British imperialism, Sir P., foaming with rage, waved a copy of *The Negro Worker* in the face of the delegation as proof of the need for the fascist sedition law.

Sir P. read extracts from the little magazine, all the while becoming more and more inflamed. Finally he threw the magazine violently to the floor and exclaimed:

"Thousands of copies of foul and obnoxious tract is pouring into the Gold Coast!"

The Sedition Bill, which gives the Governor in Council power to prohibit the importation into the Gold Coast of books, newspapers and documents, is a direct attempt to suppress the rising tide of Gold Coast natives against the destitution, misery and disease that the British imperialists have imposed upon them.

The imperialist landlords in West Africa have been "fighting" the agrarian crisis on the Gold Coast by throwing thousands of workers out of jobs, at the same time raising the taxes on the already overtaxed natives.

The attempt to stifle *The Negro Worker* and the native press on the Gold Coast is a result of the mass meetings and protest demonstrations in behalf of the Scottsboro boys and against British oppression. These demonstrations were organized mainly through the efforts of the revolutionary Negro press.

On March 17th the fascist Sedition Bill was passed in the Legislative Council. Only the Governor and white members of the Council voted it against the unanimous opposition of all the African members. In spite of the mass protest against the bill which have even forced the support of the reformist lackeys of Britain, the bill was passed.

As much as they fear this dissatisfaction against the bill, the imperialists fear the revolutionary propaganda of *The Negro Worker* and other literature more. Of course, they cannot see that the bill only adds more fuel to the fire kindled by the revolutionary movement and in spite of the bill or thousands of such bills *The Negro Worker* will break through the barriers of government censorship.

The Same
(By Langston Hughes, *Negro Worker*, October 1935)

It is the same everywhere for me:
On the docks at Sierra Leone,
In the cotton fields of Alabama,
In the diamond mines of Kimberley,
On the coffee hills of Haiti,
The banana lands of Central America,

The streets of Harlem,
And the cities of Morocco and Tripoli.

Black:
Exploited, beaten and robbed,
Shot and killed.
Blood running into

Dollars
Pounds
Francs
Pesetas
Lire

For the wealth of the exploiters—
Blood that never comes back to me again.
Better that my blood
Runs into the deep channels of Revolution,
Runs into the strong hands of Revolution,
Stains all flags red,
Drives me away from

Sierra Leone
Kimberley
Alabama
Haiti
Central America
Harlem
Morocco
Tripoli

And all the black lands everywhere.
The force that kills,
The power that robs,
And the greed that does not care.

Better that my blood makes one with the blood
Of all the struggling workers in the world—
Till every land is free of

Dollar robbers
Pound robbers
Franc robbers
Peseta robbers
Lire robbers
Life robbers—

Until the Red Armies of the International Proletariat
Their faces, black, white, olive, yellow, brown,

Unite to raise the blood-red flag that
Never will come down!

The Negro and the Century of Alexander Pushkin
(By William L. Patterson, *Negro Worker*, April 1937)

The celebration of the centenary of the death of Alexander Sergeyevitch Pushkin passed in a blaze of glorious tributes to his greatness. The Soviet Union, land of Socialism, leader of all progressive mankind and of real democracy, leader of the forces fighting for peace in a world ravaged by petty wars which the insatiable war-mongers, indulged by capitalist democracy, are frantically seeking to fan into another bloody world war – this socialist fatherland without pausing in the midst of its monumental national-international work of socialist construction paid tribute on a scale never before conceived of to the memory of one of the world's greatest men of letters – a poet of revolution, of progress and of freedom.

The world was literally forced to follow suit. There was nothing else to do. Pushkin's greatness cannot be denied. Living, he sang of liberty over the heads of tsars to their serfs, without fear of the consequences. Tsarist Russia, that prison house of nations, resounded with his appeals for freedom. Dead a hundred years – the freed sons and daughters of those serfs now in their socialist fatherland, together with millions of colonial peoples and the exploited masses of the countries, see that his songs of freedom have a world-embracing note. Love of freedom is universal. He who sincerely demands it for himself must demand it for all men.

The hundredth anniversary of the death of Alexander Sergeyevitch Pushkin, great-grandson of Ibrahim Petrovich Hannibal, Negro godson of Peter the Great, has passed. The Union of Soviet Socialist Republics has immortalized Pushkin. Only a socialist state could truly evaluate his greatness. Pushkin's immortalization reflects in all its glory the magnificent cultural force that is the Soviet Union. Pushkin immortalized lifts the prestige of the Soviet culture to the stars, ennobles it as through it his fame, which tsarism sought to suppress, gains international recognition.

Only a socialist country founded on the principle that culture is the heritage of all men could make so glorious a celebration in honour of this or any man of letters. The great works of Heinrich Heine are burned in the public square in Berlin, revealing the barbarous essence of Nazi culture. Though Shakespeare's works are preserved he is but a name to millions of Britons and not even that to the millions of its colonial slaves, while Coleridge Taylor,[15] its greatest musician, a Negro, is comparatively unknown. The names of great Frenchmen and Americans lie buried and almost unknown because their ideas transcended the range of capitalist culture. The failure to bring them even to the masses at home expresses its vast and insurmountable cultural limitations.

But Pushkin who said:

"The rumour of my fame will sweep through vast Russia" did not embrace sufficient territory, lofty as was his vision. The world – save only that part ruled by benighted fascism; the most reactionary section of finance capital – joins those he prophesised would some day know him, the "haughty Slav and Finn and savage (now cultured WLP) Tungus and Kalmuck riders of the plain" (no longer nomads WLP), to do him honour. Thus is reflected the splendour of the Soviet era. Here is the irrefutable proof of the universality of its culture. No prejudices of race or nationality, of colour or language exist to stay the spread of culture in the land of socialism.

The theories of Aryan superiority, of the omnipotence of the Anglo-Saxon, of the supremacy of white Americans are one with Pushkin's fairy tales. No! Not with those fairy tales for they, marked with genius, will live forever. These theories, birth-marked pseudo-science out of barren intellect, are one with the barbarous instruments of physical torture which fascism and its bastard brother reaction would resurrect but which progressive humanity has labelled for the limbo of the unnecessary human ills. The day of their extinction must be hastened. Pushkin, the African-hued poet of freedom and democracy, made mockery of them. The Soviet Union systematically persistently and relentlessly wars against them at home and abroad. Its perpetuation of Pushkin's memory deals a smashing blow at the fascist myths of racial-national superiority. This is the great significance of Pushkin's centenary to the Negro people.

Western Europe, England and America recognize the genius of Pushkin. They too are celebrating the centenary. This is as it should be. But do they pay more than lip service to this genius, fearful that otherwise the splendour of Soviet culture will expose the nakedness of their own? For them to do more officially than formally to acknowledge him is impossible. Their attitude, torn by conflicting interests, emerging from their antagonistical social relationships with its false superior

---

[15] Samuel Coleridge-Taylor (1875–1912), an English composer whose father came from Sierra Leone.

race ideology raises an interesting question? How do they account for Pushkin's literary superiority over his contemporaries?

Never in that Western world have we seen a black man acclaimed as truly great, always there are qualifications. Where Negroes of mixed blood have achieved a position of eminence, it has always been attributed to the fact that the blood of white men flowed in their veins. Here, Messrs, ethnologists, anthropologists, and biologists of capitalist society, you conscious and unconscious weaves of hoary myths, here, gentlemen is a great man, you acclaim his genius in that he had mixed blood, a preponderance of white blood and a few drops of African. He moved in a white world. If greatness comes from white blood, then his "pure" white contemporaries should logically be even greater than he. Yet an analysis of the literary works of his period shows that Pushkin was infinitely greater than his "pure" white contemporaries. Messrs, wise men, give us the answer to the riddle. From whence came his greatness?

The absurdity of the racial-national superiority theories is nowhere more conspicuously exposed to ridicule than through this man. Genius depends not on race or colour, it appears in all places, subject to laws as yet unknown. But who can say what flowers of genius have already been cramped by lack of opportunity, smothered the conditions bred of ignorance, arrogance and oppression? Those who accept his genius take onto themselves certain obligations. The acceptance of the genius of the "poet of freedom" is compatible only with the demand for equality of opportunity for all men. This equality of opportunity must be fought for, the myth of racial-national superiority must be destroyed. The formal attitude toward this question of many of the Westerners who accept him must be overcome.

There is however yet another side to the picture. If Western Europe, England and America impelled by the Soviet example have honoured the genius of Pushkin, unlike the Soviet Union they have carefully concealed the closet where lie the bones of the beautiful Creole who was his mother and those of the full-blooded African Hannibal, who was his great grandfather. They are true to their colours. But it is because of this background that the Negro people, who know him for the greater part only as a name and to whom his genius is but hearsay, nevertheless revere him as their beloved son. Certainly, this attitude is not entirely correct.

Why do black men turn to the lineage of this titan of Russian letters to find consolation? Because the dehumanising influence of capitalist racial-national ideology would rob them even of their identity with mankind. Because they seek to prove their worthiness, to be accepted in society by showing their racial identity with great men of the past. Whereas of itself this is of course not to be condemned, it is nevertheless infinitely better for them to express this identity by claiming kinship and moving forward with those who have declared relentless war upon false racial-national ideologies and their formulations, with those who have declared relentless war upon degraded elements in of capitalist culture. This is the task of the Negro people today.

Pushkin was not a Negro, despite the presence of some Negro blood and marked Negroid features. Pushkin was Russian, made so by his environment, but such men as he belong to the world. His kinship to black men is not to be found in the African blood that flowed within his veins, despite the opprobrium placed upon all possessing Negro blood by Western Europe and America and the lumping of them all together, nor his kinship with all white races to his preponderance of white blood. The spiritual life of Pushkin was moulded by the societal relations of his time, by the tremendous disparity between the position of the feudal landlord rulers of tsarist Russia and its starving serf masses. It was a product of, but transcended, his environment, for Pushkin's was the universal language.

That Negroes claim kinship with Pushkin is as it should be. He is an inseparable part of them as they are an inseparable part of humanity. No less have they kinship with the genius of other lands and other Historical periods. No less have their own geniuses spoken for all humanity. These men whatever their race or colour belong to the world. They have bequeathed their greatness to society. Between the Soviet world and the capitalist world lies a vast difference in the treatment of this question. The acknowledgement by Soviet society that true culture is the heritage of all men and its corresponding actions gives to the masses of the world in general and of the Soviet land in particular their first taste of these hitherto forbidden fruits. The capitalist world seeks to confine culture to the narrow ranks of the intelligentsia which capitalism creates as the ideologists of its greatness and splendour. It uses its culture as a means of proving the "backwardness" of the masses and thus of "justifying" capitalist exploitation and oppression. The incomparable loftiness of Soviet culture lies in its universality. Herein is its significance to black men. What a contrast in the culture of the two world!

Let black men then claim kinship with Pushkin through his lofty humanism. Let them claim kinship with Pushkin who found great interest in and expressed the deepest sympathy for the French Revolution, the Pushkin who followed the national liberation movement of Greece, Spain, Serbia and Romania, the national heroes of which he reflected in his works; the Pushkin who, if living, would today seek to go to the aid of Republican Spain, would champion the cause of Soviet democracy. This Pushkin must of course not to be separated from the artist or his art. But through his genius the Negro people can express their kinship with all democratic elements of the present as well as of the past.

Chapter 6

Anti-Colonialism and Anti-Fascism

The rise of fascism in Europe, especially the invasion of Ethiopia by Italy in 1935, influenced the cadence of anti-colonial politics in African American publications in the 1930s. The mid-1930s saw a race-conscious, black middle class embrace an internationalist and left-wing intellectual milieu, especially around the anti-fascist causes of Ethiopia and Spain. Ethiopia galvanised black communities from across the political spectrum, thousands wished to volunteer to go to fight for Ethiopia, though a range of factors, including Ethiopian ruler Haile Selassie's acquiescence to pressure from the US government, meant that only two African Americans eventually travelled to Ethiopia. This did not stop activists and campaigners from organising relentlessly to oppose the fascist invasion. Black nationalist, Communist and moderate organisations and individuals sought to infuse the various campaigns with their political world view. As George Padmore's 'Ethiopia and World Politics' article attests, the USSR was less than impressive in its defence of Ethiopia and this impacted on the communist led 'Hands off Ethiopia' campaign in the USA. The slogan 'Ethiopia's fate is at stake on the battlefields of Spain' was the Communist Party slogan in 1937 and many activists saw a related battle against fascism in the fight against Franco. The connections between fascism in Europe and Jim Crow at home are consistently trumpeted in these writings. The radical press of the period is littered with references to 'home grown fascism' in relation to racism in the USA. Louise Thompson's 'Southern Terror' should be understood in relation to this wider narrative.

<p align="center">Southern Terror
(By Louise Thompson, <i>The Crisis</i>, November 1934)</p>

"Birmingham is a good place for good niggers – but a damn bad place for bad niggers."

Thus spoke the officialdom of Birmingham, Ala., to me last May, and in the course of my experience there I learned what they meant. I was arrested as I went to enter the apartment of a woman whom I had known in the North. It so happened that the red squad was raiding her apartment at the time, and as I knocked at the door it was opened by a policeman who brusquely ordered me in. I did so and was immediately placed under arrest. As they fired questions at me, one officer interrupted to ask:

"Gal, where you from? I know you ain't from around here 'cause you don't talk like it."

"My home is California," I answered.

"California hell! You're one of those _____ yankee _____, that's what you are!"

And with a few more remarks quite in keeping with the above they loaded me into the "black waggon," along with the other persons in the apartment at the time, and off to the city jail we went. I was promptly locked up, with no chance given me to communicate with friends or an attorney. My attempts to question the procedure met with laughter or taunts from my jailers.

"Held for investigation," I learned later from my cellmates.

I spent the night with fourteen other Negro women held on charges ranging from drunkenness and pickpocketing to murder. One of the women was demented, and the two of us kept vigil that night, she, walking the floor and raving: I, wondering what was to happen to me on the morrow and what my friends would think when I did not return home that night.

The long night finally ended. Breakfast of huge soda biscuits, beans and a colored water which passed for coffee. Then I was called out, again taken for a ride in the patrol to the identification department for fingerprinting and "mugging" for the rogues' gallery. Though I was being accorded the treatment of a criminal I had yet to know what I was being held for, and when I would be permitted to communicate with the outside world.

During the cross examination which followed, my questioners were inclined at first to make a joke of the affair, taunting me about "my comrades," slyly alluding to some intimate relationship with the men arrested with me, and the like. But upon my refusal to answer any more questions until I had an opportunity to consult an attorney, their taunts turned to open threats which ran something like this:

"What about turning this gal over to the Ku Klux Klan? I reckon they know how to handle her kind,"

"Yeah, or a little tar and feathering might help."

"How about talking to her through the rubber tube. She might be glad to talk then." (I later learned that "talking through the rubber tube" meant beating with a rubber hose in the third degree.)

Again, one officer turned to me, pointing his finger and said: "See here, gal, you're arrested now, see. And you say 'yes sir' and 'no sir'." I was told later by some of the women prisoners that I was lucky not to have been slapped down when I refused to obey.

Eleven-notch Gun

Later in the day my friends finally succeeded in getting an attorney in to see me, after reading in the papers of the raid. He immediately prepared a writ of Habeas corpus to force the placing of a charge against me or my release. And again I rode from the city jail to Jefferson county courthouse where the Scottsboro boys are imprisoned. There I was turned over to the prize red baiter and "nigger" hater of the plainclothes squad, Moser, who boasts of eleven notches in his gun for helpless Negroes he has shot down. These were his words of welcome:

"So you're one of those _____ reds what thinks you are going to get social equality for niggers down here in the South. Well, we think Communists are lower than niggers, down here – fact is, we don't even allow them to 'sociate with white folks, let alone have white folks 'sociating with niggers. We know how to treat our niggers down here and we ain't going to stand for no interference from you _____ yankee reds. We ought to handle you reds like Mussolini does 'em in Italy – take you out and shoot you against a wall. And I sure would like to have the pleasure of doing it."

With which this "protector of law and order" escorted me to the courtroom where I was to meet my attorney for a hearing on the habeas corpus proceedings. When my attorney read the writ, Moser triumphantly stepped up to the judge with a warrant for my arrest as a "vagarant." Vagrancy is that convenient catch-all which serves all purposes.

My bail was set for $300 cash, my trial for ten days hence. On the tenth day I entered the courtroom and took my seat on the side for Negroes to await the calling of my case. Surrounding the judge were a group of officers and others, whom I learned later to be members of the White Legion. From time to time they would suggest to the judge or prosecutor questions to be asked the Negro prisoners appearing before the bar of "justice." The word "nigger" rang out from lips of judge, solicitor, officers, White Legionnaires every second. Any attempt on the part of a Negro prisoner to dispute testimony against him was met by,

"Nigger, do you dare to dispute the word of a white man," or simply by loud bursts of laughter. Here was "southern justice" undisturbed by any militant interference!

My case was finally called and I stood before Judge Abernathy. The White Legion boys drew a little nearer, the police officers stepped up to testify. All eyes were focused upon me. The judge then listened to the testimony of the arresting officer, embellished with a few points to win the laughing approval of the crowd about the bench. Meanwhile the judge fingered the documents which disproved any charge of vagrancy against me, my status as a representative of the International Workers Order, the articles of incorporation which permit my organization to operate under state law, cancelled checks for my weekly wages. He looked at me intently and then asked of the crowd about him:

"Wonder where this gal is from? Looks like she came from Mississippi – that's the way they mix up down there. Course it's got nothing to do with the case, but I'm going to ask her where she was born as I'm mighty interested in how these mixtures turn out." And to me, "Where were you born, gal?"

With no further questioning, the case was dismissed with the Judge declaring,

"You can't arrest the gal for being an octoroon."

"No, she can't help that," was Moser's parting shot.

I was not yet entirely free for another warrant was produced to arrest me on the charge of concealing my identity. A few days later, however, this second case was thrown out of court without my having to appear again.

The Bourbon authorities learned that the workers throughout the country were ready to apply their weapon of mass pressure against my arrest – and their experience with the Scottsboro case, with the Herndon case, made them cautious. They wanted stronger grounds to prepare another frame-up against a Negro engaged in working class activity.

The White Legion

Thus did I learn from first hand experience of the kind of "justice" meted out to Negroes in the South, of the unswerving determination of the servants of the State and of vested interests to keep the Negro people in utter subjection. And more, of the treatment of those who would help the Negro people in their fight for emancipation from this oppression. All the others arrested with me were white, yet they fared no better than I did, for as Communist suspects they are bitterly hated and granted no more constitutional rights than are given Negroes in the South. Being a Communist in the South is synonymous with being a fighter for the rights of the Negro people, of being a "nigger lover," of trying to bring white and Negro workers and poor farmers together – of fighting against lynching, of challenging the southern ruling class' traditional manner of treating Negroes. John Howard Lawson, prominent Hollywood playwright, who came to Birmingham to write up the terror was arrested as he left Jefferson county courthouse fingerprinted and "mugged" and ordered from town. When he returned later with a delegation of liberals he was arrested again and charged with libel for telling the truth about the terror of Birmingham's police and White Legion.

A word or two about the White Legion, this openly fascist organization in Birmingham whose stated purpose is to fight communism and any move to lift oppression from the backs of the Negro people. Its membership fee is $5.00, which of course precludes any worker members. As a matter of fact it recruits its members from the officials of the city, merchants and other middle class elements. It maintains an office on one of the main streets of Birmingham and displays in the front window Communist leaflets and any material from the Negro or revolutionary press which advocates equal rights for Negroes. One week they displayed a picture of Langston Hughes with his poem *An Open Letter to the South*, in which Hughes appeals to Negro and white labor to unite in struggle for a better world. The comment scrawled along the margin was: "If this bird thinks we are going to have social equality in the South, he's crazy!"

During the height of the terror against the Negro and militant white workers, the White Legion issued highly inflammatory leaflets seeking to provoke white against Negro workers. One such leaflet included this statement: "How would you like to awaken one morning to find your wife or daughter attached by a Negro or a Communist!" It wound up with an appeal to pay the membership fee so that the White Legion could handle such situations in the traditional manner. During the planning of action against the class-conscious workers of Birmingham, one wing of the legion was for riding through the Negro neighbourhood and shooting indiscriminately into the homes of innocent Negroes, but cooler heads in the gang realized that such an extreme form of terror was a bit premature.

"Social Equality"

The southern press also played its part well during the reign of terror which did not end with our arrests, but went on in a series of raids upon the homes of workers over the entire city. The mining strike was at its height in Birmingham and for the first time Negro and white workers were militantly picketing together. The daily press came out with scare heads of "red violence" and "red plots" and references to "social equality." One paper carried a story of a raid upon a Negro home which produced a "highly inflammatory" document – it was the Bill of Civil Rights calling for full political, economic and social equality for the Negro people. Yet those papers which went beyond the borders of the state carried not a line of the raids, the arrests, or the general terror.

That the press, the White Legion and the government officials always link the "reds" and Communism with the Negro question is not a mere coincidence. First of all, the International Labor Defense through the Scottsboro case has aroused the Negro people and rallied to their defense workers over the whole world. And it is the Communist Party which has analyzed the Negro question as that of an oppressed nation of people, defined the alignment of class forces for and against the Negro people's struggle for liberation, and begun the organization of white and Negro working masses together. Revolutionary leaders in the South are boldly defying all that the southern ruling class has striven to perpetuate, and terror and jail bars do not stop them. Down in the heart of Dixie, the Black Belt, some 8,000 sharecroppers have organized a militant Sharecroppers union to fight the starvation program of the A.A.A which deputy sheriffs' bullets have been unable to stop.

It is another matter, however, when organizations within the Negro group come forward as vehemently against any show of militancy on the part of the Negro masses and with as great enmity against a revolutionary program and revolutionary organizations as is expressed in the White Legion of Birmingham. Such organizations disregard the economic roots of the Negro's oppression, and through collaboration with the ruling class seek to restrain the masses of Negroes from militant struggle. Such organizations accept the present system of capitalism and are willing to be satisfied with what hollow reforms may come without and fundamental change.

Revolution Called Necessity

But it is impossible to take one step in the direction of winning for the Negro people their elementary rights that is not revolutionary. Capitalism developed in America upon the super-exploitation of the Negro, to destroy the enmity and to unite Negro and white labor is a blow at American capitalism. So it is that the southern ruling class is not going to budge from its position of exploiting and oppressing the Negro people. And behind the southern Bourbons stand the amassed strength of American finance capital U.S. Steel, Wall Street investments in the plantations of the South, and the like. Any organizations among the Negro people which do not point out these class alignments must therefore become the voice of reaction in the midst of a people struggling for freedom. So it is that the leadership among the Negro people must pass into new hands – into the hands of working class leaders, the Angelo Herndons,[1] who will not be stopped by jail, by a desire to cling on to jobs, by death itself for leading the Negro people through the final conflict to complete emancipation.

Ethiopia Unity Rallies Harlem
(Editorial, *The [Harlem/Negro] Liberator*, 15 March 1935)

Abyssinian Baptist Church literally rocked with the spirit of militant struggle against Italian fascism, for the defense of Ethiopia at a mass meeting called by the Provisional Committee for the Defense of Ethiopia last Thursday, March 7th.

3,000 persons jammed every available seat and overflowed into aisles and vestibules to voice their indignation and opposition to the arrogant attempts of Mussolini to turn the last remaining independent Negro country in Africa into a Italian "protectorate." And they had slushed through a nasty night which ordinarily would have crimped a meeting.

Harlem had never before witnessed such a united front. Followers of Garvey, the Communist Party, a noted historian and minister, lodge and labor union – all united around a single program: the independence of Ethiopia from imperialism.

A. L. King Speaks

Mr. A. L. King, president of the N.Y. division, Universal Negro Improvement Association, and chairman of the committee was the opening speaker. He outlined the aims of the Committee and introduced the representatives of organizations participating. He was followed by

---

[1] Angelo Herndon (1913–1997), African American Communist organiser who was arrested in Georgia in 1932 on the charge of inciting insurrection and sentenced to 18–20 years imprisonment. His case became a cause célèbre before he was finally released in 1937.

J. A. Rogers, noted Negro historian, who pointed out that this was not a fight against the Italian people. "The Italian people are not unfriendly to Negroes, as experiences during my travels prove," said Mr. Rogers, "This threatened attack on Abyssinia is a result of other forces operating within Italy."

He further presented, with the aid of a map, facts to prove the boundary "dispute" was just a smokescreen for Mussolini's real motive, stating that the real motive for the drive into Ethiopia was rich minerals.

James W. Ford, Communist leader, was the next speaker. There was wild cheering when he pledged the support of the Communist Party to the united front represented at the meeting. Another burst of cheers greeted the statement.

"If we could stop fighting among ourselves ... long enough to unify our forces against our enemy – we would advance. Unless we do this we perish! But I don't believe we are going to perish. We are going to stick together!"

Ford called for material aid to the Abyssinian people instead of volunteers. He characterized those who talked about volunteers as "people who want to talk but do nothing."

"We Must Unite," Says Reid

Opening his speech with congratulations for Ford and the Communists, Mr. Arthur Reid, the next speaker stated: "There was some fear that the Communists would not come through with flying colors in this meeting, but the speech of Mr. Ford has stilled that fear. The Communists have proven that all of us can work together. They have come through!" A wave of applause greeted this opening shot. Mr. Reid told the audience that Marcus Garvey had envisioned such a meeting many years ago and that was the coming true of his dream. "We must unite," continued Mr. Reid, "and after we unite we must fight."

Reverend A. Clayton Powell Jr. spellbound the audience when he told them that "this is a struggle against fascism! Fascism is eating into the very vitals of our people! Sometimes obstacles are good things in our path," he said. "If there were no obstacles there would be no fight! No fight, no victory; no victory no crown."

Boycott Movement Squashed

As the meeting was about the close, a woman arose in the audience to introduce a resolution against buying from Italian merchants in Harlem.

At this point Mr. King took the floor, stating that such a resolution was premature, that "We will have to wait and see how these people act and meet them "half way." The resolution was withdrawn.

Resolutions and cablegrams were adopted to be sent for Cordell, Hull, Mussolini, Mayor La Guardia, the Italian consulate and Ambassador. The cell for a parade in defense of Abyssinia was greeted with a lusty cheer and flag waving. Other speakers were Professor Huggins and Mr. Kole, an African student. $112 was contributed for the work of the Committee.

Parade on March 30th

A Giant Parade of 50,000 persons is being prepared by the Provisional Committee for the Defense of Ethiopia to take place on March 30th. It is expected that every important Negro organization in Harlem will have a section as will several workers' organizations composed of Negro and white workers.

The Committee meets each Monday at 9 pm at the above address.

Ethiopia and World Politics
(By George Padmore, *The Crisis*, 5 May 1935)

The Italo-Ethiopian conflict is but a reflection of world politics, and of the new groupings and alliances taking place among the European powers, in preparation for a new world war. Therefore, in order to clearly understand why Italian fascism has chosen this moment to launch an attack upon Ethiopia, it is first of all necessary for the reader to get a complete picture of the present European political situation. Briefly, present day Europe can be described as fascist; for England, France and the small Scandinavian countries, are the only nations in Europe still adhering to democratic institutions.

The principal features of fascism are, aggressive nationalism, and the desire for territorial expansion. This is particularly true of Germany and Italy. The imperialistic ambitions of Italy are, however, more threatening to the peace of Africa, than that of Germany, whose primary interest at the moment is to fully re-arm, and to break through the diplomatic isolation which is being developed around the Third Reich by France, England, Russia and the Little Entente.

Italy's territorial designs are in two directions, Central Europe and Africa. Since it is easier for Mussolini to achieve what he is after in

Africa, than in Europe, the danger of war against Ethiopia is very great. Furthermore, it is clear that all the big powers on the League of Nations Council – Great Britain, France and Soviet Russia – would rather prefer Mussolini to make war in Africa than disturb the *status quo* in Europe. We shall deal with this question in greater detail later on. Let us first examine the relationship of forces in Europe at the moment.

Two Main Camps in Europe

Since the war, Europe has been divided into two main political camps, the Versailles and the Anti-Versailles. Those nations which emerged out of the war victoriously, are the supporters of the Versailles Treaty. Those who lost, are the Anti-Versailles, with the exception of Italy, whose special position we shall deal with later on. The Versailles group acquired what they now have at the expense of those who lost. For example, small states like Czechoslovakia, Yugoslavia and Romania, either gained their entire independence or added much territory (Romania) as a result of the break-up of the Austrian-Hungarian and German empires. Apart from the disappearance of the Hapsburgs and Hohenzollerns, Poland, Finland, Estonia, Latvia and Lithuania also gained their independence as a result of the war and the Russian Revolution, which led to the break-up of the Tsarist Empire.

Poland also acquired a strip of German territory known as the Corridor, which runs through Greater Germany and East Prussia. This was granted to Poland, then a staunch-all of France and a member of the Versailles camp, in order to give her an outlet to the Baltic by the way of Danzig. The German African colonies were divided up between England, France and Belgium under mandates of the League of Nations. So much for those who gained by the war.

The sufferers from a territorial point of view were, Germany, Austria-Hungary, Bulgaria and Russia, for Romania annexed Bessarabia. For years the Soviet Government refused to recognize the right of Romania to Bessarabia, but they have recently settled this question in Romania's favor in order to make it possible for Russia to win the support of the Little Entente against Germany. Similarly, Germany has "recognized" Poland's claims to the Corridor in order to win her support against Russia. This is an example of high diplomacy!

After the Treaty of Versailles, the victor nations formed a united front called the Little Entente under the leadership of France, in which they agreed to help each other defend what they won in the event that Germany, Hungary or Russia ever attempt to regain lost territories by means of arms. France supports the Little Entente because she, too, needs allies in the event of another war with Germany. England while paying lip service to the League, pursues her traditional policy of balance of power.

Russia and Italy

The position of Russia and Italy towards the Treaty of Versailles requires special mention. Russia emerged out of the war as a new type of state, a Dictatorship of the Proletariat or Workers' Government. As such, the early leaders, Lenin and Trotsky, refused to enter into any alliances or diplomatic entanglements with capitalist states. While the imperialists looked upon the world as divided into two camps – Versailles and Anti-Versailles, the Soviet leaders looked upon the world as divided into two different kind of camps – the Imperialist camp, and the Anti-Imperialist camp, represented by the Soviet Union. This characterized the early history of Russia's foreign policy. But since the defeat of the revolutionary movement in Germany and Central Europe resulting in the rise of Hitlerism on the one hand, and the threat of war in the East on the other hand, the present Soviet leaders have changed their foreign policy, as they no longer have any faith in the ability of the workers of Europe and America to defend Russia if attacked. So with the object of safeguarding the Revolution, the Kremlin has made an alliance with France and the friendship with the Little Entente. And since they are also afraid of losing what they have, they all find it possible to collaborate in defending the *status quo* or to use diplomatic language. "Peace" for the *status quo* can only be changed by war. Russia can therefore be considered a member of the Versailles camp.

Now let us examine Italy's position. Although one of the victor nations, Italian fascism is hostile towards the Versailles Treaty. The reason for this can be traced to pre-war diplomacy. Before the war, Italy was an ally of Germany, but when hostilities broke out. Italy hesitated to join the Central Powers. Finally France succeeded in getting the Italians to come over on the side of the allies. Thanks to the services of the well known French professor, Marcel Cachin, who is now the leader of the Communist Party of France, Aristide Briand, another old socialist, was able to bribe the Italians to join the slaughter. Funny old world this. While men like Lenin and Trotsky were dodging the French police for fighting against the war "comrade" Cachin, was acting as chief recruiting agent for his bourgeoisie. Well, in order to get the Italians to support them, the French signed a secret treaty with them promising them rich booty in Africa and elsewhere. It is very important for Negroes to understand this for the failure of France and the other allies to live up to their promises, today has direct bearing upon the Ethiopian situation. In other words, as war is again being prepared, France is trying to pay Italy her arrears by giving her a free hand to grab Ethiopia so as to win her support in the future.

London Treaty of 1915

In the secret treaty of April, 1915, in London, Italy was to receive some of the German colonies and spheres of influence in the Balkans. But after the war, England, France and Belgium grabbed the colonies, and the Little Entente states gobbled up whatever was to be had in Europe and left the Italians in the cold. Here is where trouble began. Italy seized German-speaking Tyrol in southern Austria and part of Dalmatia and Fiume from the Serbs in 1920. But these small bites could not satisfy the Italians. When Mussolini came to power, he started to attack and denounce the Treaty of Versailles, but knowing that Italy is no match against France, he turned his attention towards the Balkans. It was not difficult for him to intrigue in the inner affairs of Jugoslavia and the other Balkan states, for jealousies are great among them. Mussolini incited national minorities against the dominant ones, and played off one power against the other. He flirted with all the discontented nations – Austria, Hungary, Germany and Bulgaria from time to time. He demanded the right of expansion in the Balkans; he wanted colonies; he wanted to turn the Adriatic into a Roman lake; he wanted everything. Not without reason, Italy is now suporting the rebel forces of Venizelos, to overthrow the Greek Government, so as to break up the Balkan Entente which exists between Greece, Turkey, Jugoslavia and Romania. Mussolini has his fingers in every intrigue in Europe. All because he is dissatisfied with things as they are.

Hitler Prepares for War

Since Hitler has come to power many changes have taken place in the realignment of forces. Hitler is a fascist dictator like Mussolini, and like the Italians, dissatisfied with Europe as it is. In this respect both men are one, but nonetheless, their interests clash. For example, Hitler wants to get hold of Austria in order to use it as a stepping stone into the Balkans. He also wants colonies in Africa, but chief of all to expand East, i.e., Soviet Ukraine. Mussolini also wants Austria, failing which, he is interested to keep Hitler out. It is here where the interests of the two dictators cross swords.

The difference between Hitler and Mussolini is this: Mussolini is a great boaster. He knows that his war machine cannot stand up before the combined forces of France and the Little Entente, so with this knowledge, he is looking towards Africa, for war is the only way out of the crisis, which is getting worse and worse daily. Hitler on the other hand, has a formidable war machine at his disposal, thanks to the Kaiser's generals who perfected the Reichswehr, under the benevolent protection of the Republican-socialists. To this army Hitler's man "Friday", General Goeering, has added an air force potentially, if not actually the equal of any in Europe. This war machine all Europe is afraid of, in so much so, that the British Government has recently issued a White Paper which spells the end of all attempt to arrive at an agreement of "collective security".

Since it is clear to everybody outside a lunatic asylum, that Hitler intends to strike out East and into Central Europe as soon as the generals say "go", he has thrown all those who stand for the *status quo* into alarm. In this pre-war atmosphere, Mussolini sees his chance to offer his support to the highest bidder, and to cash in before the war begins, so that Italy will not be left in the cold as happened after the last slaughter.

The Deal Is Put Over

As France is more in need of Mussolini's support than Germany, Pierre Laval, the French Foreign Minister, paid a visit to Rome in January, and there came to terms with Mussolini. What are the terms? France agreed to give Italy a slice of the French Sahara about the size of England, a portion of French Somaliland, and part of her shares in the Abyssinian railway, which runs from Djibuti, the port of French Somaliland to Addis Ababa, the capital of Ethiopia. But the most important part of the deal is that, Mussolini has a free hand to grab as much of Ethiopia as he can.

The pact of Rome is the most glaring example of the united front of white Europe against black Africa. It should serve to open the eyes of Negroes the world over, that white nations, regardless of their political systems, have no scruples in joining hands in assigning parts of Africa to whichever one stands most in need of colonies. This was the policy adopted by the Berlin Conference of 1885. The Rome Pact is just a continuation of that policy. In other words, Africa is not worth while for whites to fight over. They share it out by mutual agreement. However, there are some white people who will be consoling the blacks that it is better to sacrifice Ethiopia, than to disturb the peace of Europe. Already this is the tune of sections of the European press. They openly say that the white man's continent is more important than the black man's.

Now let us turn our attention to the seat of conflict

Preparations for War

Mussolini's aggressive attitude towards Ethopia dates back to the time when France and Russia failed to get Poland to support the Eastern Locarno Pact. He figured, and correctly so, that France would have to come to terms with him, so he began to provoke Ethiopia, knowing that France was in his hands and could not protest. Neither would England, for since 1925, an agreement existed between Great Britain and Italy for mutual spheres of interests in Ethiopia. Italy is to have special economic rights in the east, and fredom to build a railway to connect the Italian colonies of Eritrea and Somaliland; while England is to enjoy the right to control over the waters of lake Tsana, the source of the Blue Nile, which supplies water to the British-owned cotton plantations in Anglo-Egyptian Soudan. The only other big power on the League Council is Soviet Russia, but Litvinov[2] dares not raise his voice in protest, although Ethiopia is a member since 1923, and Article 1 of the Covenant "guarentees" the sovereignty and integrity of member states. The League is no more than a farce.

For instance, when the first clash took place of Wal-Wal, the Emperor immediately appealed to the League for justice, but instead of receiving a hearing, pressure was brought to bear upon him to withdraw his charges against Mussolini. Not having one colored member on the council he was forced to do so, as the Ethiopian Ambassador at Geneva could not find a single statesman among the big powers to support his country's appeal. Even Mr Litvinov refused to raise his voice in protest out of fear that it might offend Laval, and antagonize Mussolini. Ethiopia was therefore left to fend for herself, and negotiate directly with Mussolini who is trying to terrorize and intimidate the Emperor by dispatching troops to the frontiers while negotiations are taking place in Addis Ababa. However, Hailie Selassie has publicly declared that such bullying methods will not intimidate him to sacrifice his country's rights.

---

[2] Maxim Litvinov (1876–1951), the Soviet delegate who refused to condemn Italy at the League of Nations meeting in April 1935 where Haile Selassie appealed for support.

The Racial Aspect

Apart from the economic motives, and the necessity for fascism to find a way out of the crisis, the racial aspect looms large. It is well known that the Ethiopians and the Japanese are the only two colored nations which have ever defeated white powers at arms. This has not been forgotten by the Italians and for that matter, by the white race. Not without reason, the Rome correspondent of the *London Times*, in a dispatch writes, "Mussolini is not only defending the rights of Italy, but he is upholding the prestige of the whiter race in Africa" while Vernon Bartlett, the diplomatic editor of England's "great" liberal paper *News Chronicle* shouts that "Great Britain cannot afford to jeopardize her friendship with Italy simply in order to defend Ethiopia on the basis of abstract justice." The gentleman, however, lets the cat out the bag when he says, "if a small nation like Holland is threatened, then that is different. Ethiopia is not a civilized nation." What Mr. Bartlett means is that Ethiopia is black, for surely this man, one of the foremost British journalists, knows that the Ethiopians were Christians when his ancestors and those of his Dutch friends were running wild in the forests of the North countries. But the prize goes to a fascist paper, *Affari Esteri*, which has just published the following appeal: "It is time that the white nations of Europe should abandon their long suffering toleration towards the only African state which is still autonomous, and proceed to settle all questions connected with the Abyssinian problem. Abyssinia is a gander to the white race. The young Abyssinians are inspired with the idea of 'Africa for the Africans' and are already combining with Japanese immigrants in the country to combat the white man's influences in Africa."

We can continue to quote many such statements, not only from the fascist press, which are to be expected, but from liberal and democratic papers, which under one form or other are trying to prove that blacks are unfit to rule themselves, and Italy will civilize them. Even the French press which is not as a rule hostile towards Negroes, has become rather chauvinistic since a young white colonial official was killed in the course of a tribal feud along the French Somaliland-Ethiopian frontier. We mention this fact only in order to show that the most liberal whites can adopt a hostile attitude towards colored peoples when it suits their purposes. About this let us have no illusions.

Ethiopian-Japanese Friendship

Much of Ethiopia's present difficulties can be traced to her friendly relations with Japan Within recent years, the Emperor, realizing that his country is surrounded by colonies owned by England, France and Italy, all of whom would like to see Ethiopia backward, if not reduced to the status of a colony like the rest of Africa, has been trying to modernize his realm. This is no easy task, for apart from external intrigues, Haile Selassie has had to face formidable opposition from the great feudal Rasses (chiefs), as well as the dignitaries of the Coptic Church, who wield great influence. The Emperor has few reliable counsellors and every fool knows that no white nation is going to lend him capital, for a strong black state in Africa would be considered worse than bolshevism. It would inspire the blacks in other parts of the continent to do likewise, for the white man has spread the slander abroad that the Negro is biologically unfit to govern himself, which unfortunately, many so-called black intellectuals seem to believe, to judge from the cynical delight they take in ridiculing every attempt made by black men to build a modern state

In order to find the means of carrying through his program of reform, the Emperor has given certain preferential privileges to Japanese who not only need markets for their textiles and other commodities, but lands where they can cultivate raw cotton so as to become independent of the white powers, England and America, from which Japan now buys most of her cotton lint. This is what the white man does not like. A colored nation trading with another at their expense. This is intolerable! England and France dare not interfere, for they have enough problems of their own – England in the far East, and France in Europe, to antagonize Japan; so Mussolini has been assigned the task to intervene in Ethiopia and break up the ties between herself and Japan before it is too late. But Mussolini is playing with fire. Not only will the Ethiopians, despite all his air force, make him break his teeth if he attempts to bite, but Hitler is awaiting the first opportunity to march into Austria and attack his rear.

The danger of war in Africa is great. In this hour of danger, it is the duty of every black man and woman to render the maximum moral and material support to the Ethiopian people in their single-handed struggle against Italian fascism, and a not too friendly world.

The Abyssinian Situation and the Negro World
(By William L. Patterson,[3] *Negro Worker*, June 1935)

The national independence of Ethiopia must be maintained at all costs. It can be, there is no doubt of that. The question before those who are sincerely opposed to the imperialist provocation of Mussolini is how under their present organisational weaknesses this can be accomplished. What under present conditions are the correct tactical measures?

The Negro world is outraged over the criminal attack of the imperialist fascist state of Mussolini against Abyssinia. In every country in which Negroes are to be found discussions are taking place in their mass organisations around the question of finding ways and means of aiding the Negro empire. This is an evidence of their desire for freedom for themselves, as well as for freedom for black people on an international scale. It is precisely from this point of view that the Negro masses desperately desire national independence, that the tremendous protest movement has greatest significance. It is precisely because of this that the correct practical direction must be given to this indignation.

Everywhere the Negro reformists, forced into action by this mass indignation are seeking frantically to gain control of each protest demonstration. For what reason? They are seeking thus to save the ruling class of "their" country. They are seeking to prevent these actions from turning back upon the "home" bourgeoisie which in every imperialist country is outrageously exploiting and oppressing the Negro people and from which exploitation they receive a share. They are seeking thus to justify their right to the crumbs that fall to them from the exploiters table.

The imperialist overlords, everywhere, are well aware that so long as this mass anger is guided in its expression by the Negro reformists it will be directed into utopian "go to Abyssinia," "die for Abyssinia," etc. channels or into other such impractical avenues which hold no danger for Italy or for any other section of the imperialist world. Yet armed to the teeth these great bandits are each of them plundering millions upon millions of coloured people.

---

[3] William L. Patterson (1891–1980) was a leading African American Communist and head of the International Labor Defense.

Greeks Bearing Gifts

Fascist Germany, openly the most chauvinistic imperialism of all, offers to "help" Abyssinia with arms and military advisors. The bloodthirsty butchers who follow Hitler, have expelled all Negro workers from Germany or are preventing them from finding employment there. They have declared Negroes to be lower than some animals and lower than all other human beings. What hypocrisy their offer to help contains.

Japan with the blood of Korea and Formosa long on her hands and even now engaged in slaughtering the Chinese and Manchurian peoples has already penetrated Abyssinia for the purpose of "helping" the Ethiopian people.

These helpers of Abyssinia must be judged not only on the record of their exploitation, oppression and butchery of the masses at home and abroad but primarily by the need for the raw material wealth of the African empire and their need for new markets. They are no less desirous than Italy to control the iron, coal, gold, cotton, etc. of Abyssinia and to use its markets for the sale of their finished goods. They care nothing about the lives involved in carrying out their adventures or of enslaving peoples. Take the example of Mr Firestone's slave rubber plantations in Liberia as proof of this.

Let the Negro masses not forget the record of blood letting of robbery and of exploitation of Germany in the Cameroons, Togoland, East and Southwest Africa before she was in turn robbed of her black colonies after the World War. Let them not forget that it is upon the basis of an agreement with France, who has also butchered millions of African natives in the Congo, that Italy now turns towards Abyssinia in order to extend her colonial possessions. Let them not forget that it was America through its ambassador at Rome, Washbura Childs, who financed Mussolini and helped the fascist murderer to power. Even now America, also on her way to Fascism, is lending millions to this fascist gangster. Pressure upon these co-conspirations of Italy's can force a change in the plans of the leading conspirator in Rome.

All of these imperialist despoilers of black womanhood and legal lynchers and murderers of black men will encourage the anti-Italian feelings of the Negro masses at this moment. Millions of white workers in these countries are now desperately struggling against hunger and unemployment, against wage cuts and the lowering of their standard of living, below the subsistence level. These white masses are the exploited and oppressed classes of the Imperialist nations. Their complete victory depends upon this historic alliance. That is why these imperialist powers will welcome this opportunity to divert the attention of the Negro masses from the struggle at "home." Yet the struggle against the imperialism already oppressing them is the method by which the Negro people everywhere can best help the oppressed and enslaved masses of Abyssinia.

America is not only the land of Scottsboros. Scottsboros exist in every imperial country. It is against the misery and degradation at "home" that this justifiable nationalist anger of the Negro masses must be turned. Turned in any other direction, i.e., other than against imperialists, it plays directly into the hands of the oppressors of Abyssinia.

Solidarity Actions of Italian Workers

How correct are the tactics of the heroic Italian workers who under the leadership of the illegal Communist and Social Democratic Parties are calling for the defeat of their "own" imperialism. "Not a man, not a penny for the fascist African adventure," is their cry, and those under the Communist influence have been called for the defeat of Italian imperialism calling directly upon the army for revolt.

These splendid demonstrations of international working class solidarity on the part of the Italian workers, their fight against the criminal war plans of their white ruling class throw back into the cowardly traitorous face of Messrs George Padmore and Company the lie that white workers will not fight side by side with the black for the liberation of the black masses. All of the revolutionary working class organisations of Italy are redoubling their heroic efforts in spite of all the fascist terror to organise broad mass actions of the working people against imperialist war and against the Abyssinian adventure.

Necessity of Decisive Action

Now it is more imperative than ever that the decisive action of the Negro people be aroused at "home." They must become an inseparable part of every strike for wage increases, every hunger march, the struggles for relief and unemployment insurance at the expense of the bosses and the state. The Negro farmers and share-croppers must everywhere intensify their struggles linking them up with the struggles of white workers and farmers. The fight for the right of self-determination must become a real and living thing. Why are the Negro reformists silent concerning the necessity of struggle against these things? Why do they not explain the relation of all this to the attack upon Abyssinia? Who are they protecting?

Protest, strikes, demonstrations, meetings, all forms of mass action, all forms of struggle must be employed now to drive back every manifestation of reaction to concretely defend democratic rights and to demand that the enforcement of constitutional and civil guarantees for the Negro people be exercised. To fight for daily needs, that is the practical fight to aid Abyssinia.

The fight for the lives of the Scottsboro boys so gloriously carried forward to an almost complete victory, must be linked up with the struggle for the defence of Abyssinia's national independence, the late Ernest Thälmann heroic leader of the German working class, for the lives of the Raeggs in the prison hell of the fascist butcher Chiang Kai-shek. It must become part of the struggle for the freedom of all class war prisoners. This message must be carried into every Negro lodge and church.

The struggle for the defence of the Soviet Union, the land where every nationality now has full and complete equality, the only country truly seeking peace and concretely marking out the road against imperialist wars, is an inseparable part of the struggle against Mussolini's imperialist war in Africa.

Actions of this kind are necessary United front mass actions against the imperialist butchers at "home." This is the road to Abyssinia's liberation. Italy would not have gone forward in this criminal adventure if she were not certain of the support of France and other imperialist powers.

The Negro masses must go forward to a united front with the white workers, the struggles for bread and work, for full equality and for their right of self-determination. This pressure will defeat the imperialists African intrigues.

The Negro masses must go forward to a united front with white workers against misery and oppression and against imperialist war.

Boycott Hearst
(Editorial, *The [Negro/Harlem] Liberator*, 16 September 1934)

"Mussolini's Italians will do in Ethiopia what Englishmen have done in South Africa; what the French have done in Northern Africa. Mussolini's men will bring 'civilization' to Ethiopia, as Mussolini's predecessor, Julius Caesar, brought civilization to France two thousand years ago."

THIS is the propaganda of Mussolini. But it is the voice of William Randolph Hearst – who is Mussolini, Hitler, and American reaction rolled into one – speaking in the *Daily Mirror* (Smut) on August 30th.

The sort of "civilization" that the English and French imperialists took to Africa and the sort that Mussolini intends to take to Ethiopia is slavery, destruction and death for innocent free people.

But the vile monster Hearst is not through, he continues

"American citizens of the colored race must remember that the Ethiopian government that Mussolini will soon attack is not a NEGRO government . . . Better remain in the United States and help build real civilization here.

The Ethiopian people themselves have answered this vicious lie by specifically recognizing fraternal brotherhood with the American Negroes who already aroused in defense of Ethiopia.

The American "colored man" certainly is going to remain in America and help build a "real" civilization. But it will not be the kind of "civilization" in which Hearst and his class will be kept in power by the exploitation of the workers and the lynch oppression of the Negro people.

It will be a civilization in which the negro masses and white toilers fighting together will establish self-determination for the Black belt and full economic political and social equality for Negroes throughout America. THIS FIGHT FOR FREEDOM MEANS FIGHTING IN SOLIDARITY WITH TOILERS AND ANTI-FASCISTS EVERYWHERE FOR THE DEFENSE OF ETHIOPIA.

It is said that the Hearst press (*Daily Mirror*, *New York Evening Journal*, *New York American*) has a circulation in Harlem of more than 50,000. These newspapers which play Negroes up as "ape-men", "rapists", should be kept out of Harlem.

NEGROES IN HARLEM AND ALL OVER THE COUNTRY SHOULD **BOYCOTT HEARST!** THIS HITS THE ANTI-NEGRO FASCIST WAR-WHOOPER WHERE IT HURST MOST – IN THE POCKETBOOK.

HEARST SUPPORTS MUSSOLINI'S ENSLAVEMENT OF ETHIOPIA!

DON'T BUY – DON'T READ – HEARST.

Stay Out of the Nazi Olympics
(Editorial, The Crisis, September 1935)

THE CRISIS joins other publications in opposition to American athletes taking part in the Olympic games in 1936 in Berlin. Upon the grounds of poor sportsmanship and discrimination, America, of course, cannot raise a very sincere howl, for she has given the Negro athlete in this country copious doses of both.

If memory does not fail THE CRISIS, there was talk of the poor treatment of Tolan, Metcalf and other colored athletes in the 1932 Olympic games in sunny California, which at last reports was not in Germany. This, too, while the pair of negro runners was carrying the Stars and Stripes to victory. Just two months ago when Jesse Owens did lone battle against the whole University of Southern California team, winning four first places out of four starts, a hotel refused to allow him a room in which to stay. Then there is Weir of New York, barred from tennis; Ward of Michigan, barred from the Georgia Tech game on his own campus; all Negroes kept out of organized big league baseball; no Negroes in amateur or professional golf or tennis. The complete list would be a long one.

It is fair to the A.A.U. to say that it has refused to hold its national track meets and boxing tournaments in sections of the country where Negroes would not be allowed to compete. But the A.A.U. will not admit Negroes to regional competitions in sections where the color line is drawn. Hence, no Negro amateurs come out of the South.

We do believe, however that the American Olympic committee ought to withdraw our team from the Berlin Olympics because the games are being held in a country whose government is founded officially upon suppression of religious, political and social liberty, and upon terror and brutality. We ought not contribute anything, either in money or prestige, to such a government. Keep American athletes at home in 1936. In the meantime, if we just have to work up a lather over discrimination in sports, let us address ourselves to the color line in our own backyard.

A Stirring Ballad of Ethiopian People
(By Langton Hughes, *The [Harlem/Negro] Liberator*,
1 October 1935)

EDITORS NOTE: We present below the ballad by Langston Hughes, Vice President of the League of Struggle for Negro Rights.

It has been set to music by Thelma Brown and Nora Holt and submitted to W. C. Handy, author of the famous "St Louis Blues" for publication.

Bow your head in prayer.
Lift your soul in song.

Let the war be short
And the Freedom long.

I have been a slave.
I've been beaten down.
But you cannot keep me
On the ground.

Ethiopian warriors
With your spears of gold,
Don't let Mussolini
Get into your fold.

Ethiopian Women
Offer up their lives
On the field of battle
As a sacrifice.

Where the might Nile's
Great headwaters rise
And the black man's flag
In bright freedom flies.

All you colored peoples,
No matter where you be,
Take for your slogan:
AFRICA BE FREE!

All your colored peoples
Be a man at last.
Say to Mussolini,
No! you shall not pass!

There's nobody knows
The trouble I have seen –
But when I rise
I'm gonna rise mean.

Carnera thought that
He would have his way –
But the big Brown bomber
Just said Hey! . . . Hey!

> Mussolini's men
> May swing their capes –
> But when Harlem starts
> She's a cage of apes!
>
> We would have this world
> To be fine and Free,
> But when I say free
> That means you and ME.
>
> So get together, women!
> Get together, men!
> Let us tell the world
> Fascism must end.
>
> Although Mussolini
> Wants his peace of mind,
> The peace we want
> Is for all mankind.
>
> And that peace we want
> Means EVERY man is free,
> Listen Mussolini,
> Don't you mess with me.

Political Highlights of the National Negro Congress[4] (abridged)
(By James W. Ford, *The Communist*, May 1936)

We come now to another high light of the National Negro Congress, viz., the involving of sections of the entire Negro population in the fight for peace, and against fascism and war; and the influencing of world opinion in favor of Ethiopia and in the problems of Negroes everywhere. As an oppressed group, the Negro people have carried on an age-old fight against lynching and for civil rights and decent human relations. Now their attention is riveted on the menace of fascism to their

---

[4] The NNC was a Popular Front organisation formed in 1935 as the successor to the League of Struggle for Negro Rights. It was an impressive organisation bringing together civil rights, labour and religious groups. The conference in February 1936 had over 800 delegates representing 551 organisations. The Socialist A. Philip Randolph was President and the Communist Ben Davis was National Secretary. The NNC folded in 1939 in the wake of the Nazi-Soviet Pact.

individual and collective life, which is so clearly seen in the attack of Italian fascism on the last independent Negro state, Ethiopia, as well as in the fascist methods used against Negroes in this country. The Negroes are developing a higher understanding of these issues, higher than ever before, and are taking an advanced position among the progressive, liberty- and peace-loving forces in the fight against fascism.

The Congress emphatically showed this trend. Special sessions were held on the topics of "Fascism and War" and "Civil Liberties, Lynching, and Terror". In the general sessions of the Congress exceptionally clear discussions were heard and in the final session important resolutions were adopted on fascism and war. Practically the entire Congress was vigorous in its condemnation of fascism and war and in its willingness to fight against the twin menace. A fairly accurate description of the danger of war and of the fascist forces was given by A. Philip Randolph:

"War looms on the horizon . . . already fascist Italy is on the march to subjugate the ancient kingdom of Ethiopia . . . France and Germany are in a state of truce, awaiting the hour to strike for another conflict . . . Italy and England are in competition for place and prestige in the Mediterranean and Africa, while Japan threatens to close the open door to American investments and advance her claim to the adoption of a Monroe Doctrine over the Pacific which may bring 'Uncle Sam' and 'Nippon' to grips . . . Meanwhile Tokyo proceeds on its long conquering trek of China . . . Japan is restive in the face of the constant growth and power of Soviet Russia and is steadily resorting to provocative acts of war . . . Hitler seeks to serve as a spearhead of modern monopoly capitalism against the workers' republic."

The Lie is Given to Mussolini's Demagogy

The declaration of Mussolini that the Ethiopian war was necessary so that Italy might take the great civilization of Rome to the desolate land of Ethiopia was never more dramatically given the lie before an American audience than on the opening night of the Congress, when Lij Tesfaye Zaphiro, special envoy of the London Legation of Ethiopia, spoke to more than 6,000 people. A highly cultured young man, speaking in perfect English, calm and deliberate, he said:

"We have been called barbarians, not able to govern our own land. But Ethiopia is not the only country today in which barbarism exists.

"This war is not unlike the American War of Independence. Ethiopia is fighting for life, liberty, and the pursuit of happiness in her own land. We are fighting to preserve our independence and integrity. Ethiopia's defeat may mean the downfall of the collective security system and perhaps the end of the League of Nations. If Ethiopia wins, as she will if she is supported, it will strengthen the League of Nations and show that world sentiment must be respected."

Compare this analysis and attitude towards the collective security peace policy of the Soviet Union with the barbaric actions of Mussolini, who rains bombs and poison gas down upon defenseless men, women, and children – "a barbaric people"; or with Hitler, who takes advantage of the situation to prepare a barbaric war on a world scale; or with the Japanese militarist clique, in their drive to bring the entire Chinese people under the heel of Japanese imperialism and to penetrate into Soviet territory; or with the most reactionary forces in England, France, and the United States, that actively urge on this slaughter.

[...]

World-wide Interest in the Congress

The presence of Mr. Max Yeargan, from Capetown, South Africa, Secretary of the South African work of the International Committee of the Y. M. C. A., brought additional international interest and significance to the National Negro Congress. Mr. Yeargan, an American Negro, who has spent the past fifteen years in Africa, traveling and observing the ravages of imperialism, painted a vivid picture of the conditions of Negroes in Africa. He said:

"The capitalist trusts divide up the spoils and partition the territories of the world among themselves. This phase of imperialism has manifested itself in every part of the African continent. Britain, France, and other European countries have taken much of the land ... Various new forms of labor are forced on the people, and labor is drained out of the country ...

"Imperialism, then, means annexation of land and confiscation of labor ... It destroys the culture – the basic social fabric of the people's life. In South Africa, through the color laws, Africans are kept out of many phases of skilled labor and on the lowest level, industrially. Laws limiting freedom of assembly make it difficult for them to organize to defend themselves. Other legislation prevents their moving about freely ...This Congress has the opportunity and responsibility to make it possible for all organizations here represented to subscribe to a minimum program – to fight for those things on which the organizations are in agreement."

The Congress was duly influenced by the active participation of these representatives from abroad. The Congress condemned any form of discrimination against foreign-born Negroes in the United States and opposed any attempt to deport or drop them from relief or employment; it advised better relations between foreign-born and native-born Negroes and went on record to support people of African descent in their struggle for economic and political freedom in their respective countries.

[. . .]

Hence, the National Negro Congress in the United States occupies an important place in the life and struggles of Negroes everywhere. That is why the Congress adopted a resolution on an International Congress of Negroes, as follows:

"Whereas, the exploitation and subjugation of the Negro masses is general, and world-wide in scope, and Negro toilers in one nation are not free so long as their brother toilers elsewhere are subjected to the degrading horrors of exploitation, and "Whereas, a deeper sympathy and class-consciousness of all Negroes throughout the world can best be developed by an International Congress of Negroes, be it resolved, that immediately upon the establishment of this Congress upon a permanent basis, it work for the fulfillment of such an International Congress of Negroes."

[. . .]

The National Negro Congress did not adopt a Communist program. But we Communists stand one hundred per cent behind it in its effort to unite the Negro people upon a common program people, against all forms of discrimination, against fascism and war, for equal rights, and on issues which are in the interests of all the toiling masses of the country in advancing the general fight against capital. Today the tactic of the united front is bringing together large masses of Negroes; yet the consolidation of the organized united front among the Negro people is still weak. The responsibility for this must be lodged with those who stand in the way of unity. And as for those people who are so simon-pure in their proletarian outlook that they cannot or do not care to concern themselves with the problems of the miserable life of the Negro people, let them remember the picture of an entire Negro people, so poignantly depicted by the Negro poet, Paul Lawrence Dunbar:

"A crust of bread and a corner to sleep in,
A minute to smile and an hour to weep in,
A pint of joy to a peck of trouble,
And never a laugh but the moans come double
And that is life."

I Visited Spain
(By Edward E. Strong,[5] *The Crisis*, December 1936)

Mr. Strong attended the World Youth Congress at Geneva, Switzerland, last summer and spent some time in Spain. He gives here an account of what he saw and his interpretation of his observations.

There is no Civil War in Spain. To have a Civil War there must be a fundamental irreconcilable cleavage between two major sections of the population within a country. In Spain no such cleavage exists. Out of the population of 23 million people at least 22 million are solidly supporting the government. The rebels represent the landed aristocracy and the royalists, who constitute a negligible percentage of the population. The present struggle is tantamount to a foreign invasion of Spain under the leadership of international fascism. Documentary evidence in possession of the government proves conclusively that German, Italian, Portuguese and Spanish fascists planned the present uprising two years ago. Moreover, four-fifths of the fascist army is composed of African troops, the Foreign Legions and other imported mercenaries. If the rebels spoke for the Spanish people and had their backing, it would be possible to secure Spaniards to fight for them. Having no support from the masses, however, this is impossible and, excepting for the professional army that went over to the rebels, they have been forced to depend entirely upon imported troops.

For the Spanish people the issues involved in this struggle are clear. They are fighting economic tyranny, political terror, and religious domination. A fascist victory will mean a renewal of the intolerable conditions under which the Spanish people have lived for centuries. For centuries the peasants could neither read nor write their names; for centuries streets in villages and cities went unpaved and other necessary reforms were not made. We visited village hovels that were inferior to the worst of Mississippi shanties. On the other hand we were in villas and mansion owned by the nobility that contained tapestries, rugs, paintings, libraries consisting of thousands of dollars. For sheer gaudiness, extravagance and uselessness these Spanish palaces far exceed anything to be found on New York's Park Avenue, Chicago's North Shore or Boston's Beacon Hill. Until the establishment of the Republic in 1931

---

[5] Edward Strong (1914–1957) was a Texan-born African American civil rights activist. He was active in both the NAACP and the Communist Party and in 1936 was elected head of the youth division of the National Negro Congress (NNC).

surplus wealth went into these non-essentials, thus making impossible the social reforms beneficial to the masses. For this state of affairs the fascists are fighting. They would like to keep the nobility in their luxurious mansions and the peasants in their pitiable hovels. The objectives of the Spanish fascists and the southern landlords in our own country are identical – to keep the masses of underprivileged peasants tied to the soil in complete subjugation and ignorance. To conceal their real purposes the fascists are crying "wolf-wolf, Red-Red" but only the blind and Mr Hearst can fail to understand the basic internal questions confronting the Spanish people – a reversion to feudalistic slavery as represented by the fascists or continuation of economic, political and social reforms already initiated under the government.

Darker Peoples Involved

It can no longer be maintained that the Spanish conflict is one that concerns only the Spanish people, for questions are involved that have long since transcended the boundaries of the country and are of vital concern to the entire world and to the American Negro in particular. A fascist victory will lend additional impetus to the already rapid drift toward another world war, intensifying the present armament race. Encouraged French fascists would initiate a similar uprising in France thus threatening French democracy. Italian fascism would be in a position to consolidate its recent gains in the Mediterranean and would renew with additional vigor its efforts to subdue Ethiopia.

A victory for the Spanish fascists would be a tremendous blow to the interests of dark people, colonial and semi-colonial nations the world over. Recently we have seen a revival of race superiority theories, doctrines of manifest destiny, new ideas of the Nordic Myth and persistent determination on the part of Germany and Italy to intensify exploitation of colonial countries. With these race-hating doctrines the rebels are in one hundred percent accord.

The Spanish government, as contrasted with the attitude of the fascists, unequivocally stands for racial equality and equal opportunities for colonial people. The supporters of the Spanish democracy carried on a most intense campaign in behalf of the Scottsboro boys and Angelo Herndon. Greater interest was manifested in these cases in Spain than in any other country in the world. Huge Scottsboro mass meetings were held in the major cities; pamphlets were written and distributed by the hundreds of thousands; meetings were held by women in factories and shops; delegations visited the American Ambassador in Madrid, who, however, refused to receive them. During this same period fascist newspapers were condemning the Scottsboro boys and pronouncing Angelo Herndon a troublemaker.

The Spanish masses were overjoyed at seeing two American Negro youths in our delegation. (Negro representatives who attended the Worker's Olympics in Barcelona prior to the outbreak of the conflict tell similar experiences.) Speakers at receptions and other affairs given for the delegation never failed to mention their interest in the problems of the American Negro and to point out the similarity in the conditions of the two people. Upon visiting the Somosierra front in the Guadarama Mountains General Galan, commander in charge, threw his arms about one of the Negros in a heartfelt embrace. In this action of the general there was more involved than the typical Spanish custom of greeting a person. It was a symbol of unity between the masses of Spanish people fighting for freedom and of the Negro people of America who are waging a fight basically the same. General Galan expressed his action as such and sent to the American Negroes his deepest greetings. He further expressed his "hope for an early emancipation of the southern Negro from under the economic lash of Bourbon rule." (Remember the fascist Hitler policy towards Negro athletes at the Olympics.) This was the attitude of other leading government officials that we interviewed as well as the Spanish masses in both villages and cities.

Americans Misinformed

In the United States many illusions and misconceptions exist concerning events in Spain. The first and most pronounced is that all church property has been destroyed and that all priests have been ruthlessly murdered. We visited the St. Maria Cathedral of Barcelona and the Bishop's palace which were intact just as they have been for the last six hundred years. However, another cathedral in Barcelona that we saw had been burned to the ground. It was burned because it had been occupied by the fascist forces at the beginning of the outbreak. The only church property that has been destroyed is that used as barricades and forts by the fascists as centers of pro-rebel anti-government propaganda.

In the Basque province of Northern Spain the church has never participated in fascist political activities and today the priests are saying daily mass and services are regularly attended. Here complete separation of church and state has been successfully achieved. This is the object of the government throughout Spain – exactly the same as in our own country where there has always been a separation of church and state.

The Constitution of Spain guarantees religious freedom, permits religious teaching in the churches, private schools and in private homes, but provides for lay teaching in public schools.

The attitude of the Spanish Catholics is expressed by Ossorio Y Gallardo, former Minister of Justice in King Aphonso XIII's government before the declaration of the first Republic in 1931, staunch Catholic and firm Liberal who opposed the dictatorship of the Gil Robles government 1934–36, and now supporter of the new republic. He says:

"I want to correct a completely mistaken legend which is current today. Believing in a religious conception of life I have the moral right to proclaim to all that the Spanish have respected freedom of thought and speech as much as the freest of countries. A Catholic should respect and obey the church. But the church, the immortal depository of the most elevated doctrine, the most pure and most generous that has ever lived across the centuries, ought not to be confused with this ecclesiastical degeneracy of many of the Spanish archbishops, who stored up jewels and riches for personal motives, who brought the name of God into election fights and thus insulted it, who even exposed the blessed sacrament and proclaimed that by this gesture God would see that the 'lefts' should lose the elections. It should not be confused with those who lowered God to the class of a belligerent, reduced Him to the status of a conqueror and thus blasphemed His divinity; it should not be confused with the religious orders in Spain who amassed millions even if it was in no way to the profit of their members; it should not be confused with those individuals, whether laymen or ecclesiastics, who fired upon the people from their church towers, thus denying the sacred character of these buildings and giving a good reason to the destruction which followed. The church should not be confused with those priests, who participate in the battle, rifle or machine gun in hand, thus deserting their duty which is to pray and work for peace among all and not to shoot upon people. That is why a man like me, without changing one jot of my belief and the doctrines that I have propagated for a quarter of a century, come today and place myself whole-heartedly on the side of the government of the Peoples Front and swear that I will use my heart and brain so that it may succeed."

The masses of Spanish Catholics are with the government and are not in sympathy with large sections of church officials who have seen fit to support the fascists in order to maintain church domination of the government and the special privileges of a priestly class.

Ultimate Government Victory

Ideas all too prevalent in America relative to the destruction of foreign property, alleged disorder and confusion in the cities have absolutely no foundation. All foreign property is carefully guarded by government militia and on this property are to be found huge signs calling upon the population to respect it. In Barcelona the American flag still waves proudly over the American Telephone and Telegraph Company. Rather than confusion the delegation was amazed at the lack of it. It would be incorrect to contend, however, that such a conflict could exist without a minimum degree of disturbance to the normal life of things.

Though the struggle in Spain will be a long, hard one, ultimate victory rests on the side of the government. The major reason in assuring this victory is a united people determined to maintain their freedom from suppression regardless of the price that must be paid. The only hope for a rebel victory (except that Germany and Italy send a complete army into Spain which is always a possibility; the fascists will stop at nothing in their efforts to win), lies in the annihilation of 22 million people. This the fascists will not be able to do. Time is on the side of the government. Every day the conflict is prolonged weakens the position of the fascists and strengthens the hand of the government. At the beginning of the outbreak four-fifths of the army went over to the rebels and the government was left without a disciplined trained group for defense of the Republic. But this handicap has been largely overcome as successful steps have been taken towards organizing a democratic people's army with a consolidated disciplined leadership. While the government is training thousands of men for the newly created people's army the rebels are forced, to a greater extent than ever before, to depend upon African troops. But their hold on the Moroccan troops is none too secure. When being pressed into service they were made many glowing promise which the fascists will not be able to keep. They were told that the opportunity had finally arrived to get even with their own enemies of the mainland who, for centuries, have exploited them. Being unable to differentiate between the present government and previous ones, the Moroccan troops have attacked with a will. But the iron fist with which they are being ruled is rapidly convincing them that the fascists, though coming in a new guise, are the same exploiters of old. That this is true is proved by the uprisings that have occurred in Spanish Morocco against the rebel rule and the threat of Moroccan leaders to withdraw their troops from the conflict. Moreover, there will be on short easy victory with rewards of "wine, women and money" as the fascists have so ardently promised. Instead of wealth and riches the Morrocan troops are finding death from a very formidable foe in the newly mechanized government army. To add further to their discomforts will be the terrific winter of the Guaderrama Mountains. Being used to a warm climate the African troops will not appreciate spending the cold winter months settling a war that is not of their choosing and will be in no mood to accept the tyranny of fascist generals. Once becoming convinced that they are "chasing butterflies" and that there is no possibility of illusory promises made to them being carried out, the Moroccan troops will refuse to fight. That this may happen is more than a possibility.

Additional proof to support the opinion that ultimate victory rests with the government is to be found in the heroism demonstrated in the conflict by the Spanish women and youth. Women militia, organized in all parts of Spain, were to be seen on the barricades fighting side by side with men. All secondary schools and institutions of higher learning have closed, professors and students are fighting in defense of the republic.

The prolongation of the conflict has been due to the overwhelming superiority of fascist equipment and the inability of the government to secure adequate armaments. Indeed, this has been the major government weakness and its ability to secure sufficient arms will largely determine how quickly the rebels will be crushed.

Walter Garland Tells what Spain's Fight against Fascism Means to the Negro People
(By Richard Wright,[6] *Daily Worker*, 29 November 1937)

After braving for a year the inferno of fascist fire, Lieutenant Walter Garland, just recently returned from Spain, told just what the heroic fight for Spanish democracy means to the Negro in America.

In an exclusive interview with the *Daily Worker* yesterday Garland revealed the courage and understanding of today's American youth who went to Spain and helped create the "miracle of Madrid."

Twice wounded in action, the 23 year-old Negro from Brooklyn rose in the short space of a year from the rank of private to that of lieutenant in charge of the American Training Base in Loyalist Spain.

---

[6] Richard Wright (1908–1960), famous African American author, poet and essayist. Most notable for his path-breaking novel *Native Son* (1940). Wright was a member of the CPUSA from 1933–1944.

At Negro Congress

Until a year ago Walter Garland lived a life of "quiet desperation" in Brooklyn, earning his living in the orchestration department of the NBC studios on the Lucky Strike program. Of five children, two girls and three boys, he was the oldest son. Though his father is living his mother died before he could hardly remember. Garland was hardly out of grammar school before he had to go to work and help carry the family responsibilities.

But the National Negro Congress, especially the Brooklyn Division which he joined shortly after its formation, gave Garland new perspectives and most important of all, courage and a method of action.

The first and most important discovery of Garland's life was his recognition that what was happening to him was what was happening to the oppressed the world over, whether in Ethiopia, Spain, or China.

To Meet the Enemy

Distressingly he had watched fascist Mussolini butcher the unarmed Ethiopians. He reasoned that it would only be a matter of time before these brutalities descended upon the Negro in America, unless the spread of fascism was halted. And Garland did the only thing that a man who saw as he saw could do: HE WENT TO MEET THE ENEMY!

In January he arrived in a democratic Spain with her back to the wall, a Spain desperately trying to stave off the hordes of fascism until it could organize its industries, government, and army.

"They put us through about four weeks of intensive training and shipped us to the Madrid sector," said Garland. "This was my first taste of war. Franco was trying to encircle Madrid, to cut it off from the rest of the nation.

To Save Madrid

"You can imagine what effect the capture of Madrid would have had on the Loyalist population. We wanted to save Madrid at all costs.

At that same time the Loyalists had no trained reserves to relieve us. We stayed in the trenches for 130 days."

Garland went into the front lines as a private but was soon promoted to Section Leader.

"Most of the officers of the old Spanish Army, being sons of the rich, had gone over to the insurgents. When there was any occasion to fill a vacancy in the ranks, men were moved up from the bottom.

"One of the reasons for this," said Garland, "was to build a people's army to ensure loyalty to the worker's cause."

Hit on 8th Day

On his eighth day in the front lines, Garland was wounded – a bullet through the stomach. Luckily, his cartridge belt deflected the force of the bullet and the wound was not fatal.

He spent eight weeks in a hospital at Chenchun and was then sent to an officer's training school. He emerged as a lieutenant and was placed in charge of training a machine-gun company.

In June in 1837 Garland took his company into a reserve position on the Jarma Front and stayed a month. Then, in the broiling heat of July, he was ordered to Brunete.

"It was a desperate period," said Garland. "We didn't have much time; the fascists were pressing us. In order to get into a position as fast as possible, I took my men over an exposed area. All but two of us got over safely. One of the boys got hit and I tried to drag him to safety and got a fascist bullet in my hand. It wasn't much of a wound, but it was enough to keep me out for 12 days.

Back July 18

"On July 18 I went back into the trenches and stayed till the end of the Brunete campaign."

Garland came out of the inferno of Brunete a hero of Loyalist Spain. His quick adaptation from civilian to military life, his understanding of the world-wide issues involved in the struggle, was the reflection of the ultimate hope of a Loyalist victory.

Garland estimated that more than 100 American and West Indian Negroes are now fighting in the ranks of the Spanish Loyalists. He stated that the heroic records of many of these men were due to the fact that there existed no discrimination towards them.

Names Negro Heroes

"They gave all of us a chance to put our abilities to use," Garland said. "For instance, a young Negro from Brooklyn, Burt Jackson, was promoted to a lieutenancy and is now in charge of the Loyalist Topography

School. There is Oscar Hunter, who is a political commissar. Abe Lewis, another American Negro, is quartermaster at a training base.

"The Spanish Government is stronger today than ever. It is going to win. The capitalist press in this and other countries usually play up the gains of the fascists. That's where their interest lie. But the interests of the Negro and other oppressed groups lie with the Loyalists," Garland continued.

On the home scene what interests Garland most is the development of the People's Front Against War and Fascism in America – comprising of the Negro people and progressives of all other races.

"The National Negro Congress is certainly doing fine work," he said. "The hope of the Negro lies through its activities. There's one thing that every Negro ought to do. He ought to get into the National Negro Congress and fight reaction in all of its forms. If they do, then maybe we won't have to go through with what the Spanish people are going through now."

Support the Spanish People
(Editorial, *Negro Worker*, February 1937)

Six months have passed since General Franco, supported by Hitler and Mussolini launched the war of destruction and extermination against the Republic of Spain and the Spanish People. Six months of the most barbaric destruction of people's homes, of structures of art and culture. Six months of snuffing the lives out of women and children by the German and Italian bombing planes. This, is the record of the fascist brigands who seek to establish their domination and extend the slave system of fascism over the Spanish people.

Superiorly armed and equipped, the fascist hordes approached the gates of Madrid over two months ago. But there they have been checked by the heroic resistance of the toiling masses. Like Mussolini, who used the Eritrean and Somali Natives as the shock troops and spearhead in the Italian war of conquest of Ethiopia, so Franco has used the Moors in the brunt of the fight for Madrid. But this time it did not work out as in Abyssinia. The Moors and Foreign Legionnaires have been checked. German and Italian troops have taken their place in the attempt to capture Madrid. But they too are being successfully stopped.

The International Brigade, composed of volunteer anti-fascist fighters of all nations and races appeared in time to give effective aid in stopping the fascist onslaught.

Among these volunteers who have offered their lives in defence of Spain from fascist barbarism, are a number of Negroes and other colonials. These colonials, fighting in the ranks of the Government forces, realize that the fight for freedom in Spain is very closely connected with their own struggles against tyranny and the ever increasing world fascist menace. They realize further that a defeat of fascism in Spain, means not only a victory for the Spanish people, but a decisive curb to the fascist ambition of war for colonial annexation and a tremendous setback in Mussolini's attempt to consolidate his occupation of Abyssinia.

The Negro people must not limit their support of the Spanish people who today are battling the same enemy the Ethiopians fought and are still fighting to a mere handful of frontline fighters. This support must be extended to cover as well other means of material aid in the form of MONEY, FOOD, CLOTHING, MEDICINES, AND NURSES AND DOCTORS. Negro nurses and doctors and others with special qualifications should offer their services to the Spanish Aid Committees which have been set up and join the groups going to the assistance of the wounded and those of the fighting front.

This humanitarian aid to those who are offering their lives to repel the common scourge of all humanity – Fascism – will serve to cement the bond between the Negro people and all other elements fighting for freedom.

Conclusion

The radical black press of this era also reported widely on, and made connections to, the struggles in the Caribbean, India, Haiti, Liberia and South Africa. There are extensive rewritings of radical black history, and the history of the enslaved. The day-to-day reports of police brutality and blacks' deaths in both the north and the Jim Crow south are ubiquitous, as are assertions of black pride and interracial class unity. The writings selected for *this* volume bear witness to a particularly inflected black internationalism. It is an internationalism which has much to tell us about the politics of race and solidarity in the contemporary world. Internationalism has been a distinctly unfashionable term in the realm of post-colonial studies. Frequently conflated with the implicated universalism of the West, and its varied deployments in the insidious workings of globalisation, it has often seemed a woolly and banalising term that works precisely to silence the discrete politics of place and identity which are located within literary and historical post-colonialist paradigms. Apparently, it is only in the slippages and gaps, the interstices, of colonial discourse that we can productively locate challenges to colonial rule. In such a dehistoricising formulation the 'totalising' concept of internationalism is suggestive of a politics of appropriation which potentially eschews the lived experience of race. It is thus a term which demands that marginalised subjects sacrifice their precarious experiential politics for an abstract notion of solidarity which silences difference. The material re-published in this volume demonstrates the limitations/vacuity of the dominant varieties of narcissistic high post-colonial theory of the 1990s by foregrounding class conflict, transnational solidarities, the strategic nexus of anti-colonial and anti-racist politics.

The writings in this volume make apparent both the possibility and the desirability of a concept of internationalism which is precisely predicated upon the assertion of difference, but not 'difference' as politics in and of itself. There is nothing silent about race in these visions of international solidarity. McKay, Briggs, Harrison, Domingo and Padmore are committed to placing race not just at the centre of anti-colonial politics but at the centre of class politics also. This is a *process* that E. San Juan identifies in a different context as one of:

> class conflict in which identities are articulated with group formation, where race, gender and ethnicity enter into the totality of contradictions that define a specific conjuncture, and in particular the contradictions between the social relations dominated by private property and the productive forces . . . (San Juan 2005: 85)

The determined effort to pursue the interconnectedness of a global system of oppression, an effort which is illustrated and exemplified by these radicals and their writings, demands an understanding of colonialism and anti-colonialism as dialectical processes of capitalism. As such, they are processes which necessitate making links to other groups who are exploited and oppressed. It is the insistence on the shared *structures* of oppression rather than on the shared *experience* of oppression that empowers this political position and its analysis of race and colonialism. The *experience* of Russian Jews, Irish colonial subjects, Caribbean peoples, Ethiopians, Liberians, Haitians and Spanish Republicans is not what is claimed by these writers. It is the connections forged in *how* these different groups have been oppressed, the nature of their oppression and their resistances to those oppressions which inaugurate the politics of solidarity evidenced in these writings. The attempt to forge those links opens up a space in which the specific nature of racism in the USA between the wars is attested in all its complexity. It is a space in which that specificity is mobilised to imagine global resistance to colonialism and capitalism. These sometimes sectarian, sometimes doctrinaire, sometimes outraged, and always ambitious writings illuminate an extraordinary moment of revolutionary intent.

Works Cited

San Juan, Jr, E. (2005), 'From Race to Class Struggle: Re-Problematizing Critical Race Theory', *Michigan Journal of Race & Law*, 11 (1), Fall, 75–98.

Index

Entries in **bold** indicate material that is authored by the person named. For articles from individual publications see the contents list.

Abyssinia *see* Ethiopia
Africa, 11, 12, 27, 34, 59, 67, 68, 74–6, 77, 82–4, 86–8, 105, 108–9, 112–14, 118–20, 126, 128–9, 135–7, 140–1, 144, 148, 157, 158–9, 160–1, 181, 182–5, 194–8, 204, 212–13, 232, 234, 235, 237
African Blood Brotherhood (ABB), 6, 8–10, 45n, 50n, 108, 128, 130, 177n
American Federation of Labor, 4, 44, 69
American Revolution, 24, 26, 60, 91, 134
Attucks, Crispus, 91

Bagnall, Robert, 141, 151, **157**
Barbados, 38–9, 142, 196, 204
Bolshevism, 1, 8, 10, 13, 15, 23–57, 58, 64, 108, 136, 159, 173, 229, 235
Briggs, Cyril, xi, 7, 9–10, 17, 23, **26**, **34–8**, **59**, **62**, **66–7**, 82, 85, **90**, **108**, **125–7**, **128–31**, 142, 167, 258
Britain, 24, 29, 30, 31, 32, 36, 37, 38, 48, 52, 61, 62, 65–9, 88, 89, 113–18, 126, 130, 134, 135, 169, 179, 181, 185, 189, 192–9, 213, 228–30, 233, 234, 235
Brown, John, 162
Bullitt, William C., 36–7
Burroughs, Williana, 7

Campbell, Grace, 7
Caribbean, 5–9, 12, 15, 29, 31, 36, 39, 98, 102, 112, 116, 120, 123, 129, 137, 139, 158, 161, 165–7, 169, 177–8, 188, 189–90, 190, 196–9, 204, 212
Casement, Roger, 59, 76
Chicago Defender, 85, 86, 141, 154, 164
China, 72, 102, 135, 136, 137, 159, 172, 179, 188, 244, 253
Collins, Michael, 79
Communist International (Comintern), 8, 9–10, 13–14, 43, 46, 49, 51, 177
Communist Party of United States of America (CPUSA), 9, 10, 13, 14, 17, 45, 56, 177, 185n, 191, 210n, 220, 225, 226, 227
Congo, 30, 40, 237
Costa Rica, 122, 127
The Crisis, xi, 14, 17, 58, 166

The Crusader, xi, 5–7, 9, 17, 58, 167
Cuba, 89, 120, 127, 187, 205, 206

Daily Worker, 7, 15, 252
Davis, Benjamin, xii, 243n
de Valera, Éamon, 60, 77, 79, 133, 169
Denikin, Anton, 35, 38
Domingo, W. A., xi, 7, 11, **28–30, 31–4, 39, 88–90, 97–100**, 122, **163–8**, 168–71, 258
Douglass, Frederick, 61
Du Bois, W. E. B., xi, 2, 17, **41–4**, 60, **64, 65**, 99, **122–5**, 138, 140, 141, 154, 165, 166, 167

Eastman, Max, xii, 51
Egypt, 30, 36, 59, 67, 87, 88, 100, 112, 158, 159, 179, 193
The Emancipator, xi, 39, 163
Emmett, Robert, 76
England *see* Britain
Ethiopia, 2, 14–15, 84, 85, 131, 220, 216–18, 226–46, 248, 253, 255, 256, 258

Fascism, 13, 14–15, 216, 226, 227, 228–35, 237, 243–4, 247–9, 252–7
Ford, James W., **180–2**, 227, **243–6**
France, 29, 31, 36, 37, 48, 59, 83, 86, 88, 113, 125, 126, 130, 135, 172, 179, 205, 228, 229–31, 232, 235, 237, 239, 245, 248
French Revolution, 24, 26, 41, 218

Garland, Walter, 252–5
Garrison, William Lloyd, 162
Garvey, Marcus, xii, 2, 6, 10–12, 17, 47, 57, **74–8, 111–14**, 122–73, 196, 226, 227
Germany, 24, 25, 48–9, 82, 83, 89, 116–17, 135, 136, 137, 172, 186, 188, 228, 229–30, 232, 237, 241, 248, 251
Grenada, 189–90
Griffith, Arthur, 74, 77–8, 79

Haiti, 2, 48, 86, 101, 110, 120, 123, 135, 136, 137, 179, 188, 197, 206, 213–14, 257
Harlem/Negro Liberator, xi–ii, 7, 182n
Harrison, Hubert, 2, 6, 11, 15–16, **38–9, 40–1, 96–7, 100–2, 103–11**, 258
Hearst, William Randolph, 116, 140, 239–40, 248
Herndon, Angelo, 223, 226, 248–9
Hitler, 230, 231–2, 235, 237, 239, 244, 245, 249, 255
Hoover, J. Edgar, 12
Houston Riot, 4–5
Howard, Perry, 164–5, 167, 170
Hughes, Langston, 15, **199–200, 204–5, 206–10, 213–15**, 224, **241–3**
Huiswoud, O. E., 7, 10, **177–8**

India, 29, 36, 48, 51, 52, 59, 64, 66, 73, 89, 98, 100, 108, 112, 116, 134–5, 159, 172, 180–1, 190, 192–4, 198–9, 257
Industrial Workers of the World, 4, 30n, 38, 171
International Congress against Colonial Oppression and Imperialism, 118, 171–3
International Labor Defense, 185n, 211, 225, 236n
International Trade Union Committee of Negro Workers (ITUCNW), 12, 186, 187, 177n, 188
International Workers Order, 210–11
Ireland, 2, 8, 10, 29, 37, 58–81, 100, 104, 110, 112, 126, 130, 133, 169, 190, 193–4, 198–9

Jamaica, 7, 89, 122, 123, 138–9, 141, 163–4, 169, 170, 178, 196–8, 204
Jews, 32–4, 35, 41–2, 46, 50, 55, 61, 80–1, 132–3, 208, 258

Jim Crowism, 4, 85, 86, 90, 100, 141, 142, 151, 191, 206–7, 210, 211, 257
Johnson, James Weldon, 142, 167

Katayama, Sen, 50
Kipling, Rudyard, 53, 96–7
Kolchak, Alexander, 33, 35, 38
Ku Klux Klan, 12, 45, 80, 86, 141, 143–50, 151, 155, 157, 160, 161, 221

League of Nations, 30, 40–1, 95–6, 229, 245
League of Struggle for Negro Rights (LSNR), 201–3, 241, 243n
Lenin, V. I., 10, 23, 30, 34, 38, 43, 49, 113, 179–80, 230
The Liberator, xi, 41
Liberia, 11, 59, 86, 119, 123, 135, 136, 188, 237, 257
Lincoln, Abraham, 99, 140
L'Ouverture, Toussaint, 91, 120

McDonald, Ramsay, 183, 189
McKay, Claude, xii, 2, 6, 7, 10, 23, 41–4, **46–57, 69–74, 102, 114–18**, 122, **137–41**, 167, 177n, 258
MacSwiney, Terence, 77
Markievicz, Constance, 69
Marx, Karl, 1, 43, 61, 115
The Messenger, xii, 1, 9, 17, 58, 163–9
Mexico, 101, 135, 136, 137, 206
Miller, Kelly, 141, **157**, 165
Moore, Richard B., 7, **118–21**, 167, 171n
Morocco, 36, 87, 102, 179, 214, 251
Moton, Robert, 60, 167, 204, 205
Mussolini, 14, 222, 226, 227, 228, 231–6, 239, 240, 241–3, 244–5, 253, 255, 256

NAACP, 13, 17, 42, 44, 138, 140, 141, 151, 154, 165, 211, 247n

National Negro Congress (NNC) 243n, 245, 246, 253
Negro Worker, xii, 1, 13–14, 17, 180n, 212–13
Negro World, xii, 6, 11, 17, 128, 131, 139, 140, 167

O'Connell, Daniel, 59, 65, 76
Owen, Chandler, xii, 9, 17, **93–6**, 123, 125, 141, 150, 151, **168–71**
Owens, Jessie, 241

Padmore, George, xii, 2, 13, 17–18, 180n, **182–7, 189–90, 192–9**, 220, **228–35**, 258
Patterson, William L., 17, **215–19, 236–9**
Phillips, Wendel, 91, 162
Pickens, William, 141, 151, 165, 168
Pushkin, Alexander, 31, 215–19

Randolph, A. Philip, xii, 9, 17, **93–6**, 125, **131–7**, 141, 151, **158–62**, 163, 239, 243n, 244
Robeson, Paul, 15
Robins, Raymond, 36
Reed John, 49
Rogers, J. A., **79–81**, 227
Russia, 24–6, 31–4, 35–8, 39–40, 43, 49–57, 61, 65, 81, 95, 98, 108, 113, 126, 133, 159, 187, 206–10, 215, 218, 228, 229, 230–1, 233, 244
Russian Revolution *see* Bolshevism

Scottsboro, 13, 185–7, 203, 211, 213, 223, 222, 225, 238–9, 248–9
Selassie, Haile, 220, 233, 235
Shaw, George Bernard, 52, 72–3
Sinn Fein, 59, 60n, 67, 69–72, 79n, 101, 130, 133–4
Socialist Party, 6, 9, 18, 27, 28–30, 38n, 99, 118n, 171, 191
South Africa, 39, 89, 102, 119, 179, 181, 182–3, 186, 198, 239, 245, 257

Spanish Civil War, 1, 14–15, 180n, 210n, 219, 220, 247–56
Stalinism, 13, 18, 177
Stribling, T. S., 117–18
Strong, Edward, **247–52**

Thompson, Louise, 7, 17, **210–12, 220–6**
Trinidad, 13, 30, 38, 142, 189–90
Trotsky, Leon, 32, 39, 40, 55, 61, 113, 230
Trotter, William Monroe, 60, 138
Tulsa riot, 45, 104–6, 129
Turkey, 108, 179, 231, 232

Washington, Booker T., 3, 11, 48, 60n, 138
Washington, George, 112, 113
Wells, H. G., 74–5, 76
West Indies *see* Caribbean
White, Maude, xii, 7
Wilson, Woodrow, 4, 30, 32, 37, 40, 60, 61, 83, 205
Wobblies *see* Industrial Workers of the World
Woodson, Carter G., 153, 166, 168
World War I, 4–5, 8, 24–5, 31, 40, 41, 42, 48, 66–7, 82–3, 96, 97–8, 139, 159–60, 172–3, 229–30
Wright, Richard, **252–5**

EU representative:
Easy Access System Europe
Mustamäe tee 50, 10621 Tallinn, Estonia
Gpsr.requests@easproject.com